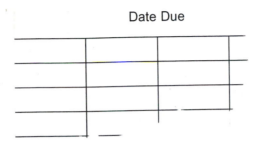

# NOAH'S RAINBOW
## A Father's Emotional Journey from the Death of his Son to the Birth of his Daughter

*David Fleming*

Baywood Publishing Company, Inc.
AMITYVILLE, NEW YORK

**Baywood Publishing Company, Inc.**
26 Austin Avenue
PO Box 337
Amityville, NY 11701
(800) 638-7819
E-mail: baywood@baywood.com
Web site: baywood.com


Library of Congress Catalog Number: 2005053577
ISBN: 0-89503-315-1 (cloth)


**Library of Congress Cataloging-in-Publication Data**

Fleming, David, 1967-
   Noah's rainbow : a father's emotional journey from the death of his son to the birth of his
   daughter / David Fleming.
      p. cm.
   ISBN 0-89503-315-1 (cloth)
      1. Bereavement--Psychological aspects. 2. Grief. 3. Fetal death--Psychological aspects.
   4. Stillbirth--Psychological aspects. I. Title.

   BF575.G7F63 2005
   155.9'37'0924--dc22
   [B]

                                                                        2005053577

*For Kimmy*

CRISO

# Table of Contents

# Acknowledgments

Several years ago, long before I knew what I was getting myself into, I stood in front of my son's gravestone and boldly promised Noah that I would fulfill my duty to perpetuate his spirit by writing his story and sharing it with the world. Since then, many people have gone to extraordinary lengths to ensure that a father would not have to go back on his word to his son.

First and foremost on that list is my wife, Kim. Many of the words, insights and lessons contained here are products of her tender heart and remarkable mind. Her strength and selflessness touched every aspect of this book: from the creation, to the writing, the editing, the marketing and even the actual sale of the manuscript. Early on I realized that if this book was going to help other bereaved parents, it would have to recapture exactly what we went through after Noah's death. The only way to do that, however, was to re-visit, for weeks at a time, the most intensely painful and personal moments of our lives. That is far more than anyone has the right to ask of a mother who has lost her son; yet Kim's support never wavered. And without her tireless effort, vision and unending encouragement, the book you are holding—a father's promise and a son's legacy—never would have come to fruition.

I'd also like to thank my kids, Noah, Ally, and especially Kate. While she didn't get mentioned in the book, Kate's ability to nap soundly in Daddy's lap while he typed away at the final few chapters was as crucial a contribution as any to the completion of this project.

Like any grieving parent searching for guidance on coping with the loss of a child, I am also grateful to everyone at Baywood Publishing Company. Not just for their support of this project, but for remaining a beacon of hope in the publishing industry. In particular, I'd like to thank my editor, Dr. John Morgan, who handled my absurd amount of questions, concerns, and e-mails with remarkable grace. I'm also indebted to literary agents David Halpern and Byrd Leavell, both of whom gave their time and expertise to this project.

Gary Belsky, my friend and an executive editor at *ESPN The Magazine*, added his deft touch and perspective to the manuscript. His enthusiasm helped carry the project to its completion. Thanks, as well, to Gary, John Papanek, Gary Hoenig, Neil Fine, Steve Wulf, Chad Millman, Jon Scher, David Cummings, and everyone else at ESPN's award-winning magazine for supporting me both as a father and writer.

As you might imagine, with someone whose career began at the Mason (Ohio) *Pulse-Journal,* I have many people to thank for their role in my development. As a young reporter at *The Cincinnati Post,* it was my great fortune to fall under the tutelage of former *Post* sports editor Mark Tomasik, an exceptional editor and an even better person. Because of the odd timing of Noah's death and my departure from *Sports Illustrated* in August of 2000, I've never properly thanked many of my former colleagues. To the incomparable Stefanie Kaufman, to David Bauer, Larry Burke, Richard Demak, Gabe Miller, Hank Hersch, Peter King, and far too many others to mention here: thank you for six years of thoughtful guidance and support.

During this process I drew inspiration from Kim's grandmother, Jean Thompson, and Chris Crawford of KinderMourn. More than a decade ago I was also profoundly affected by the grace and dignity shown by the family of Kristin Renneker. Thanks, as well, to my entire extended family during this process, but, in particular, I'd like to mention my mom and dad and my older brother, Greg, each of whom acted as a sounding board for many of the passages in this book.

My neighbor and friend, Teresa Farson, guided me on matters of faith and was one of the first people to believe in the manuscript. The advice and assistance from author and colleague Joe Menzer helped move this project from an idea to a reality. Thanks also to my buddies Jak Farson, Mike Burns, Chad, and Scott Orhan.

Finally, I owe a special debt of gratitude to the people portrayed on the pages of this book. For the last several years our friends and families have performed countless, selfless, and often-times anonymous, acts of compassion on our behalf. Not the least of which was a willingness to be a part of this book: to have their actions annotated while under the most difficult circumstances so that others might learn from our experiences, both positive and negative. Should this book help other bereaved parents, after Noah and Kim, these are the people who deserve a bulk of the credit.

Even as I write what are the last few words of this book, I know it remains impossible to comprehend or communicate the love and support I've received—and continue to receive—as a husband, a father, a brother, a friend, and a writer. I know that memory and space preclude me from chronicling every last kind act I've benefitted from during the last five years. But I wish I could, I really do. Because each one saved my life in some small way.

And for that I remain eternally grateful.

*"Every night, when I go to sleep, I die.*
*Every morning, when I wake up, I am reborn."*

— *Mohandas Gandhi*

CRITERIA

# CHAPTER 1

# The Sharp Heart

The first thing they hook you up to when you check into a maternity ward is a fetal heart monitor. It's not much more than a flat plastic paddle attached to a long cord. The whole thing is then plugged into a small machine near the bed that monitors your baby's heartbeat and broadcasts it back to you in three ways: a whooshing drum beat, a set of green fuzzy numbers and a jittery printout that looks like the results from a polygraph examine. It's a truth machine. Indeed.

For whatever reason, though, when no fetal heartbeat registers, the machine goes silent, the paper goes blank, and the numbers are replaced with what now seems like a cruelly ironic little symbol for a heart. It sits there frozen on the screen, pumping at you, flashing at you, mocking you, like a stale yellow traffic light. The sound and printer go dead with a moaning whir and all that's left is that heart.

That puke green, electronic heart. That cheap, misshapen, god-forsaken, square heart. A heart with corners. A sharp heart. The same one I still see every time I close my eyes. The one that has forever been tattooed on my psyche.

It was early August 2000 when my wife, Kim, entered the hospital 41 weeks pregnant. Without professional prodding, it seemed our son, Noah, was perfectly content to stay exactly where he was, snoozing and getting rounder by the day. "He's such a Fleming," Kim joked. And for the longest time, after checking into the hospital in order for Kim to be induced the next morning, we listened to the reassuring pump and whoosh of the fetal heart monitor. It made it feel like our boy was right there in the room with us. His strong and noisy heart filled the air—loud, clear, and steady; never dropping below 135 beats per minute.

1

It went on like that for six hours. Now, there are a million things that can go wrong during a pregnancy, but for some reason, when we made it to the hospital, only hours away from reaching the finish line, in our hearts it seemed only natural to relax a bit, to celebrate and think, "We made it." It's such a great feeling. As we filled out paperwork and phoned our friends and family, Kim and I sat side by side in that hospital room, holding hands, playing kissy face, laughing, hugging, and daydreaming about having our son here in less than 24 hours.

"We'll be a family tomorrow," I said, walking over to check Noah's printout. I held the paper in my hands, so proud of that strong and steady chart. It looked like the most magnificent mountain peak known to man.

*Dave, get away from there.* Kimmy, will Noah be taller than me? *Everyone is honey.* Will he have blond hair? *Brown.* He'll be tough and funny, right? *He might be sensitive and serious.* When would he get married? *I don't know.* What school would he go to? *Miami, maybe.* How about Stanford? *Okay.* Will I like his wife? *Yeah . . . and she'll adore you.* I want to backpack through Europe with him the summer before he goes off to college. You think he'll want to go with me? *Maybe, if you can somehow manage to stop acting like such a complete dork right now.*

Oh, what a glorious six hours.

Then, suddenly, Kimmy winced.

That is where everything began to turn sticky and confusing—gelatinous almost; where the world we knew before Noah was slammed shut behind us and sealed forever.

Although her contractions were coming up mild on the monitor, Kim was bent over in pain and in progressively more anguish. You must understand something: Kimmy is about as tough as they come. This wasn't normal. I was shocked, in fact, when the next time the nurse came in with more paperwork, Kim asked if she could have a shot for the pain.

In the time it took for the nurse to get the shot and come back, Noah's life had begun to slip away. In those 200 seconds, the kaleidoscope of color and smells and sights all went grayish and blurry—as if everything was suddenly wrapped in sticky plastic, the ceiling melting and swirling into the floor, the colors of our lives mixing into some new kind of reality. This all took two, maybe three minutes tops. That's all it took for our world to change—completely and forever. Two hundred seconds. Two hundred terrifying seconds. The length of a short song on the radio. A few TV commercials. That's it. That's all the time and warning we got, and then our entire being was twisted inside-out; as if someone had yanked our guts out from the navel; like untangling an old, bunched-up sock.

Another burst of pain burned in Kimmy's side.

She sat up and winced, bent sideways, squeezing my hand until I was sure the bones would snap like dry twigs.

Seconds before, we were talking about what college Noah might attend. Now the fetal monitor, which had been steady and strong like a drum, was suddenly wobbly and warped and jumping all over the place like a slot machine. The numbers, those ugly green fluorescent numbers, jumped to 210 then down to 15 and back up again and down with increasing randomness.

There was no pattern. No steady beat anymore. Not from any of our hearts.

Just when we thought it couldn't get any worse, just when our thoughts made that leap from "No biggie, the monitor's just slipped off" to "WAIT . . . IS SOMETHING WRONG?" the sounds and symbols disappeared all together.

Nothing.

Then 188.

Both our eyebrows rise.

Back to nothing.

Jesus.

Now 55.

111.

32.

. . .

Nothing.

Goddammit.

Silence.

A steady beat.

His heart beating again, ours too.

135 . . . 133 . . . 140 . . . 131 . . .

Breathe. Inhale.

Atta boy. Good boy. Thank you.

Our hands come together. We squeeze. Total silence on the outside; screaming in our heads. Our eyes lock. We are reading each other's minds. *Something's wrong.*

22 . . . — . . . 74 . . . — . . . 221

Back to that stupid green heart. Ba-bump. Ba-bump. Ba-bump.

— . . . 118 . . . — . . .

Nothing.

Nothing.

Oh Jesus.

Nothing.

No numbers, no sound. Just that heart.

Nothing on the screen. Forever.

Nothing, forever.

Looking back, that may have been the hardest moment to take. Because in retrospect we realized that in these few short minutes, Noah was fighting for his life. Fighting, suffering, struggling in his own little net, daddy's little warrior.

"Oh, he just wasn't meant for this world," they will say, patting their own heart.

"Ya know, at least he didn't suffer," they will say, dropping off a casserole.

They weren't there, though. He fought. He struggled. He gasped and moaned and cried. He may have been meant for another world, but Noah battled to be here. He wanted to be here. He suffered. He thrashed. He kicked. He was in pain. I have to admit that. I have to come to grips with that if I ever want to get better: my son was in great pain as he fought for his life.

He was bleeding to death.

That is essentially what happens with a placental abruption. The placenta, which supplies blood to the baby, tears away from the wall of the uterus, and the baby bleeds out. Imagine what it would be like if someone unplugged the aorta from your heart. Placentas have life spans. That is another lovely detail we learned. Placentas can get old or tired or used up. They can die. Partial placental abruptions are not uncommon. A pregnant mother sees a little blood while at home, she drives to the hospital, gets some clotting medicine, stays in bed for a while, then has her baby.

But full placental abruptions where fetal death occurs are extremely rare. Lightning strike rare; 1-in-5,000,000 rare. It's the Powerball of pain. It's so rare, in fact, very little research has been done. There are no celebrity benefits. No marathons. No bake sales. No research grants. No one trying to cure it. Trust me, Kim is an expert now; can quote *The New England Journal of Medicine;* statistics, studies, proteins with long names. She knows more than most doctors, although we've learned that's not always saying much.

"Okay," said the serious and confident neonatologist we saw after Noah died. "Now, you had a placental abruption at 41 weeks that resulted in fetal death."

"The fetus' name was Noah," I always want to interject. But who am I kidding? I don't have the guts anymore, don't have the energy or the confidence.

"And you were at home . . . ?"

"No we were in the hospital."

"In the hospital?"

"Yeah, on a heart monitor waiting to be induced."

Stunned silence. Always stunned silence. Nurses. Doctors. Even the gray-haired expert who has seen it all takes off his glasses and rubs his eyes. He adjusts his ugly, blue and burnt orange Tommy Hilfiger tie. He buffs off a spot on his giant mahogany desk the size of a Civic.

"Oh . . . I see . . . hmmmm."

There are very few known causes for placental abruptions, other than extreme high blood pressure and cocaine use. And if there are next-to-no known causes, then there are even fewer ways to prevent, predict or counteract a full PA once it starts, other than almost immediate detection, which we most certainly did not get.

The nurse came back in, finally, with the pain shot for Kimmy and immediately we asked her about the heart monitor. She made a cursory glance over her shoulder and saw the screen.

Heart. Heart. Heart.

"Hmmm," she mumbled.

Then it jumped.

212 . . . — . . . 42 . . . — . . . 117 . . . —

Heart. Heart. Heart.

"See?"

The nurse shrugged.

"Probably just slipped off your tummy," she said.

We squeezed hands. Our lungs refilled with air. *Just slipped off your tummy.* Happens a lot.

The shot went into the IV, but it gave Kimmy no relief. As the nurse lifted Kim's gown and fiddled with the fetal monitor, Kim relaxed a little bit and sunk back into the bed. Her body was no longer as tense, but the pain was still there, still white hot.

The nurse kept fiddling. Kept adjusting while looking over her shoulder at the monitor, waiting for the numbers to climb, to get steady—for Noah to come back. I wait, still, to this day. A minute went by. Then two. Her adjustments got more physical, moving and pushing Kim's tummy.

"These stupid monitors," the nurse said.

We have developed the technology to clone a human being, to keep men alive with artificial hearts and send go-carts to Mars, but the fetal heart monitor, well, those little contraptions are still run on Radio Shack technology and held in place by equal parts elastic bands, gel, and luck.

Nothing. The nurse kept working, but the screen stayed blank.

She fiddled with it some more.

She pushed. Adjusted. Added more gel.

Nothing.

Nothing but that puke green, cubed heart flashing in our faces.

"Come on little one, where are you?" she said.

There was a little panic in her voice now.

Nothing was working.

"Let me go get another nurse who's better at this," she said. " Let's see if she can help. It takes a certain touch, you know."

She walked to the door, but as soon as she hit the hallway she started running. Her white sneakers squeaking on the floor. Panic setting in. You could tell. She tried to hide it, but we understood. Kimmy and I looked at each other in silence, knowing. Something wasn't right. We're in trouble. We know it. No one has to say anything. Our hands squeeze together. They are soaked in sweat. We know it.

Almost as quickly as it closed, the door swung open again. It was another nurse; this one blonde and southern, her eyebrows already pinched into a V. Faking calmness. All "Hihowareyous?" and "Isthisyerfirstbaby?" as she messed with the monitor. More blue gel. More pushing. Sliding. More worried, nervous over-the-shoulder looking.

Nothing.

The other nurse bounced from foot to foot in the background.

"Hmmm. Well. Gosh. Maybe he flipped over. That happens. Come on little fella, where you hiding at?"

And then suddenly, Kim, who had been quieted a bit by the pain medication, exhaled and sat up in bed as if awakening from a nightmare. She smiled a puzzled smile.

"Oh wow," she said with a hint of hope, "I think my water just broke."

"He's coming tonight," I thought. "He just can't wait to get here. Okay. Okay. That's why the monitor was all screwy." It's weird looking back how we tried to talk ourselves out of the stark reality that was as clear as that green heart on the monitor—the one that was screaming at all of us in a way no one was hearing: NO HEART BEAT NO HEART BEAT NO HEART BEAT.

"Okay sweetie," said the blonde nurse. "Let's check."

She stopped with the fetal monitor for a second, smiled warmly at Kim, and pulled back the bed sheet.

Bright red blood.

A giant pool of it. Crimson—inky almost—horrifying in its volume and its contrast to the pure white bed sheets. The most blood I have ever seen. Bright. Bright. Soaking into the sheets now, almost pinkish and shiny on the edges. I swallow. I shiver. I stumble back and grab hold of the armrest on the chair next to me. The nurse immediately pulls the sheet back over Kim, turns and runs out of the room. The little black-haired nurse follows her. They say nothing. They just leave. Running. No faking it anymore.

We're all in deep shit.

I reach out and touch Kimmy's cheek. She doesn't know. She is looking at me. Those sweet blue eyes wide open, asking, pleading. Her face, framed by thick, sweaty brown hair, is a question mark.

"It's okay Kimmy," I say. "There's blood—a lot of blood. They went to get a doctor."

Kimmy is fading a bit. I lean in close to her.

"You okay? Hang in there, sweetie. A doctor's coming. Coming right now, sweetie. Hang in there. Two seconds. HANG ON KIM, sweetie, hang on."

I kiss Kimmy on the cheek. Now I'm the one who is faking calm. The images are swirling again. Colors mixing, like blood seeping into those sheets. The net tightening. All those warnings: *If you ever see even the tiniest bit of blood call your doctor or come straight to the hospital,* echoing in my head.

Kim asks me to go check on the nurses. I walk briskly out the door and down to the nurse's station. They are leaning over a phone, wildly leafing through a giant phone directory, searching for numbers on the gray pages.

They are so frantic they don't see me there, standing above them.

Blondie puts her finger on a number and looks up.

"Is that amount of blood normal?" I ask.

"We are trying to reach the doctor right now, okay Mr. Fleming?"

I used to be daddy or proud Poppa or future diaper changer. Now, all of a sudden, I'm Mr. Fleming.

Blondie looks down. They ignore me.

I walk back to Kim's room, and on the way I list to the side of the hallway for a moment, like someone on a ship that's just been hit by a big wave. I realize later what that was. It was the tidal wave reaching land; the sonic boom hitting me; the signal that nothing will ever be the same again.

Nothing.

Forever.

Boom.

I get my balance back, take my hand off the wall, and keep going.

I am back at her side. We hold hands. The nonverbal communication is stunning in its completeness and clarity. Glances. Sighs. Looks. Smiles. Squeezes.

We know.

Do we know?

We know. We know.

Tick.

Tick.

Tick.

That green heart. The jagged heart. Ba-bump. Ba-bump.

Then the door busts open, and behind a giant clumsy ultrasound machine on wheels is a tiny female doctor in blue scrubs and a funky, paisley operating room hair-cap.

Everyone moving with a sense of purpose now; the machine wheeled into place. The plugs, the switches, the gel, everything one-two-three like a drill, including shoving me out of the way.

"I understand you've had some bleeding and trouble finding your baby's heartbeat," said Doc Paisley. "What I'm going to do now is check the baby with the ultrasound to see how he's doing, and we'll go from there. . . ."

She starts with the wand over Kimmy's stomach. The lights flick off as she tilts the screen toward her so she can see. Moving quickly she tries several different angles and locations.

There is nothing.

No heart beat.

No movement.

Nothing.

On the screen, Noah is face down, limp, sluggish. Nothing. He's not moving. Lifeless. This is very hard to watch. He looks limp. A blob. He's gone. Is he gone? He can't be gone.

I will pray and cry and beg and scream and vomit and curse and pound my fists through walls for the next six months and finally go half-crazed at Christmas trying to find some peace with this, but Kim and I both know it, or are starting to understand it: He's gone.

The doctor has seen enough.

She stands, shoves the machine away, nods to the nurses, and they start rolling Kimmy's bed toward the door.

"Your baby is in trouble, okay?"

We nod.

"We need to take you in RIGHT NOW for an emergency C-section."

"Right now?" I ask.

More nods.

Kim and I glance at each other. That's all the time we get. This isn't the movies. One glance. I grab hold of the railing of the bed by her foot. I will help push the bed and stay with Kim and be the hero and will the outcome to be different. We hit the door. The doctor slides in front of me. I give her the go-go-go nod, like, "Come on, time's a wasting."

She puts her hand firmly on my chest. I lose my grip on the railing. This memory goes into the gallery, next to the frozen green heart on the monitor, the unused car seat that stays in the trunk for months and that look on Kim's face—me forced to let go of the railing, the cold metal bar slipping out of my fingertips like losing the grip of someone who is dangling off a ledge.

"You can't come with us," the doctor says. "You just can't. Stay here. We will keep you informed. You can't come. We'll take good care of her. I promise."

I'm not listening; I move to my right and tiptoe above the doctor.

"I love you Kimmy. Hang in there. I love you sweetie . . ."

What more do you say? I hadn't rehearsed this. There's no time.

Just a few minutes before we were discussing godparents and Christmas presents and whether or not he'd be a fullback on the football team or a center on the hockey team. "Both," I said, "and an artist." Now it's as if I'm looking through the wrong end of a pair of binoculars, and Noah is getting farther away instead of closer.

My throat swells. My tongue is thick and sticky now. I shake my head. Rub my eyes. But I'm in a fog. I can't focus. The bed is rolling. The doctor turns to grab on where I was just holding it. Taking my place. I can't think, can't speak. I swallow. The bed is moving. Almost out the door now.

"I love you Kim . . . be strong . . . everything is gonna be . . . I love you . . ."

Kim gives me a flat smile and a nod of her head. Determined. Scared. But strong. She is the fighter. I am nothing like her.

"I love you," she mouths to me.

Then she's gone.

I stand there, frozen. The tart, muddy, acrid smell of blood flows up my nostrils and stings my brain, like ammonia. *That's Kimmy's blood.* I can't breathe. Won't breathe. Have to avoid that smell. That very thought. Feel sick. I want to go back. Press pause. Erase. Rewind. *That's Noah's blood.* The room is empty. Silent. Still. The overhead lights are still dark from the ultrasound machine. Can't see too well. The sick, greenish glow from the fetal monitor is the only light in the room. I do not move. My hands and arms are heavy at my side. I can't move. I am alone, paralyzed with confusion.

Did that just happen?

Wait.

No.

Stop . . . no . . . wait.

What just happened?

The door is closing.

Wait.

Did that just happen?

Wait. Stop. No.

Wait.
Wait.
Please, wait.
The heavy, wooden door swings shut.
I am plunged into darkness.

CおBの

## CHAPTER 2

# God Descends as a
# Child Ascends

I fell backwards into the door as it shut behind me, staring back into the cold, empty hospital room. The only light, from a tiny bulb above the sink, drew me across the room and into the bathroom where I was startled by my reflection in the mirror. It was me, alright. But it wasn't. I seemed to be reflecting only in shades of black and white. I ran some cold water over my hands, splashed it on my face and massaged it into my eyes. Then, from behind a towel, I looked into the mirror one more time.

"I have faith," is what I said. "I have faith. I have faith. I have faith."

But it was more a question than a statement. More prayer than proclamation. In truth, it was a shallow, meaningless stab into thin air. If I meant it, I meant it only as an answer to the kind of cosmic pop quiz I believed God had just thrown at me. And that by displaying a burst of faith (even a quasi, fake, watered-down version) God would somehow forget all of those trespasses and unkept promises he was about to punish me for, change his mind, decree me worthy and return my wife and child back to me unharmed. All I had to do was impress him with my faith and he'd overlook all those unforgivable deeds throughout my life that were now rapidly . . . unspooling . . . inside . . . my . . . head.

(What an odd combination of spiritual mind-washing and hubris, I later thought, recalling these first few torturous moments alone. My wife and child are fighting for their lives, and my first reaction is to wonder what *I'm* being punished for. Or what I did to deserve this.)

Thankfully, the frozen face before me blinked.

Unsettled, I moved away from the mirror and back into the room. There were lights from the parking lot coming in through the windows, and my eyes had adjusted enough to notice just how hollow and antiseptic a room like this becomes without a bed and a patient.

Feeling useless and alone, I moved to the gap where Kim's bed had been and, without thinking, bent down to the floor. Using the damp brown paper towel from the sink, the one that smelled of dust and reminded me of middle school back home in Michigan, I began cleaning up the droplets of blood that had breached the side of Kim's bed. The blood did not come up in a clean, easy flick of the wrist. None of this would. Down on my hands and knees, the harder I tried to wipe it up the more the blood—Kim's blood, Noah's blood, which, in turn is my blood too—smeared and swirled into the cold tile floor where it dried in brown streaks like wood stain. On my hands and knees, heaving, convulsing in agony, the unthinkable hit me: It may already be over. I may have already lost everything. Noah was in trouble, I got that . . . but so was Kimmy, I suddenly realized. So was Kimmy.

* * *

We met during the first week of Kim's sophomore year at Miami University, a picturesque little yuppie training ground of ivy-covered red-brick buildings and shaded slant walks, plopped down in the cornfields of southwestern Ohio. Our first date was to the Cincinnati Zoo to see a panda. Chiachia, though, was asleep in a mud puddle, and I had to rush Kim back to campus because, I later found out, she had a second date lined up for that evening. (As you can see, I've let this go.) Our next date went much better. It was a canoe trip in Indiana where, at the end of the float, Kim's sorority had arranged for a photographer to shoot pictures of the water-logged couples, or at least the ones who were still speaking to each other.

Sun-burnt and smiling, we wrapped our arms around each other and posed for the keepsake. The picture dude paused and leaned out from behind his camera. "I've been doing this a long time," he said. "And I can tell, I mean I can just tell, you guys have been together a long time, right?"

Kim was an overachiever in pursuit of a Marketing degree and then a prestigious job with a Fortune 500 company in New York. A native of Detroit, I attended school courtesy of a wrestling scholarship that, after a robust five years, four letters, and one torn ACL, somehow resulted in an English degree. Despite the lack of any actual writing experience, I landed an internship at a weekly newspaper in Mason, Ohio.

Manhattan and Mason. Business and English. Democrat and Republican. Kim came from a nuclear family; mine had been nuked by divorce. She was the president of her sorority; I was the captain of the wrestling team. She has two sisters; I have three brothers. We were both middle kids. She has brown hair. Mine is blonde. See took life too seriously; me, not enough. She was organized. Me? Not so much. On the day before a business trip, I once had to drive from New Jersey to Ohio to renew my driver's license before it expired. Kim studied all night for her accounting final and still flunked the damn thing. I once slept through the first half of a Poly Sci exam and aced it.

We fought. We laughed. We laughed some more. (If there is a language to our relationship, it is laughter.) We argued. We talked and talked. She opened up about her mother, who died of pancreatic cancer when Kim was just a baby. (Her dad remarried eight years later.) I talked about my parents' divorce.

Kim's experience in her Catholic elementary school choir tells you everything you need to know about her. The nuns decided she had a terrible voice and told her to just mouth the words during recitals. "Yeah, right," thought Kimmy. That only made her sing louder. Then, during a wedding performance, a nun actually snuck over and yanked Kim off the riser. Kim had that same song played at our wedding, but she didn't sing it. (Thank God.) As for me, when I was about the same age, I begged my teacher to excuse me from class because of a stomachache. But because I had been such a troublemaker, she didn't believe I was really sick and told me to sit there for once, and be quiet. Eventually I passed out. They rushed me to the hospital, where an emergency appendectomy was performed minutes before the stupid thing burst.

Kim and I challenged each other. We complemented each other. We mocked and made great fun of each other. I called her by her last name, Sachs, until I discovered her borderline infatuation with the department store Nordstrom. After that she was Nord. She called me Flem for the first five years of our relationship. We liked ourselves better when we were together. The first time I told her I loved her was by a dumpster behind the Miami bar called Ozzies. We fit like pieces of a jigsaw puzzle. Without question we were the kind of couple other couples hate.

We dated for the rest of college. When Kim took that job in New York, we were half a country apart for more than three years. Eventually I moved on to *The Cincinnati Post* and, after a story on a giant catfish caught an editor's eye, to *Sports Illustrated* in New York.

Once there, all I needed was a VISA card with a high enough credit line, and I was off to the jewelers. After eight years of dating, we got engaged on the beach in Hilton Head during a family vacation. We walked for what felt like miles as Kim waited while I worked up the nerve. Afterward I told her, "I have one goal for our life together: in 50 years I want to come back here, to this very spot and watch our kids and our grand kids run around on this very beach . . . that's it . . . that's all I want out of life."

We spent our first year of marriage in New York. I had been promoted to staff writer when Kim, a rising star at Westvāco, a paper company, became one of the youngest women to be appointed regional manager. So we packed up our fat, yellow Lab, Scoop (that was now pushing 130 pounds), and moved, pretty much sight unseen, to Charlotte, North Carolina. There, halcyon days of fun, love, travel, and work, fueled by the disposable income and limitless free time of a young couple without kids, unfolded effortlessly for another four years.

During our travels we always sought out wishing wells and fountains, tossing away fistsfulls of dollars in loose change for what we thought was a simple, altruistic wish: happy and healthy children.

In the fall of 1999 we decided to start a family. We were just sitting watching TV one night when Kim turned to me and, before she could say a word, I said, "We're ready for more, aren't we?" Three weeks later Kim was pregnant. After our first ultrasound—the one that confirmed it was a boy—I was mesmerized by the picture in the palm of my hand. Overwhelmed by the notion that that tiny life was the actual, physical manifestation of our love. We were in a bagel shop at the time, and Kim leaned over and grasped my hand oh so gently, whispering ". . . hold it together there, daddy."

Once we got my sappiness in check, we breezed through the rest of Noah's pregnancy without a single complication. Not one. Not a hitch. Not a warning. Not a single, elevated test result. Nothing. Kim loved her doctor, Leedylyn, and the appointments became like minidates for us. Even his name came easy. I loved Holden, but Kim vetoed that one. Too artsy, she said. Yeah, like that's a bad thing. Kim liked Christopher but was afraid I'd shorten it to 'Topher. (She was right.) On a lark, after watching the movie *Clueless,* we started shouting out names while the credits rolled.

"Jon."

"Jake."

"Austin."

"NOAH!" We both shouted at the same time. We looked at each other. And that was that. For all we know, our son is named after a craft services guy from Hollywood. It took me less than a day to shorten his name to Mo. I also called him Baby Boy and just The Boy.

Kim stuck with Noah. Only later would we discover the significance of our choice.

A few months later, at the grandiose baby shower our neighbors threw, I pointed out for everyone the traits I hoped they would pass along to my son. I joked with Kim's dad, Ed, a doctor from Dayton, Ohio, who had briefly attended Notre Dame, that if he tried to make Noah a Fighting Irish fan, I would get a restraining order. Everyone howled. Except Ed.

"We are ridiculously blessed," I said in closing.

Later that day we posed for pictures in front of baby strollers, tiny football jerseys and in between balloons and color-coordinated table cloths. On the giant blue, yellow, and white cake were the same words we had painted on the walls of Noah's extravagant nursery: *I see the moon and the moon sees me, God bless the moon and God bless me.*

We looked so tan, confident, and rested in those pictures. The perfect couple. Perfect families. Perfect house. Perfect jobs. Perfect friends. Perfect marriage.

Perfectly oblivious.

*　*　*

There were two empty, brown faux wood chairs in Kim's room, but for some reason I felt more comfortable on the floor. I was unbalanced, wobbly, and I suppose it seemed safer down there. The one time I did stand was to hit the nurse call-button on the wall to ask for an update on my wife.

"I'm, um, checking on my wife . . . and baby," I barely whispered.

"Yes Mr. Fleming," crackled some anonymous voice, so loud I stepped back several feet at the sound. "We haven't heard from the doctors yet, Mr. Fleming. As soon we know something, somebody will be in to see you."

"Mr. Fleming?"

"Yes."

"You okay?"

"Uh-huh," I grunted. ". . . well, I need . . . I really need some news on my wife. . . ."

"I understand, Mr. Fleming. As soon as we have some news, we'll come in or the doctors will come in. It won't be too much longer."

Back down on the floor, images swirled in my head: that pool of blood, the picture from our canoe trip, Noah's limp body on the ultrasound, Kim's wonderful flat smile that only I could decipher, the nurse's panicked face, our wedding, the Noah flag I so confidently flew from our porch before leaving for the hospital, the first night in our new house when we ate pizza and camped out on the carpet using bath towels for blankets, the hospital bed being pulled out of my grasp. The blood. The emptiness. The icy, metallic sound of the nurse's amplified voice.

*I'm losing it. This must be what it feels like. I can't hold it together. Can't stop it. Stay strong. For her. What if? Don't even think it. Yeah, but what if? A funeral. A wake. The aftermath. Oh God. Just wait for the news. Hold it together. For Kim. Don't fall to pieces now. Not now. What would Kim be doing right now? She'd be strong. So think of her. Think of what she's going through. Be strong. For her. Can't you even do that?*

I was too far gone. I couldn't reel myself back in. The idea of Kim and Noah, mother and child—dying, suffering, in pain—I was unraveling. My legs were tucked up underneath me, and I was rocking back and forth. The blood. Cold bodies. Darkness. Choking. Crying. Gagging. I was patting at myself, pawing my chest for air. Losing it. Quicksand. About to crash. Unspooled. No breath.

"Help me," I gulped.

My chin hit my chest. "Give me strength," I begged.

No sooner had the words left my mouth, when an immense feeling of warmth and peace came over me, as if I was lost in the snow, on the verge of freezing to death, and someone had come up and wrapped me in a down comforter. I suddenly felt washed in calm power. It was an amazing, unique and visceral sensation—one I will never forget. I actually hugged myself, rubbing my shoulders and looking around above and behind me for someone or something. It was that incarnate.

After that night there would be plenty of horrific memories to contend with. On the opposite end of the spectrum, however, was this equally powerful and glorious epiphany that had come just as I was about to go under. For me, the concepts of faith, spirit, hope and God had always held such ethereal qualities. I believed that I possessed them. I believed that I believed. But how could one know, especially such a natural cynic and accomplished skeptic as me? After all, you couldn't capture them in your hands. Couldn't feel them or take their picture. They were just . . . there—or not. The very concept of faith, after all, is belief without proof.

But that feeling, that was as physically moving and unforgettable as a bear hug. I was drowning in the self-absorbed notion that I was being punished. The world had forsaken us; God had glanced over a list of five million soon-to-be-parents, pointed His mighty finger, targeted us for tragedy and then, I don't know, ordered lunch or something, leaving us to fend for ourselves.

But that warmth was the unmistakable contradiction of that. God had just slapped me across the face.

*I'm still here.*

He had neglected to bring any answers with Him. No peace or strength or wisdom, either. No simple solutions or quotations or revelations that solved everything in a snap. I had just experienced the physical manifestation of my faith and, well, I was still a wreck; never more than two breaths away from going catatonic. If my prayer for strength had been granted, I had been given just enough to keep my head above water. What I felt was balance; or perhaps just a possibility of balance in all of this. Horror and hope. Ignorance and enlightenment. Darkness and light. Life and death. Hot and cold. Tears and laughter.

God descends to a hospital room while down the hallway a child ascends to God.

Balance.

Just enough, in fact, to get me back on my feet. I stood and waited for the news. Ready for it. Waiting to lead. I felt, perhaps for the first time, more like a husband and a father than a son or a brother.

"Be with them," I pleaded, trying to correct my earlier thoughts. "Be with them. Not me."

When the door opened, I didn't have to search for answers; they were right there on the doctors' faces; the bowed heads, the slumped shoulders, the shuffling feet. They were still in their blue OR scrubs, their masks crumpled and knotted around their necks. I stood and watched as they solemnly marched toward me. They didn't have to speak. I knew. Deep down I knew.

Of course, I had held out hope that this would end with a happy call over the nurse's intercom: "Mr. Fleming? Whew . . . well little Noah sure did give us a scare there, but everything is fine, and you can come down to the nursery and see your son."

But I knew. Something gurgled up inside me. Something so strong, so savage and raw, I knew I wouldn't be able to contain it; that it would rise up from my gut and straight out the top of my head, splitting me in half.

Oh God, had I lost them both? Jesus no, I shivered. The doctors formed a circle around me, each one grasping one of my hands. The doctor who had performed the initial ultrasound, still wearing her purple, paisley hair-cap, looked up into my eyes.

"We're here for you," said the other one, the one I didn't recognize. "We're here."

Then Paisley spoke. "We performed an emergency C-section on your wife. Her placenta had abrupted, or torn away from the uterus . . . it had given out and the baby was rapidly losing blood . . . the placenta is what nourishes the baby with blood, and when that gives way it's like an open artery . . . we got him out just as fast as we could, and we tried everything we could to save your baby . . . we used all of the life-saving techniques . . . we worked as hard as we could . . . we did everything . . . to . . . revive him . . . but we just didn't get to him soon enough . . . your baby . . . your baby died . . . he's gone."

It suddenly felt like all the forces of nature were conspiring to drag me down into a pool of mush on the floor. My head bowed, and it felt like my face began to melt. The doctors squeezed my hands, tugged hard on my arms, brought me back a bit.

I pinched my lips together and bore my eyes into Dr. Paisley.

"And my wife? Is she okay?"

"She needs you now," said the other one.

I nodded my promise. Oh, my precious Kimmy. Alone. Lost. Confused. Torn open. Empty. The strength I was given, I would tell her about it, transfer it to her. I promised. For once, I would be the strong one, and she would lean on me.

"She's okay. She has lost a lot of blood . . . has been through a traumatic operation. With placental abruptions there is always the worry that the mother's blood doesn't clot . . . everything looks okay right now . . . we did not have to perform any other procedures other than the C-section . . . but we will be monitoring her very closely."

"She needs you now. She needs you to be strong for her," said the other one. "You need to stay strong for her."

"I understand," I said. "Can I see her?"

"We can take you to see her right now," said Paisley. "She's in a recovery room . . . she needs to rest and recover . . . but you can see her."

The hallway was so bright. It was ablaze, blinding and foreign. I didn't recognize anything. None of it looked familiar. I passed doctors, nurses and parents during the long walk that took me the length of the Labor and Delivery floor. The parents avoided me, literally diving to the side of the hallway to get out of my way. Hospital workers stared at the floor. At the nurses station, everyone suddenly got very busy. All I saw were the tops of heads.

I had just stepped back into the blinding, harsh light of the real world where I was now the father of a dead son, and no one, it seemed, would look me in the eye.

### CHAPTER 3

# The First Drop From an Ocean of Grief, Released

Kim was slipping in and out of consciousness. Her head had sunk deep into the pillow where her pale face was nearly camouflaged by the white pillowcase. Her chest and stomach were a tangled mass of blankets, wires, tubes, and monitors. Machines pumped and clicked; monitors beeped and hissed. I was afraid to touch her. I stepped around her IV and bent down at the top of the bed, carefully reaching my right arm across her chest. I nudged my left shoulder down onto the mattress and nestled my nose in close to her ear. Perfect puzzle pieces snapped back into place.

In a moment, Kimmy recognized that I was there. Without the strength to lift her head or even turn her body, I felt her twist her face toward me. I backed up. My palm rested on her cheek. I bent down and kissed her wet, clammy forehead.

Her sad, tired eyes blinked.

Then she mouthed the words, "I'm sorry."

I shook my head violently. "Don't say that, don't ever say that," I said through a whispered scream. "You saw what happened. You were right there. He was gone so fast. It's no one's fault. God took him. He took him and there was nothing we could do." I shook my head at her. "Don't you think that. Don't ever think that again. Okay?"

She nodded. Her head rolled back, and she looked at the ceiling for a moment, and her eyes shut again, squeezing out a tear that slide down the side of her face.

"I need to tell you something," I said.

She turned and stared into my eyes, focusing.

"I asked for strength, Kimmy, when I was alone, and I didn't know what was happening. I asked for strength, and it came to me. I felt it. It helped me. I felt it. Just ask. Ask for the strength. You have it. I know you do."

I didn't tell her everything was okay, because it wasn't. We both knew that. "Everything's gonna be fine" would have been a lie. We were in uncharted territory now. We had no idea what feelings or pain was coming next and no clue if, or how, we would get through it. Our survival instinct had been reduced to nothing more than the next breath. All I could think to do was let Kim know she had the strength to move forward and face this—and that I would be right next to her.

She scrunched up her face and nodded. A machine clicked. A tube moved. She exhaled. Her chest rose and lowered, and she was back asleep. It was only then that I realized there was a nurse in the room with us. I looked up at her. She smiled. I smiled back. I put my head back down into Kim's pillow.

The nurse got up and left the room. Out in the hallway I could hear talking. After a few moments she came back in. She moved gently to my side and placed a hand on my shoulder.

"Mr. Fleming," she said.

"Yes?" I said, looking up from the bed.

"I'm so sorry for your loss."

". . . thanks."

There was a long awkward pause. She stood there frozen for what seemed like a few minutes. She wanted to say something.

"Would you like to see your son?" she whispered. "We can bring him in for you now if you'd like."

"Okay, sure, yeah. Like, you mean right now?" How do you answer something like this? My god, what would he look like? Would he be ashen and cold? Stiff? Will it smell? It's a corpse, right? A dead body. Like on TV? Do I want to hold a dead body?

Then instincts of a deeper nature took over. I ached to see him, to hold him, to smell him, to touch and kiss him. My son. Run and get him, I thought, I can't wait another second. Whatever condition he was in, I couldn't have cared less. Go get him. Run. "Yeah, please, that would . . . yeah, please."

I stood at the foot of Kim's bed, watching her, waiting for my son. They had begun cutting her stomach open before the anesthesia had kicked in and when Kim winced in pain everyone halted. "GO GO GO," she screamed at them. "GO!" My wife, my dear sweet, brave wife. She was pale, unconscious, her hair soaked in sweat, her eyes blood-shot, her stomach still bleeding with a tangled web of tubes—a dozen, maybe more—criss-crossing her body.

The door opened.

The nurse wheeled him in using a regular bassinet. It all just seemed so torturously normal. He was wrapped in blankets. He had a little knit hat on. His skin looked pink. He had footies on. I had always thought the gap between the living and the dead was some huge, easily distinguished chasm. Instead, the difference was barely perceptible.

Like any first-time dad, I stood there nervously waiting to cradle my son. I wiped my hands on my pants. I folded my arms. I stood up straight. I had practiced a thousand times during the last nine months. And as the nurse transferred him to me I made sure to support his head, to get my left forearm under his body, to retuck his little feet under the white cotton blanket he was wrapped in.

Noah's body was still warm when the nurse gently handed him to me, and I realized that I was cradling my son for the first—and probably last—time.

The first wave of life-changing sorrow was bubbling up inside of me. I had promised to be strong for Kim—and I kept my word. But it was coming, there was no doubt. Like driving down the highway and spotting dark, ominous storm clouds in my rearview mirror, I knew it would be here soon enough. I sensed it like a dense tumor in my gut; one that would turn my heart cold, swell in my throat and finally, like an overinflated innertube, it would build and expand, engulfing my head until it burst out in violent, exhaustive waves.

The sky was darkening.

The wind was swirling.

The temperature was dropping.

The grief would be hitting soon. I knew it.

As I adjusted him in my arms, Noah's tiny, blue and pink knitted hat slipped down off his head and awkwardly covered half his face. It had curled his left ear up and smooshed down his right cheek. *Oh, that might hurt.* So, like all clumsy new dads, I fumbled with it, using two free fingers of my left hand like tweezers to try and readjust the hat. Of course, I only ended up making it worse. Without thinking, I gently pulled it off with my right hand, scrunched it into a ball in my fist and tucked it into my pants pocket.

That was the first gift I received from my son.

For during the next several weeks that hat never left my pocket. When reality had set in—when the doctors explained the lightning-strike odds of what had happened; when I had to sign a death certificate instead of a birth certificate or fight off the hard sell on a "family-pack" burial plot from a cemetery salesperson or watch as Kimmy tucked my son's blankie under his arm before we shut his coffin—I reached into my pocket and was sustained, comforted somehow, by Noah's little cotton hat.

Without a hat, the little rascal's thick brown hair was exposed. In the back, just like his old man, his hair was sticking straight up. My mind had been racing up until that point, but for a moment it slowed, and I began to focus on my sweet baby boy. He was so warm against my chest. He was big. Oh so big. That was part of the problem, I suppose. He was almost eight and a half pounds and 21 inches long with pudgy little cheeks and a full head of thick, brown hair just like his momma.

The sweetest, pudgiest little boy on the earth. My little fullback.

I was drawn to him. I needed him closer to me, so I raised my son to my face and showered him with kisses. His hair, his cheeks, his ears, his forehead, his hands, the tiny, beautiful tip of his perfect nose. For several minutes I did nothing but kiss him. As I did that, the thought that ran through my head was no different than any other parent who gets to hold their child for the first time.

"He's perfect," I cried.

Perfect feet, perfect little chubby forearms and fingers, nose, ears, eyes . . . all of them perfect. When you look at the detailed features of your child for the first time, say, the way his ear is a perfectly shaped swirl of delicate flesh, the word miracle does not seem to be too strong to describe how a baby is conceived, grown, and delivered unto our world. So I was within reason, then, to think that God had given me a perfect child. He had granted me a miracle, made me an angel and then, as if to torture or punish me, He neglected to turn him on.

That was the notion that kept running through my head in those first few moments.

*Someone turn him on! How could we get this close? Turn him on! Flick a switch! Push a button. Give him a shot. Someone, please! This can't be happening. Why would You let us get so close and then yank him away? Who would do such a thing? You waited for the most painful time and then took him from us? Who are You? Are You getting Your jollies from this? Is that it? What kind of a God—if there even is one—would do something like this?*

That's when the storm clouds had arrived and the innertube burst, and I began to howl. Now, I have cried many times before. Cried after losing wrestling matches in high school. Cried during sad movies. Cried when a friend tried to kill himself. Cried, I am utterly embarrassed to admit, during a particularly bad stretch of work. But I was not so much crying then as I was wailing. I never would have guessed that I was capable of the sounds, the heaves and the waves of emotion that came over me at that moment. But, again, I was no longer the same person.

It was a guttural, confused, tortured moan. There weren't tear drops as much as a stream. The snot pushed out of my mouth and drained down my face and soaked the collar of my shirt. I didn't care.

In my arms and next to my cheek, I could feel the warmth, the life, perhaps the very soul departing from Noah's body. His life was evaporating against my skin, and I was powerless to hold on to it; like water leaking out of cupped hands. The darkest moment of my life and the greatest moment of my life were somehow occurring simultaneously.

At that moment, at the moment when I realized that Noah had indeed died, that no one could—how did I put it, turn him on?—I crumbled. I was reduced to dust. I felt it happening. I felt like skin over a hollow frame, and I was about to fold up like a discarded overcoat on the floor. The David Patrick Fleming who had existed up to that point was now gone. My crying took on the tone of a wounded animal.

As I continued to weep, one tiny tear, like a single raindrop at the beginning of a huge thunderstorm, welled up in the corner of my left eye. It slid down my cheek and dropped, with a tiny splash, into the crease between Noah's perfect, tiny, little nose and the corner of his closed eye. And then, as quickly as it had fallen, it disappeared.

I first thought that I had imagined things. Or that there had been a mistake and he was actually alive; that it didn't really happen (as crazy as it sounds, on some level I would cling to that notion for several months until it nearly destroyed me), and so I looked up and all around to see if anyone else had witnessed what I'd seen. Was I going mad?

Kimmy, though, was still in and out of consciousness. The nurses had left us alone. So I looked back down at his sweet face and an enormous feeling of calm fell over me. That would happen several times in the next few days and periodically over the next year or so—the scales of my life tipping between despair and hope—and the effect always seemed heaven sent. I stopped crying. I stopped howling. My chest stopped heaving. I focused. I wasn't alone. My son, or at least his soul, his golden soul, was right there with me.

Because my Noah, my perfect, beautiful, baby boy had absorbed that tear into his own eye. The first tiny drop from an ocean of grief, released.

## CHAPTER 4

# Families Arrive, With Baggage

After Kim had stabilized a bit and test results confirmed that her blood was beginning to clot, they moved her to another room down the hall. That was the place where mother and child are supposed to be reunited after a C-section. Instead, our room was full of cold, gray shadows and lurking, unanswerable questions. Kim was still coming in and out. I sat next to her, my hand up under the side of the bed, rubbing my thumb back and forth over the soft skin on top of her hand. It seemed like the only place not connected to a tube, needle or monitor.

On the table next to Kim was a white phone. With my other hand, I reached over and brought the phone to my lap. The movement woke up Kim. She looked at the phone, then looked at me. The corner of her mouth frowned. We had stepped away to some other place the last few hours. Now the reality and responsibilities of the real world were slowly seeping back into our new life.

We both knew what I had to do. Kim blinked. She looked away from the phone. Her eyelids closed. Her head turned away.

I stretched the phone cord across the room, leaned against a wall near the door and dialed the numbers to her parent's home in Ohio. By now it was close to midnight. The last time we had talked to anyone was around 9:30 p.m. just to say good night. "We'll call ya in the morning when your grandson gets here," we said. It was supposed to be so different—so completely different.

Ed answered right away. His voice was hushed and gravely.

"Uh, hello?"

"Ed?"

"Yeah."

"It's Dave."

"Hey Dave."

"Ed . . . I . . . I need to talk to you for a second, okay?"

"Sure, yeah, everything okay?"

"No. It's not . . . Kim is fine. She's okay. But . . . we lost the baby. Noah died. He's gone."

"Oh no, Dave, no, oh no, no, I'm so sorry."

"Kim had a . . . um . . . placental abruption," I said, struggling to remember a term that I would probably never be able to forget. "She started to bleed really bad. They did an emergency C-section, but they couldn't save him. He's gone. I guess they didn't get to him quick enough. They couldn't save him. They say they tried. But it was . . . too late."

Ed whispered the news to Kim's mom, Janie. In the background I could hear her cry out.

He came back on the phone. "Kim is okay?"

"She's fine. I mean she's okay, physically. She's sleeping right now. They're making sure her blood is clotting. So far the tests coming back are all good." I started to cry. "She is so strong, Ed. She is so strong."

"You're strong too, Dave," Ed said. "You need to be strong for each other. You'll need each other more than ever right now. This is going to be hard on you two . . . and your marriage. Very hard."

"Okay."

"What can we do?" said Ed.

"Kim needs you here, I know she does," I said. "We need you here."

"Of course."

Then I asked him to call the rest of Kim's family. Her older sister, Karen, is a former school teacher who lives in Chicago. She's married to Jason, a good guy who, on family vacations, always seemed to be up and at 'em while I slept til noon; or dressed in pressed slacks and oxfords for dinner while I wore cut-off shorts and a Pearl Jam t-shirt. Their son, Connor, was almost one at the time. The Con-man is a tender-hearted tornado. He's a riot. Kim's younger sister, Kristen, whom I first met when she was just an eight-year-old pip-squeak in ponytails, was only days away from beginning her freshman year at Miami. I love Karen and Kristen like my own sisters. They were my first real confidants in the family. They are loyal, strong and smart women and always quick to laugh.

"Sure. Of course. No problem. Have you called anyone else?" Ed asked.

"No not yet. This was my first call."

"Okay then. I'll let you go . . . go be with Kim. You need to take care of her now, okay? And yourself."

"I will."

"Hang in there, Dave, okay? Be strong. Take care of each other."

"Yep."

I repeated that phone call a few times to other family members. I called my brother Bill, an FBI agent, who had recently moved back to our hometown with his wife, Laura, an attorney, and their two young daughters, Megan, who at the time was 5, and Emily, 3. I also called my mom. Then I called my dad, who is an Episcopal priest (as well as a retired VP of human resources for a company in Detroit.) I asked him if Noah needed last rites; if there was some kind of time limit. I didn't know. In the movies, it always seems like they're rushing in a priest to perform the service just before—or right after—someone dies. But Dad said it didn't work that way. He would perform last rites for Noah when he got into town. He asked for Noah's full name.

"Noah William Fleming," I said. The William Fleming on the other end gulped back tears.

"Is there going to be a funeral?" he asked.

There was a long, hushed pause.

"I . . . I . . . Dad . . . Kim and I haven't even talked about that . . . she's still out of it . . . ," I said, starting to unravel.

"Okay honey, I just. . . ."

"I mean, I don't . . . I'm not sure . . . he just died. . . ."

"Okay, okay . . ."

I hung up the phone and slid down the wall to the floor. I sat for a long time in the dark with no idea where I was going to find the energy and the tools to deal with it all. Noah's death was just the beginning. Last rites. Family. Friends. Funerals. Work. Marriage. The future. Eating. Sleeping. Talking. Breathing. How? I half expected all of this to be put on hold. But the world just continued on, faster than ever.

I had one more call to make that night, to our friends on the cul-de-sac. The last time we checked in with them they were outside in a group setting up a staggered schedule for visiting Noah the next day. I dialed the Farsons. Then I hung up. I dialed again. Then I hung up.

I was tired of ruining people's evenings.

Since moving in a few years ago, we had grown close to Jak and Teresa Farson and their four great kids: Abby, who at the time was 12, Kelsey, 10, Grace, 8, and Sam, 6. They were the rare couple we knew where we considered both of them to be our good friends. And we adored their kids. After we moved in, it took them about a week to go from calling me Mr. Fleming to Dave. They constantly scolded me for having a potty mouth.

Jak grew up in rural Indiana. He was a two-sport athlete at Purdue in track and swimming and a computer brainiac who worked for IBM before going into business for himself. Jak has a brilliant mind, endless energy and an intensely honest, loyal and simple way of looking at life. Still in shape from college track, on a whim one weekend in 1984, Jak entered the Orange Bowl Marathon. Afterward he was heading for his car when he noticed several guys in blue blazers chasing after him. Jak thought he had taken too many free Gatorades or that his entry fee check had bounced. Turns out, he had qualified for the Olympic Trials, which were the same day as his wedding. "Sorry," he said, "I'm busy that day."

Since we both work at home, Jak and I spend a lot of time procrastinating together. We fly-fish. We painted a full basketball court in the street that got us in hot water with neighborhood management. We set up an elaborate wall and lighting system that transformed our turnaround into a sweet roller-hockey rink. We spent a lot of time watching *Seinfeld* reruns, bootlegged tapes of Triumph, the Insult Comic Dog, and playing guitar instead of writing computer code or sports stories.

Jak picked up on the first ring. I could hear him walking his cordless phone to his front porch where the Farson's red-brick steps serve as the neighborhood's stoop.

"Jak?"

"Dude, what's up? Everyone's asleep."

"We had problems . . . Kim started to bleed . . . really bad."

"What?"

"They rushed her into surgery . . . she's gonna be okay . . . Kim's fine . . . but . . . but . . . they couldn't get to him fast enough. To Noah."

"What do you mean?"

"He's gone, Jak. Noah's gone. He's dead."

"No way," Jak said. "When did this happen? I don't understand. Wait. We just talked to you guys a couple hours ago."

"It came on quick. Kim was in pain. There was blood. They took her away . . . that was it. They couldn't save him."

"I'm so sorry. Kimmy's okay? She's okay?"

"Kim's gonna be okay, I think. They are making sure her blood is clotting. She's out of it. I'm just kinda sitting here with her. I don't know what to do."

"Should I come over?"

If Jak had asked 1,000 times, I probably would have said no 999 times. But somehow I just knew. Kim was sleeping, and I felt too alone for my own good; I could feel myself spinning out of control. One more push, and I'd be gone.

"Yeah, ya know what? I think that might be a good idea," I said. "Yeah. Come on over, I'll be waiting for you in the hall near the nurse's station."

It was a heavy burden to place on Jak or any friend. What can you say or do in this situation? There are no magic words. Nothing's going to help. Flowers? A card? Shoot. What could he do?

Something. Anything. A lot, it turns out. People become paralyzed in these situations worrying about what it is they can do to help. They want to be perfect. But specifics don't really matter. In the end the only thing that matters is if you do *something*. Because, honestly, every card, every nice word, every cheesy bible verse, every meal, every remembrance of Noah, every ounce of compassion, every silent prayer helped.

In a few days we would get a small, simple sympathy card from Jon, an editor at ESPN, who is also a close friend of mine. (In the last few weeks of Kim's pregnancy I had changed jobs from *SI* to *ESPN The Magazine*. In fact, the last words I said to my new editor-in-chief after taking the job was, "well, my next call will be to tell you about the newest member of the ESPN family.") It was an orange note card with a sunflower on the front. At the end of his card, Jon wrote, "Spring will come again." Four words. Jon and Kim had never met. Yet those four words, on that day, gave us hope, boosted our spirits, and helped us get through another 24 hours.

Four words can make a huge difference. Like, "Should I come over?"

I didn't want to disturb Kim, so I waited for Jak out in the hallway. Minutes before he got there, a female hospital administrator, who seemed peeved that she had to deal with Noah's death at the end of her shift, walked up and, without an introduction, pointed her finger at me and said, "Hey it's you . . . good . . . you need to make some decisions."

I stood at attention. "I what?" I said.

"You need to make some decisions," she said. "You need to sign the fetal death certificate. We're gonna need to move your wife to another room. Do you want to stay on the maternity floor or go to another part of the hospital? And, we can't hold the body forever. You have to decide what to do with it?"

"Do with it?" I said, confused. "With the baby?"

"We're a hospital, okay?" She said. "We don't, uh, deal with bodies. We can give you some time to make arrangements, but at some point, yeah, you have to do something with the body."

She waited a second then added, "Or we will."

That made it sound like Noah was going out with the morning trash. I was baffled. Did I want to scream in this woman's face or collapse into her big, meaty arms? "You're the ones who killed him, you deal with the body" was one of the responses running through my head, when from behind the woman I could see Jak loping down the hall.

"Excuse me," I said, walking away to meet Jak.

For the next couple hours Jak just hung out. I first went over everything that had happened, and I told him all about Noah. But we didn't figure out the answers. We didn't even try. We talked about sports and other stuff. We also went long stretches without saying a word. Jak didn't say much. He never really does. But he gave me someone to vent to and bounce things off of rather than just letting them rattle dangerously around inside my head.

Leaning against the windowsill near the elevators, a nurse heard us talking about the issue involving Noah's body. I was at a total loss. "I can help you with that," she said. "I can give you some options and information about funeral homes." We followed her to the nurses station and she gave me a photocopied page with names and numbers of funeral homes. She even pointed out one that she had heard good things about. All I had to do to, she assured me, was make the calls in the morning, get a feel for which one I might prefer, then ask them to come pick up Noah's body. They would take it from there.

There was a matronly mixture of confidence and empathy in that woman. She leaned across the counter and quietly asked me if I had a camera. Of course, I said. "Well," she responded, "one of the things you might want to consider is taking pictures of your baby."

"Oh I don't know," I shrugged.

"I know right now that might seem strange," she continued. "But it's been my experience, one thing parents come to regret later is not having pictures of their baby."

"I . . . I don't know," I said.

"Try this," she continued. "You don't have to develop them. You can throw the film away later if you want. But this way, at least, you'll have the option."

"Okay . . . okay," I said. "I think I'll do that."

"They're gonna move your wife to her permanent room in a bit," said the nurse. "And while they're doing that, I'll come by and take you over so you can take some pictures of your son."

"Thanks, thanks so much," I said.

As cold and thoughtless as madam administrator had been, this nurse had been even more helpful and compassionate. It was a pattern that would repeat itself many times in the next year: everything bad seemed to be balanced by something equally as good; every bit of confusion was offset by some moment of clarity; every moment of darkness would reveal some glimmer of hope.

Before leaving, Jak poked his head in to see Kim. She saw him at the door and waved him in closer. Choked up, all Jak managed to get out was "We love you, Kimmy." Kim was awake now, and we needed to use that window to discuss a few things. So after a quick goodbye, Jak was gone. The plan now was for Teresa to come back to the hospital in a few hours to sit with Kim while I worked my way through the list of funeral homes.

Jak's work, however, was not even close to being done. He had to tell his kids what had happened. He had to tell our neighbors and phone our friends. I also asked him to clean the house out of baby references and to start with the Noah flag I had so arrogantly hung out in front of our home before leaving for the hospital.

Back at her bedside, I spared Kim the stuff about Noah's body and the death certificate. I did ask her about switching floors. And Kim said, no, she didn't want to retreat to some other part of the hospital where, we both agreed, it would feel like we were hiding. She was a mom, and she wanted to stay with the moms. I asked her about the photos, and she said I should take some pictures of the boy if I felt up to it.

When the time came, the nurse led me into something that looked like a supply closet off the side of the nursery. In some of the pictures, in fact, you can see the labels across the fronts of the drawers near his bassinet. I said, "Hi" to him and touched his cheek with the back of my hand. I bent over and kissed his forehead. His body would be gone in a few days, but at the time, it felt like he would be with us forever. I tucked the blanket under his chin. I backed away. With hands shaking and no idea whatsoever if the pics were in focus or if the camera was even right-side-up, I shot half a roll. Thank goodness. The nurse, who had gently guided me through the whole thing, was right. Other than a box of keepsakes that the nurses collected for us—footprints, hair clippings, his blanket and his hospital bracelet—we have come to cherish those photos above all else.

By the time Kim was moved to her permanent room, the sun had already begun to turn the sky pink and orange. The nurses had placed a special note card on our door—a floating leaf with a single drop of water in it (whatever that means)—to signify that our child had died. Although it didn't always work. The first anesthesiologist to check up on Kim popped into the room and, with a big goofy grin on his face, congratulated "the happy new parents!"

We just stared at him.

"How'd everything go last night? Everything okie-dokie?"

We just stared at him.

"Guuuuuureat."

More staring.

"You guys just have a super day."

On his way out the door, the guy nearly knocked over Teresa. Kim was so glad to see her she began to weep. In the three years since we moved in, Kim and Teresa had become like sisters. Teresa is a model mother and one of the most deeply spiritual people we know. Yet in a world filled with the shallow, hypocritical cacophony of Bible-bangers, she is an anomaly: she has a strong faith while remaining open-minded and nonjudgmental. She also has a keen, wicked sense of humor. Teresa's hair was still wet, and she seemed physically ill with grief. We all embraced, then sat and talked softly for a while. She had only brought one thing with her: her Bible. All night Teresa had been flipping through the pages, unable to find a simple solution to Noah's death. Although she held that book tightly in her arms and close to her heart, Teresa never opened it. She didn't know the answers, the gesture seemed to say, but she knew they were somewhere close. "I don't know what to read or what to turn to or what to say," she said, lowering the book back to her lap, unopened. "Except we all love you. God loves you."

I can give Teresa no greater compliment than to say, as fragile as my wife was at that moment, I felt perfectly fine leaving Kim in her company. I grabbed my list and excused myself to the empty room across the hall. I dialed the first funeral home, the one that seemed closest to our house. By the scratchy voice and thick, southern accent on the other end of the line, it sounded like I had dialed Yosemite Sam's Funeral Home. "Yessir," said the man, after a lengthy pitch, interrupted by a hacking cough, "we'll come fix yer son, Noer, up real nice and such. It ain't gonna be no problem. You just leave it all up to us now, yahear?" I believe he then asked for my VISA number. I told him I'd have to think about it and hung up the phone without ever saying goodbye.

Then I remembered the funeral home the nurse recommended. I dialed the number. They were courteous and informative. They patiently answered all of my questions. Yes, they said, they would come get Noah as soon as I gave them the okay. We could meet later to work out the details and the costs. Now, though, was a time to be with my wife. I hired them on the spot. And a few hours later, when my cell phone rang, it was William, our funeral director, informing me that our son was now in their care. We made an appointment to meet on Saturday to work out the rest of the plans.

By then night had turned fully into day. Friends had begun to arrive on their way to work. They brought us a never-ending parade of cards, tears, and support. For most of the morning we barely had a moment alone—and I think that was their plan. It was exhausting retelling the story. But it helped to verbalize it. Each time it lost some of its sting. Every new face, every hug, every tear was comforting. Knowing that I'm a junk food addict, my buddy Mark brought us Burger

King. Even Kim's friend, whose sole response was, "this sucks" helped a little. I hadn't made the connection until that very moment: that people would be expressing their love for Noah in the only way they could now: through grief. I had never considered it to be such a pure expression of love.

The wave of friends tapered off a bit after a few hours, and we knew that later that morning our families would begin to arrive. In the time being, the nurse asked us if we wanted to see Noah one more time before the funeral home picked him up.

"Sure," we said halfheartedly. "Sure."

The nurse said she would halt any visitors until we gave her the okay. We both held Noah again, but only for a short time. Something was different. He was cold now. He had lost much of his color. And even though we held him close, he seemed to be a thousand miles away. In a short time we called the nurse to come and get him.

I would have taken him back myself, but I was a bit gun-shy about venturing back into the hallway. A little earlier I had bumped into a couple from our birth class near the elevators. She was in a wheelchair with her new son in her arms. He was behind her, pushing a cart full of flowers, gifts, and balloons. They were both sporting huge, toothy grins, and they yelled out a big happy "HEY!" in unison when they saw me. I was trying to leave a voice mail for a friend at work who had called wanting news about Noah. I hung up the phone. "Hi" . . . I said. "Congratulations." That's all I got out before my eyes starting filling with water. I waved. I swallowed hard. I shook my head. I tried the best I could. Honestly, I didn't want their kid. I wanted Noah. But the contrast and the thought of how close we had been to that outcome just cracked me in half. I held up my hand as if to say, Stop, don't come any closer. The nurse pushing the wheelchair bent over and whispered something to the woman. They just bit their tongues, nodded politely and pushed past me in a hurry, as if their baby could catch something from me. I had been marked: father of dead baby. That was something that would take some getting used to.

Back inside Kim's room, I could breathe again. I was putting the cell phone back into my duffel bag when the earrings I had purchased for Kim fell out onto the ground.

"Are those for me?"

"Yeah," I said, "Sorry . . . you weren't supposed to see them."

"Why not?"

"I don't know, I thought they'd make you sad. Like you'd think they were a consolation prize or something."

"Can I see 'em?" she asked.

"Sure." I opened the gray velvet box and showed the stones to Kim. For once I had not skimped. She smiled softly. I could tell what she was thinking. "You wanna wear 'em?" I asked. She nodded. Why the hell not, right? She had earned them. That's my Kimmy. It was her own little act of defiance. She had already begun to go against the grain. No one would tell her how she was supposed to act as a grieving mother. I leaned over and gave her a hug and helped her put the earrings on.

A bit later there was a knock and then the door to Kim's room barely crept open. It was Kim's family: Janie, Ed, and Kristen. Karen and Jason would be arriving later from Chicago. They paused at the door, taking a deep breath like someone about to swim underwater, and then they fell into the room, breaking their collapse against us with big, hearty, tearful hugs. While still holding hands, they spread out around Kim's bed and fell to their knees in prayer.

Kim and I had always wondered about the balancing act between our families. Mine was too sappy, too heart-on-the-sleeve, too touchy feely and Kim's was too guarded, too quiet, too restrained. This was the most emotion I had ever seen Kim's family express. I was relieved and touched. Kim needed this. We both did.

When Kim was an infant, her birth-mother, Kathleen, died of pancreatic cancer. From diagnosis to death took less than 9 months. Faced with the unimaginably horrific challenge of grieving his new wife while trying to raise two young girls, Kim's dad, a doctor with a new practice, did the only thing he could: he buried much of his sorrow with his wife. Although the families stayed in touch, Kim's mother's name was never spoken. Kim, in fact, barely knew even the tiniest details about her. She had only a few pictures. No anecdotes or keepsakes. She wasn't even certain of her full name. Yet out of respect for her father and Janie, who married Ed when Kim was nine (and quickly became the woman Kim happily calls mom) she never asked. But as Kim got closer to being a mother herself, naturally, the questions about her birth-mom haunted her.

Each individual, I was quickly learning, is the ultimate authority when it comes to deciding how it is they need to grieve the death of a loved one. I don't know the whole story, and I don't pretend to even understand a fraction of what Ed went through, but if that was the way he needed to act to survive, so be it. Still, I can't help but think that our eventual open, inclusive and straightforward approach to grieving Noah was, in one way or another, a deliberate reversal of the way things were done with Kim's mom. We were both worried how that would go over with Kim's family.

The minute I saw them in her hospital room, it hit me: we were not going to grieve for Noah by ourselves and in a vacuum. No. It wouldn't be that easy. Everything associated with Noah's death would first get filtered through our families, their history, and all of the deep-seated and intertwined issues we all had long before Noah ever came into the picture. Noah's death would significantly change my relationship with every member of my family.

My younger brother, Bryan, was a perfect example. The news left him hurt and confused, and he would leave it a mystery up until the very last second whether or not he would show up for Noah's funeral. Bryan was a preteen when my parents divorced and therefore took the brunt of the emotional turbulence. Since then, he seems to have spent the majority of the last 20 years punishing himself and the rest of the family for that experience. When Dad reached him, Bryan said his job tending bar would keep him in Cincinnati until the weekend. (Bill and Laura were already on their way. My other brother Greg, a sales rep who is two years my senior, and his wife, Trish, a director of a social-services clinic, were flying in from Los Angeles.) To help get him to the funeral, my parents bought Bryan a plane ticket. But he missed that flight in Cincinnati and had to drive to Columbus to catch another plane.

He called once while circling on the Columbus outerbelt looking for the airport. He later called Kim's hospital room directly to express to her what a hassle it all had become for him. Bryan's travel plans were consuming everyone's time and energy. And his behavior after Noah's death would forever alter our relationship.

Ed, though, seemed willing to meet us halfway. He was more open and emotional than I had ever seen him. In subtle ways, I think he was telling Kim that he wished he had been able to be more open about Kathleen's death. And his willingness to change, even a little, in order to ease our pain just blew me away. It meant everything to Kim—to both of us.

Ed was also tireless in his research into Noah's death. Every time I went into the hallway for something, he was grilling another doctor or nurse. And because we trusted him so much, his medical conclusions gave us a great deal of peace regarding Noah's death. Like everyone we were close with, Ed could have gone either way. But he became a positive force in our healing because he was willing to do it our way—and not his. That was an incredible gift.

Most of the time, the people I thought would be of great support and comfort never quite came through, and the family members I never even considered were the ones who helped me the most. Ed and I are fundamentally different in almost every way. I had always believed that we had two very different ideas of what it is to be a man. Yet Ed's verbal support after Noah died, along with the notes he wrote, were some of the most touching, inspirational words anyone ever offered me.

A week after Noah died he wrote:

> A famous writer, I think it was Hemingway, Dave will probably
> know, said, "Courage is grace under pressure." Both of you have
> shown more courage than I could ever imagine. . . . We will never
> know why Noah could not live but we do know that everyone did
> everything possible and that he did not suffer. I have a grandson who
> will always be perfect and will now be in the hands of God and
> the many wonderful persons who have gone before him. . . . When I
> think of Noah's death I will not remember grief and tears but the
> wonderful love and tenderness that I saw. I hope by remembering
> these things I will become a better man, father and grandfather . . .
> I believe with all my heart that should you ever think to have
> another child that there is no biological or genetic reason this
> would ever happen again. . . . Remember that love will eventually
> overcome grief, that laughter will overcome tears but the memory
> of your Noah will always be there. . . . Dave: the greatest consolation
> that I have as a grandfather and father with regard to Kim is
> that you are her husband. You give her strength and she returns it
> to you. Please take good care of yourself and also the one we both
> love so much. I know you will . . . Ed.

In the end, I guess Ed wasn't quite as cold and shallow as I had
thought him to be, and I think he realized I wasn't quite the goofball
he had once thought me to be. Our new connection was a blessing,
but also still something of a shame since it took Noah's death for his
father and grandfather to see each other more clearly. But the truth is,
none of us ever truly change unless we are forced to by adversity.

After the rest of Kim's family left the room, Ed stayed behind for a
bit. He stood at the foot of Kim's bed in silence until his face became
red and twisted with tears. Ed is not a big guy by any means, but
he works very hard to create a presence much larger than his physical
appearance. That was one of the few times he let us see him as vulnerable or frail.

"I've been through something like this—Kim you know," he said.
"And I just want you to know . . . you can get through this . . . you will
get through this . . . you will smile again . . . you will love again and
be happy again . . . you two will be stronger for this . . . I know . . . and, if
you want, you will have children again . . . I just want you to know . . .
you're gonna be okay."

Ed and Kim embraced. Even the unspoken acknowledgment of her
birth-mother's death was a huge relief for her. Ed then bolted for the
door to catch up with the rest of the family. "I always thought I was
supposed to teach you guys what it is to be strong," he said over his
shoulder, "but it turns out you guys are the ones teaching me."

I put out my hand. Now, like I said, Ed's a no-nonsense guy. He's a handshake man, pure and simple. I think at our wedding he went completely nuts and patted me on the back. But that time he brushed past my extended hand and gave me a big old bear hug.

## CHAPTER 5

# Hundred Bucks Off Your Fourth Plot

In our hospital room, I had fixed it so that my reclining chair served like an attachment to Kim's bed. That way, at night we could be close enough to hold hands and whisper back and forth. Wide awake before dawn on Saturday, I peeled myself away and went to the black duffel bag in the corner of the room. Deep down in the corner of the bag was the blue and white striped cotton jumper we had planned to dress Noah in for his trip home. I looked over my shoulder to make sure Kim was still asleep, then I brought the outfit slowly to my face sniffing that creamy, clean smell; missing the boy terribly. I dug deeper into the bag looking for his socks and his tiny white sneakers. Then I carefully transferred the entire outfit into my backpack before heading in to Kim's bathroom for a long, hot shower.

Afterwards I lifted my finger to the mirror above the sink and wrote Noah's name in the steam. I stood there for a long time examining how my zombified face reflected through the curves and corners in the letters of his name. The night before, when the rest of the family had made it into town, we came up with a plan: Laura was to stay with Kimmy while Mom, Dad, Bill and I made Noah's funeral arrangements.

I leaned over Kim's bed and kissed her on the forehead. She reached her arms up to hug me. I slipped my face deep down into her pillow. A part of me wanted so badly just to stay there.

"Good luck honey, I love you," she said into my ear. "Be strong."

"I love you too, Kimmy," I replied. "I'll be fine."

She was back asleep before I reached the door.

I was hoping everyone at home would still be asleep as well. But my mom was up, just standing in the kitchen nursing a cup of coffee, staring across the room into the woods behind our house. I walked by her into the laundry room. I set Noah's outfit down and waited for the iron to heat up. On that day of seemingly impossible tasks, I knew the first one would be the hardest.

"Do you need something ironed?" Mom asked.

"No thanks, ma."

"Just set it out honey, I'll iron it."

"I'm okay, ma, really. Thanks."

"It's no problem, I'll do it, just show me what it is."

"Mom, no. Okay? No. I'm fine."

From the beginning, everyone wanted to spare me from the details of that day. Kim wanted me to hand off the tasks to her dad. Bill offered to make all the arrangements, come get our approval and then finalize the deal. Dad had asked several times to pay for the whole thing. Mom, I could tell, was up to meet me when I got home. Just a few days earlier, the idea of giving that job to someone else would have seemed like a smart move. To the outside world, bereavement rituals seem superfluous, ostentatious and, well, a bit creepy even— until someone you love dies. Then you begin to understand their impor- tance and the comfort they bring. The minute that chore became a necessity, it took on a much deeper meaning for me. Kim carried Noah for nine months (and then some)—she nourished him, felt him hiccup, sang to him, rocked him to sleep, bathed with him and scolded him whenever he'd wedge the heel of his foot into her ribs. She was with him when he died. As for me, making these arrangements would be one of the few tangible things I would ever get to do for my son. I was determined to do it all, to do it well and, in some small way, honor Noah.

"Have you eaten?" mom asked, poking her head into our laundry room.

"No. I'm not hungry."

"You gotta eat."

"Not hungry, mom," I said, shielding Noah's clothes with my body.

"Okay. Well, whatcha doing in there? Let me do that for you."

"Mom . . . I'm ironing his clothes . . . Noah's clothes. They got wrinkly in the bag, okay? I don't want him all wrinkly. I don't want Kimmy to see him all wrinkly and wonder why I didn't iron his outfit, okay?"

Mom just smiled a soft, understanding smile, turned and left me alone. It's hard to describe, but she has always loved me perfectly, but from a distance.

It was hard to be away from Kim, but it felt good to be inside our home. As the sun began to light up the front of our house, I found strength and energy from the subtle, warm affection of my family. I was also grateful for the way they picked up on my businesslike approach. Early on in this process I recognized that people were taking their cues from us. As counterintuitive as it might have seemed, we had to lead, because even the people closest to you are paralyzed by not only their own shock and grief, but by fear and ignorance as well. They would rather do nothing than risk doing the wrong thing.

So if we talked about Noah's death, they joined in. If we avoided it, they did too. If we wept, they teared up. And if we were strong, they were strong. There were dozens of important decisions to be made that day and being weepy and spineless would only make it more painful. This was going to be the most significant thing I ever did for my son, and I didn't want to be blubbering my way through it. This was for Noah, not me. So I kept my game face on: steely stare, stiff back, clenched jaw. *Just hold yourself together today, for Noah, for your son. Be a man. And if you don't feel it, fake it.*

On the way across town in Kim's silver Taurus, my parents warned me that funerals, coffins and cemetery plots can get outrageously expensive. And they were right. As if survivors have any choice. It's not like you can wait for gravestones to go on sale. Bill, always the G-man, was particularly keen to what he perceived as a racket. "We're not gonna, you know, let things get out of hand with the costs of stuff," said Bill. "Just, you know, be reasonable. What you spend is not a reflection on how you feel about Noah. Sometimes they try and make you think that. It's shameless, but it happens. We'll help. We'll all help make decisions, okay?"

Dad offered, again, to pay for everything. I turned around to face my parents in the back seat. They are divorced but remain friendly. Mom's boyfriend is Claude. Dad remarried a lovely woman named Becky who has turned out to be perhaps the best influence on his life. "I appreciate the offer," I said, "but we're fine."

"We're his parents," I told them. (I loved how that sounded.) "This is something we'll do for our son."

It was also a great relief when we saw the funeral home for the first time. Less than twelve hours after Noah died, I had picked that place based upon an ad in the yellow pages, a nurse's recommendation and a 10-minute phone conversation. That was one of the few things I could control about Noah's death—the manor in which he would rest in perpetuity—and I wanted it to be done right, to feel right. I wanted things to go well.

The facility was actually quite impressive, full of Roman columns and new carpet, mahogany and marble. William, our funeral director, met us as we came through the door and swiftly escorted us to a conference room where we sat around a large, polished wood table. William was a quiet, proper and forthright man with a department-store suit and a banker's haircut. He was compassionate without being phony. He listened. He led without being condescending. He always waited for us to ask his opinion, but when we did he was straight-forward and spoke with an economy of words backed by experience and confidence. It was all very businesslike and efficient. William made the process as professional and painless as it could have possibly been. I liked him.

He answered my first question, in fact, before I even had to ask. Indeed, that morning they had picked up Noah's body from the hospital and transported him there without incident.

"So he's here?" I asked.

"Yes, he's here."

I reached into my backpack and handed over his outfit.

"Fine," said William. "Very good."

We then talked in general terms about how Kim and I wanted Noah's day to go. Then we began the tedious work of writing his obituary. Bill took notes the entire time, keeping track of the minutia of names and details I was sure to forget. As we went about listing all the imme-diate family members, I was taken aback by the number of people effected by Noah's death—the grief radiating out from center like ripples in a pond.

When that was done, William left to type up the form and locate some contracts. We all took a short break before the next task: looking at coffins. That was the only time I became melancholy. I was on autopilot trying to complete the day's work, and the short break gave me a moment to actually think about what I was doing. No one can ever be prepared for something like that. That goes without saying, I guess. But as a young, married man, I was especially naive. I mean, my life had been a cakewalk up to that point. I had certainly never dealt with death. My parents are healthy. My peers had been untouched by tragedy. I knew nothing of real grief, mourning or bereavement. That had changed. Sitting there inside the funeral home with a moment to contemplate the situation, my brain was like a computer that had been given too much to process: it locked up. "Is this happening?" I mumbled to myself, shaking my bowed head. "Am I making funeral arrangements for my son?"

Mom leaned in and put her hand on top of mine. "You alright honey?" she asked.

"I just . . . I just can't believe this is happening . . . ," I said looking up at them. "Are we doing this? We're really doing this? I . . . I . . . can't be burying a child. I can't."

Bill came around, and the two of us walked to the bathroom where I splashed some cold water on my face. I got myself back together in a few minutes. By the time we returned, William was waiting for us at the conference table.

On such short notice, he explained, options regarding the coffin would be limited. The choice was between something that looked like a wicker laundry hamper and a glossy white enamel number that resembled a miniature casket with airbrushed faux gold corners. A plain, normal looking wood casket would take several days to deliver, I was told. Painting over the gold corners, which looked like they had been sprayed on by a guy sporting a mullet and working a t-shirt booth in Myrtle Beach wasn't an option either. We decided to just drape some nice white flowers over the corners.

I signed all the necessary forms and paid for everything with one swipe of my American Express. (And for maybe the first time, I truly appreciated my paycheck.) I was given a nice, neat forest-green folder with all my paperwork, including an 11-page catalog of the funeral home's services, a pink carbon from my contract for Funeral and Burial Services for "infant Noah Fleming" and an itemized receipt (Death Certificates 5 @ $3.00 . . . $15.00 . . . Monticello Children's Vault $650.) The coffin, I discovered, also came with its own dignified, gold leaf certificate of warranty with a stamp of approval from the Casket & Funeral Supply Association of America (CFSA).

Surreal, it was all absolutely surreal. And it had only just begun.

All that was left to do now was scout cemeteries based on the three requests I could come up with on such short notice. We wanted Noah's plot to be near our home since we planned on spending a lot of time there. It needed to be in a quiet and rural setting; and in a place where we could erect a headstone, since I didn't really care for those ground-level plaques with the fake flower urns. William quickly compiled a list of three such places. We shook hands and were off.

The first "cemetery" was, quite literally, an abandoned lot at the end of a street. The office was a trailer; the grounds were a mixture of dirt, weeds and garbage. We circled the place three times, double checking our directions to make sure we were in the right place. We were. We didn't even bother to stop and get out. I just shook my head, and Bill gunned the Taurus to the next place. It couldn't possibly be as bad.

It was. This is the honest-to-God's truth: "Cemetery" No. 2 shared a dirt driveway with a biker bar. I swear. Although it was barely lunchtime, the bikes were lined up like shiny, chromed-plated dominos the full length of the brown clapboard building. The only discernable sign that this was in fact a cemetery was the rusted, red gate and the dozen or so scatter-shot graves. I half expected to see old rotting couches, a pickup truck or two up on cinderblocks and a pack of wild dogs. There were four mouths agape inside our car as, once again, we looped through the property without even bothering to slow down.

As we waited for traffic to clear so Bill could get back out onto the highway, no one said a word. There was a choice to be made, however. It was subtle, but significant.

It was, after all, funny. No, hilarious. A cemetery/biker bar? I mean, that must be one freakin' tough place if it has a cemetery out back, right? "Hey, if you get in a knife fight and die here at Redneck BillyJoeBob's, we'll bury you before last call." This was an absolute classic. There really was no way around it. Funny is funny, I don't care, even if you're out shopping for your son's eternal resting spot.

The choice, then, was whether or not to acknowledge it—to go ahead and have a quick chuckle or to stuff it down and stay sour and silent. It might seem trivial now, but it was major. For starters it helped reinforce my growing notion that I should just feel what I felt: to never force myself to be sad or to fake a smile. If I felt like crying when everyone else was happy, I should let 'er rip, and if I felt like laughing when everyone around me was sad, so be it. I was just going to feel what I felt. Period. It was also a chance for me to take charge of my own grief. I had just stumbled upon the concept that grief is like art: we all interpret and process it differently, and there are no wrong choices. I had to do what worked for me. The only error I could make was to conform to some preconceived notion of how I thought I was supposed to behave as the father of a dead son. Whatever path I took from that moment on, I was certain of one thing: I was not going to add to my own misery by trying to contort my emotions into what society perceives as the correct way for a man to mourn. The easiest thing in the world would have been to morph into a male cliché: stay silent and strong, show no emotion at all, stuff it all down and let it fester. That wasn't me. I grew up with three brothers in a rough-and-tumble household. I was a wrestler in college, a member of a fraternity and then a sportswriter. On some level my life had been one overtly macho endeavor after the other, so I guess I didn't feel the need to broadcast how tough I was after Noah died. I felt free to just be myself.

If we are all different and unique, then why would we presume to grieve in the same way—like sad robots? The only rule at that point was there are no rules. In such a vulnerable, shaky state, the tough part would be to trust my instincts, to be myself. For me—a person who lives to laugh and to inspire others to do so—that meant if I was lucky enough, in the midst of all that crap, to find something to laugh about, hell, I was going to go ahead and let myself laugh.

The car was still in shocked silence when, out near the main road, the bazooka blast of a revving motorcycle engine turned all of our shoulders into earrings.

I couldn't hold it in anymore. A guttural burst from my throat exploded inside the car and everyone else exhaled with their own thunderous chuckle. Still shaking my head in disbelief, I said, "Someday we're gonna look back on this and it's gonna be really funny, right? Ya know? Holy crap, was I seeing things?"

It may have only lasted for a few seconds, but even that short burst of laughter was enough to sustain me for the rest of the day. Whatever the effect crying was having on me—draining, exhausting, disabling— laughter had the direct opposite impact.

The respite was short-lived, however, when we realized we were quickly running out of options. The funeral was less than 24 hours away. My dad was freaking, to put it mildly. He wanted to call William and chew him out. I almost let him. Instead I dug my cell phone out of the glove box and dialed his number.

"William, this is David Fleming, we were in earlier planning my son Noah's funeral . . ."

"Yes of course, everything okay?"

"Well, no . . . these first two cemeteries are extremely unacceptable."

"I see."

"These will not work, they aren't even close. This is not good. I'm upset. We need to find an acceptable cemetery, right now."

"I'm terribly sorry," he said. "You said rural and close to your house were the two most important factors, and that's what I went on."

He was absolutely right. He sent us to the exact kind of cemetery I had requested. Hmmph. I took a deep breath which helped me stave off my first instinct: to pull out my I'm-the-father-of-a-dead-child-how-dare-you attitude and get all prickly and indignant with William. I had every right. I had an untrumpable, emotional Get Out of Jail Free card for every social situation if I wanted to use it. Was that the way I was intending to play this? Was that who I was? Was that going to be the lasting legacy of Noah's death, that I used it to get whatever I wanted? I had another choice to make.

At that moment I was reminded of a conversation Kim and I had the night before. We agreed the next few days were going to reveal our true character: not just how we responded to something so awful, but how we acted when the world was giving us the freedom to behave any way we wanted. It would define us as individuals and as a family, perhaps forever. It would be our legacy, and more importantly, Noah's as well.

We discovered that by working backwards, by asking ourselves, "Could this get any worse?" The answer was yes. We could behave in a way that when we looked back on those days, say, in 10 years, we would cringe at our behavior.

"You know what? This was my fault, William. My mistake," I told him. "Totally. So let me just try again to describe what I want. Let's just start over."

"Okay, fine."

"I want quiet. I don't want cars racing by or strip malls across the street. I want grass and trees. I want open air. I want clean. I want something that looks more like a park than a cemetery."

"How close does it have to be to your home?" William asked.

"You know what? Forget that. The setting is more important than the drive. Distance is far less a factor than atmosphere, how about that?"

"Well, the next place on your list is, I think, more what you're looking for. I have already called ahead, and they are expecting you. Why don't you drive down there and take a look, and if it's good, then go ahead and meet with the rep there. If not, call me right back, and I will begin working on other locations."

"That sounds good."

"I'm sorry this was a problem, but I think we're on the right track now."

"Me too. Me too. Thanks."

We drove south on I-85 for about 10 minutes, exited, and headed west for another few miles until we saw the green expanse and the stonewall gates. We bypassed the office and drove around inside. It was exactly right. I called William and told him we were set. We parked the car and wandered into the musty offices where we were greeted by someone who could have just walked off the set of *Six Feet Under*.

The woman I began calling Elvira wore gobs of thick, splotchy red lipstick that stuck to her teeth and discolored her coffee cup. She reeked from the hair spray used to construct her 1970s-style hair helmet. If her heels were one inch longer, her skirt cuff one inch shorter or her neckline one inch lower, it would have been inappropriate. She squinted at us from behind eyelids as narrow as coin slots. She looked like the sixth member of Twisted Sister. This women was so bizarre, I was worried about getting the giggles. That is, until she started in with the hard sell. From what I gathered, she had stayed late as a favor to William and was determined to make it worth her while. We had barely settled into our wood and burgundy leather chairs when she began hitting me with the idea that now was the ideal time to purchase plots for the entire family. One-stop grave shopping, if you will.

"This is a terrible time for you right now," she said. "But I would not be doing my job if I didn't express to you the importance of buying a place where all of you—your family—can rest together."

"I'm 33," I said, shrugging my shoulders and looking around to Bill and my parents.

"Oh Dan, you know better than anyone that . . ." she reached across the table and grabbed my hand. Her clammy skin made me jump. ". . . how you just never know. . . ."

"Uh, well, I just want to focus on finding something for my son," I said. "That's it. I don't want to talk about anything else."

Undeterred, she continued, "I've seen it a hundred times . . . and the only thing that can make something like this worse is realizing you and your wife would not be able to rest side-by-side next to your son."

I stared at her intently, hoping something would penetrate all that aerosol. "No," I said. "No thanks."

"Accidents happen, we don't know why . . . I see so many young people nowadays. . . ."

"STOP IT, please," said my dad. "I think David was very clear about what our goal was for today. We're here to find a gravesite for Noah. If you can help us with that, fine. If not, may we please see someone who could?"

Elvira nodded knowingly at Dad and, I swear, I could see her trying to calculate his age, life-expectancy and annual income. "Oh, of course, of course, how wonderful that your parents are here to help you. I just wouldn't be able to live with myself if I didn't explain all the options to you. You understand."

Finally, she opened a massive leather-bound book that had all the sections of the cemetery charted in giant graph paper. I put my finger down on a few, and we jumped back into our car to take a look. I could tell Dad was at the end of his tether. "We gotta hold it together, Dad," I said on the way toward the back of the grounds. "I know this woman is bugging you. I don't like her either. But let's just hold it together and get through this without any blowups."

"Sure honey, sure," he responded. "It's just that. . . ."

We all huffed knowingly, and I patted the old man on the back. "I know Dad, I know."

The first few areas were fine. Then we came across a plot near the back that was bordered on two sides by a thick batch of trees. There were no roads or buildings, only grass, trees, and sky. The wind rustled through the branches above us. It was peaceful. Behind where Noah's gravestone would be was a very young maple sapling. I could imagine that tree offering shelter and shade to him and his visitors. When the thought hit me that we could mark time by the growth of that tree, my mind was made up.

Pointing to the plot I said, "This is it, right here."

Mom and Dad shook their heads in agreement.

"We can come here . . . and watch . . . this tree grow," I said, choking back tears. The idea that the tree would grow, bloom, branch out, and touch the sky while Noah would remain a baby, frozen in time forever, began to hit home.

The three of us started walking back to the car, but Bill was stuck on Noah's plot. His chest began to heave. I went to him quickly and through my own swelling throat tried to convince him that everything was going to be okay. It was a mistake. I knew it right away. In retrospect, I should have left him alone for a little while longer, I should have let him dictate that moment. I hadn't given him the same freedom to feel that I expected from everyone else. Bill has always been a very emotionally guarded person and for him to break down like that was out of character, but refreshing. My rushing in made him feel self-conscious. Immediately he stood up and swallowed hard, choking off his emotions, almost kind of cursing himself for not being strong for his little brother.

Bill and I have always been close. When Dad left, Bill selflessly stepped in as the role of surrogate father. He was my high school wrestling coach. When I moved to New York flat broke, I lived with Bill and Laura for nearly two years. I was his best man and he was mine. I am the godfather of his first daughter and he was going to be Noah's. Noah's middle name, William, is an homage in large part, to Bill.

That abbreviated outburst, however, was the first and last time Bill showed any outward emotion regarding Noah. In fact, he hardly ever spoke his name again and, although we are still close, we have drifted apart since my son's death. Bill's method of grieving ended up being very different from mine. That was something that would take time for me to reconcile. I knew in my heart that no one was in any greater pain than Bill; that no one loved my son or felt more compassion for me than my oldest brother. Yet for the most part he remained silent and internal with his sorrow while I wound up going to the other extreme, naively expecting everyone to fall in line behind me. It was disconcerting, to say the least, to be on such a different wavelength from someone I was so close to at such a critical time. And this added to my growing sense of confusion, isolation, and detachment.

Something had gone terribly wrong in my life and I guess I just figured, in fairness, everything afterward would go perfectly as planned. But Bill had to stay true to himself and grieve the way he saw fit. A grief curve was forming. Some of our friends and family would never speak Noah's name. Some would talk about him all the time. Everyone else would fall somewhere in-between. With such an emotional powder keg, perhaps the toughest task ahead for our extended family was to respect and honor one-another's vastly different methods of mourning.

As I stood there watching Bill gag back his tears, I knew every relationship in my life was about to be redefined by Noah's death. Still, I was in pure survival mode now, with no choice but to draw closer to those who comforted and counseled me while pushing away everyone else, including Bill.

Like everything else, though, there was an equilibrium with my brothers. While Bill and I grew apart, Noah's death brought Greg and me closer together for maybe the first time in our lives. Growing up, we were too near in age and far too competitive to be tight. But when Noah died, we both finally dropped that baggage. Matching his chilled-out California personality, Greg was perfectly at ease speaking about Noah and our recovery. We didn't always talk about him. Just knowing that option was open to me eased my feelings of isolation. Some days Greg's support was nothing more than a voice-mail message letting us know that Noah was in his thoughts. Getting to speak Noah's name meant a lot to us, but hearing people we love and respect remember him was the kind of rare treat we could live off for weeks. In their home, Greg and Trish have always had an end table covered in pictures of their nieces and nephews. Right in the middle is a pressed flower in a frame with Noah's name on it.

Greg's just a California dude at heart. I mean that as the highest compliment. A stand-up guy with a laid-back personality. He has wild, funky curly hair. He was an actor when he first moved to Cali, and he landed parts in several commercials as well as *The Fresh Prince of Bel-Air*. Greg is the kind of guy who goes to a concert and ends up partying with the band on their tour bus. Thanks to my work we've been to many Super Bowls together (I'm still trying to pay off his bar tab at the Hyatt in Phoenix.) But I keep inviting him back because, just like with all my brothers, I'm a better version of myself when he's around. I was anxious to see him and grateful beyond words that he and Trish were, at that moment, flying across country to be with us.

Back in Elvira's office, there was more paperwork to fill out. More AMEX receipts to sign. More gold-leaf certificates. Another forest-green folder. And more of the hard sell—much more. She coyly pulled out a gift certificate from the top drawer of her desk as if she might get in trouble just for offering it to us. It was for $100 off the fourth plot when you buy the first three at full price.

I just stood up in midpitch, extended my hand across her desk and said, "Are we done? We're done. Thank you very much for your help."

The Taurus stayed silent most of the way home. I thought the day had gone well, and I was relieved. I had an odd sense of accomplishment, like I had just completed the first real adult task of my life. My actions had honored my son. That was all I cared about. Not the funeral plans or the coffin or the plot. There were three forks in the road that day: the decision to laugh at the biker burial ground, the decision not to play the grieving-father card, and the decision to console Bill so quickly. I had chosen correctly on two. It was a good start.

Back inside the hospital, I pushed open the door to Kim's room and saw her entire family surrounding her bed. The mood was light. People were smiling. Kim was sitting up.

I didn't say hello. I didn't wave. I didn't stop. I just walked straight to Kim's bed, put my arms around my wife and sunk my head, once again, deep down into her pillow.

㋡

## CHAPTER 6

# The Bathroom Summit

Kim was discharged from the hospital the following afternoon. We got her home with little incident, although she quickly grew tired and excused herself for the night. Soon thereafter everyone else headed up to bed. As the house grew quiet and dark, I went around turning off the remaining lights and locking up. Before leaving for the night, a family member put his hand on my shoulder and handed me a folded-up napkin.

"You guys really need to sleep," he said. "This will help."

Curious about the napkin, I made my way back to our bedroom and shut the door behind me. Inside were two sleeping pills. They were white and looked almost too small to have any effect. One was for Kim, I assumed, and one was for me. Tomorrow was our son's funeral, and neither of us had really slept or eaten all that much since he died two days before. The consensus among our family was that we needed sleep, even if it was drug-induced.

I looked around for Kimmy, but didn't see her in the bedroom. Instead, she had retreated deeper into our master bathroom. That place, with its tile floor, marble tub, and cream-colored walls, had become our sanctuary. Our home, the entire cul-de-sac, was overflowing with friends and relatives. Yet it was clear to Kim and me from the beginning that we were now different and in many ways alone. Don't get me wrong. The love, support, and compassion we received eased our suffering tremendously. In the end, though, Kim and I were the only one's who truly understood what we were going through.

The bathroom had become our quiet, private place to sneak off to when we needed to get away from everyone; get away to a place where we felt comfortable to talk, laugh, cry, or scream. There was a physical draw to that spot. It felt like a cozy, soundproof clubhouse. People did not hesitate to walk into our first-floor bedroom to check on us, but no one would dare barge into our bathroom. In there we were safe. The low ceiling and all the corners seemed to hug and support us. The smallness and plainness of the bathroom helped reduce the world to a manageable size with no surprises. Sometimes, when things got even worse, we retreated into Kim's walk-in closest.

Kim was sitting on the marble ledge next to the tub just staring into the mirror and dabbing at her wet, swollen eyes. Over her shoulder on the towel rack above the garden tub was her black maternity swim suit. During her pregnancy, one of the ways Kim loved to beat the heat and cheat gravity was to jump in a nearby pool. Noah loved the water too. Anytime after he took a dip with his mom, you could feel him kicking for joy underwater and throughout the rest of the day.

I smiled at Kim, closing the door behind me. "Hey Nord," I said, "look what I got . . . sleeping pills. Check it out."

"What?" Kim said, sitting up.

She looked into my palm then back up at me.

"Let me see. Should we take 'em?"

"I dunno," I said. "What do you think?"

"Will they knock us out?"

"You know me Kimmy, I take this, and I may sleep right through my son's funeral."

There was a deeper meaning to the joke. I was hoping we'd be on the same page with this one. My gut told me that was a watershed moment in this process. That was our *Matrix* moment. Red pill or blue? Harsh reality or safe fantasy? Do we take the pills, float off to a drug-induced sleep, don some thick dark shades for the funeral, and begin an end-around pattern with the grief? Or do we flush the pills and confront it all head-on? Do we run or fight? Do we take our own route on this rough road or the one prescribed for us?

Kim was way ahead of me. We would deal with it like every other challenge we had faced up to that point: head-on and hand-in-hand. Besides, it had been 48 hours since Noah died, and we were both just bursting with things we wanted to talk about, ask and share with each other. We weren't trying to figure it all out that night or come to grips with everything. That would take a long, long time if it ever happened at all. What we wanted was to start the process, to deal with the overpowering initial feelings and questions that had bubbled up since Noah died. The anger. Questions of blame. Confusion. The search for a reason. God's role. Our role. Where we thought Noah was now. And, if we were lucky, some tiny hint of hope. Eventually we'd get to the really heavy stuff. Right then we just needed to get that boulder moving up the hill.

"So let's flush 'em," she said with a raised eyebrow, like we were disposing of evidence.

"Yeah," I said, "let's flush 'em together."

We squeezed into the tiny toilet closet. The napkin and the pills were in the palm of my right hand, which I ceremoniously held over the commode. Kim gave me a quick nod, and I turned over my hand. The pills dropped out first, barely disturbing the water, then the napkin fluttered down on top of them. Kim reached over and sent them away with the push of the handle. Then we high-fived.

At that moment, we'd already accomplished 90% of what we needed to do that night. By flushing those pills, we had made our most important choice: we would control the grief, not the other way around. We had taken control. We would face this thing head on. We would take the tough road. We would commit to the work. Together.

Kim went back to the ledge next to the tub, and I sat on the floor facing her, touching her toes with mine. The first thing she talked about, through what seemed to be a never-ending stream of tears, was how sad it made her to think about all the father/son things Noah and I would never get to do. I was worried that when she had said sorry to me in the hospital after Noah died, that she was somehow blaming herself—which I wouldn't allow. But that's not what she meant. She was sorry that a father would never get to backpack through Europe with his son. She was sorry we would never get to burp the alphabet together, argue over *The Catcher in the Rye* or watch *Seinfeld* for hours on end.

Kim's stomach was still draining from surgery. The welts where the skin staples had gone in were still red and irritated. Noah had been ripped away from her, meaning the woman who had given birth to her and the child she had given birth to had both been taken away. But it was so typical of her to put that aside and think of others first. I couldn't be like her, but I needed to try.

I reached out both my arms and took her hands in mine. "When I called your dad after Noah died, one of the first things he said to me was how hard this was going to be on our marriage," I said. "At the time I thought that was such a weird thing to say."

"I know," said Kim.

"But I've heard that now a bunch of times. About some, like, huge percentage of people who get divorced after a child dies. I don't know. Doesn't make sense to me. But it scares me."

Kim nodded, "Me too."

I shook her hands up and down, "I just . . . I just don't see how this could harm us. I know it's gonna change us, right? But it won't harm us. I know it won't. We will get through this. . . ."

"You're the only thing I have left," Kimmy said.

"I won't ever give up," I told her. It sounds like a goofy cliché, I know, but at the time, just making the promise to never give up seemed like a monumental commitment. Because a huge part of me did want to give up, and that scared me to shivers. But now I couldn't. I had promised Kimmy. Many of the things I once guessed defined me as a man—my job stature, my physical strength, my possessions, my toughness—turned out to be absolutely worthless in the face of real crisis. What did I have left? What could I really count on? What defined me as a man? Love. The love I had for my son and my wife, the kind of love that prodded me to go on. Love for God. Love for life. Beyond that it wasn't about who I loved, but more so, who I was blessed enough to have love me. My son. My wife. My family and my friends.

I exhaled and shook my head trying to stave off the tears. There were always long pauses of silence after each bit of conversation now because, literally, we were making it up as we went along. So far I knew Noah's funeral was the next day and that we had each other. Other than that, I was lost. Confused. Clueless. Scared shitless. Angry. Navigating the days after Noah died felt like trying to put a jigsaw puzzle together in the dark. I was frightened of turning the lights on and seeing exactly what I had created so far.

"I don't know what to do," I confessed, throwing my hands up in the air. "I don't know what to do."

"What do you mean?" Kim asked.

"Well, like where do we start with all this? What do we do? What do we turn to?"

Kim didn't answer right away. I liked that because, instead of feeding each other bull, if we didn't have an answer, we didn't say anything. Long, silent pauses would become a big part of our lives.

Finally, I sat up and just blurted out, "How are we supposed to handle this?"

As if she had anticipated my question, Kim responded calmly, "All I know is that we still have each other. And I love you."

She was right. I was looking for a complicated answer when, as usual, the solution was simple and right in front of my face: us. Noah's death had been like a flash flood; it swept away everything superfluous in our life. All we had was what we could hold onto: each other. And if that was all we had left, it was plenty.

"What I don't get," Kim said, "is how people can say to us, 'God only gives you what you can handle.'"

"Uh huh."

"If God thinks we can handle this," Kim continued, ". . . if he took Noah from us because he thinks we're strong, then I want to get off this list. Put me on the weak list."

I shook my head violently in agreement, reaching for her Kleenex. That saying used to make so much sense. All of life's little refrigerator magnets and bumper stickers used to seem so brilliant. Now they all sounded like nursery rhymes. Nothing made sense anymore. Mostly because when Noah died, so did everything we used to believe in. Everything changed. We could no longer be certain of anything. The worst part was when it felt like we were spiraling out of control, being swept away by this flash flood, there were no beliefs or sayings or ideas to bring us back. I was a 33-year-old emotional infant. We were starting over, and the task itself was so daunting, it made us dizzy.

We both felt untethered: from God, the world, our faith, love, the future—all the biggies. None of it made sense anymore. I thought about trying to dig the pills out of the toilet.

Instead, the first thing we proposed during our bathroom summit was a sort of emergency list of things to believe in. While we were getting our feet back under us, we needed some things to hold on to, stuff we understood to be true no matter how confused or weary we were or what other horrible thoughts might be swirling in our heads.

"The most important thing is we have each other," said Kimmy. "This could be so much worse right now."

"I know . . . I know," I said.

Kim was trying to be gentle, to tiptoe into this issue, but what she meant was it wasn't all about us. It wasn't about how sad we were or how sorry everyone should feel for us. It was mostly about Noah. We needed to think about him first of all. He's the one who died. He's the one we needed to honor. He's the one who suffered the most. He's the one who gave up the most. He's the one who will be watching. Noah should be first. We're his parents, and parents put their kids first.

"He's our son," is all Kim had to say.

"Yeah . . . "

"He's our son, and I don't want this to all be about sadness," Kim said.

I hadn't really thought of it like that. Probably because it seemed so goddamned unfair. We were coming at the whole parenthood thing backwards. We had been given all the responsibilities and pain first with none of the profound joy, love, or growth. We got screwed is what it amounts to. But what Kim was saying is that it didn't absolve us of our duty. If anything, Noah's death gave us even more responsibility.

"We're the only ones who knew Noah," Kim continued. "Which means the only way everyone else will know him is through us and how we act." That was revolutionary to me, and the idea acted like an emotional U-turn. Society had given us *carte blanche* as grieving parents, and I was oh so tempted to snatch it up and run with it. But what Kim was saying was that I was in fact accountable and duty-bound to the most important person in our world right then: our son. I had thought giving up totally was an available option to me after Noah died. After what the world had done to me, who cares, right?

Noah does.

That's what Kim was saying. She knew what she was doing by appealing to the "guy" in me. She was giving me someone to fight for: my son. And the shame of dishonoring or embarrassing him scared me far more than facing up to his death.

"This is another one of those stupid sports clichés, but I think it's true," I said, trying to add onto what Kim had started. "Anyone can be a good person when things are great—that's easy. Anyone can be nice and believe in God and have faith and peace and all that when they have everything they want. But the true test of who we are is what we're like when something really bad happens."

Would we crumble? Would we lash out at everyone? Would we change? Would we become bitter and sad? Who we really are was about to come out. That was going to be the true test of our character; of our marriage; of our entire lives.

Kim's demeanor changed while I talked. Her eyes dried a bit. Her posture straightened. She was responding to my approach. That made me feel better. I wanted to do anything that would help her. And she, in turn, was nodding her encouragement back to me like a parent getting a wobbly child to walk to them for the first time. "More," her eyes said, "more. Go on. What else? Say it, Dave. Get there. You can do it."

"So this is the greatest challenge of our lives and how we act will define us for the rest of our lives?" I asked.

Nodding, Kim said, "And the only way people will know him is through us."

Twisting her tissue into a tight ball, Kim said one of the first cards she got from a friend had a handwritten note that said someday we would make great parents. "We're parents now," she said angrily. "Haven't we given up more than any parent has?" The thing is, when you decide to have kids, you accept it all—the good and the bad. We agreed to this whether we knew it or not. We just never imagined it. But who does? No one ever mentions this to you when you announce you're going to start a family. No one ever says, "Oh the sleepless nights, the poopy diapers and . . . the chance your child might die and destroy your entire life."

"And as parents," Kim went on, "aren't we supposed to want what's best for our kids, no matter what?"

"I guess," I said. We both knew what she meant. Heaven. If we really were parents, then we should be happy that Noah was in the best place possible. We believed in heaven. We believed Noah was there. And that he wouldn't suffer. Somehow, though, that didn't make us jump for joy. Kimmy smiled through big drops of tears that looked like water overflowing a gutter during a rain storm. We both giggled at our Hallmark moment. It was so much more painful and complicated than that, we knew, but just being able to make that statement and say it out loud was an affirmation of something. Even if it was cheesy or shallow, we had to at least try to think positively. As his parents we had to be able to be happy for him. It was something. It was one more reason to go forward. Maybe that's what we were looking for here, not so much things to believe in but a list of reasons to carry on.

"He's probably at the all-you-can-eat buffet," I said.

"I know, I know, he was pudgy wasn't he?" Kim replied.

"Pudgy? You're such a mom. Pudgy? He looked like a dang fullback."

I was curious, too, about where he was now and how he was doing. We both felt comfort believing that Kim's birth-mom, Kathleen, was waiting for our son. Kim reminded me that Nan would be there too. Nan was Ed's mother and the matriarch of the Sachs family. When she died in 1997, I was a pallbearer at her funeral.

Nan, I'm sure, believed her Kimmy could have done a whole lot better than me. I loved her for loving Kimmy that much. At my first Thanksgiving dinner with Kim's family, I tried to score points by choking down some of Nan's really awful army-boot bean casserole. Nan saw right through me and with a wink, served me up a big spoonful of seconds. Nan spent her days shopping on QVC. She was the one who instilled in Kim the shopping credo: If you find something you like, buy three. You just didn't mess with Nan. When Kim and I accidentally left one of her friends off the list for our wedding, Nan called with one simple message. "Put Francis on the list or there's gonna be trouble." We put Francis back on the list.

"I bet Nan already has him dressed in little velvet pants," I said, looking up to the ceiling with a pinched scowl on my face. "You better not, Nan."

Kim felt strongly that her mom and Nan were waiting for Noah with open arms, that they'd take care of him. It made their deaths seem more reasonable to her. That maybe their purpose was to be there when Noah arrived. "I feel my mom with him," she said. "I really do. Like now she gets to take care of the baby she never got to."

"I bet your mom just loves having Noah with her," I added. "Feels good to think of them together." I felt grateful to Kathleen, to this woman I never met but seemed to know. I really did. "I just have such a clear picture in my head of her snuggling him and holding him and making sure for us that he's not scared. I feel connected to her, but like, you know, through Noah."

A sad smile snuck across half my face. Speaking into the floor I said, "He looked so much like you, Kimmy."

"You think?"

"Yeah, he was a momma's boy," I said, smiling at her. "Your eyes. Your hair. Your smile. It's good."

"Good?"

"Well, yeah, because every time I look at you, for the rest of my life, I'll see Noah in there somewhere."

"He was a happy, fun baby, ya know?" Kim said. "He was loved."

I smiled and nodded. A long silence unfolded as we daydreamed about him. I understood what Kim was getting at: we had him for nine months; nine glorious, wonderful months, and we shouldn't forget that. Despite how the world might define a life or look at him as never "getting here" or being with us upstairs in his nursery, we knew different.

I heard his heartbeat. We watched him grow on the ultrasound. I didn't miss a single appointment during the pregnancy. I sang to him. I talked to him. And he would jump at the sound of my voice, so much so that Kim had to prepare herself for our father and son chats. I tickled his feet through Kimmy's belly until he flipped over wildly. When he got the hiccups at night, I'd put my cheek against her stomach so I could feel them. I used to watch him move while Kim slept. His elbow or heel would push across her belly like a shooting star flying across the sky. He loved to wedge his foot up under her ribs to the point that Kim would have to block him, saying to him, "no, no, no, Noah. Get your foot outta there you little stinker!" Kim swam with him, bathed with him, walked with him. Unconsciously, she used to stroke circles with her hands across each side of her tummy to calm him down. I held him in the hospital. I smelled him and felt him and kissed him. His blue eyes. His thick brown hair. His chubby cheeks. Those giant hands.

We had a son for nine months, which is longer than a lot of people get to have children. We needed to remember that. To cherish it. To be grateful for it. And to focus as much about the time we had as the time we lost.

"Okay, so last night, real late, I couldn't sleep and Greg and Trish came down and sat with me," I said. "After a while Greg asked me, just flat out, if I hated God. And I was kinda shocked by the stuff I said."

"Like what?" Kim asked.

"I said, no. I said I didn't hate God."

The fact was I actually felt thankful. The one thing I seemed to have clarity about in the whole mess was He could have easily taken Kimmy too. And then my life truly would have been over. There would have been no way to recover from that. Or He could have taken Noah months before and we never would have had the time we had with him. I wondered, of course, if I was BS-ing Greg; trying to seem more together and profound than I was in front of my big brother.

"But as I was talking," I told Kim, "I just sort of had this image of walking up to God someday and yelling at Him, you know, all indignant and everything with a score to settle. 'How could You take my son? What kind of God are You? I want some answers.' And God just wagged His huge finger down at me, disappointed, and a bit pissed too, and He said something like, 'I was gonna take your wife too, but I spared her, I spared you . . . and your son, I let you know him for nine months, and then I took him with as little pain as possible and brought him up here. And this—*this*—is how you thank me?'"

Out of the blue Kim asked me if I remembered watching the movie *Simon Birch*.

It was a movie based on the John Irving novel *A Prayer for Owen Meany* that centered around a deformed, abused child who fights through his unbelievably sad life to bring his odd sense of joy, enlighten-ment—and ultimately, salvation—to the people of some small town. Months ago Kim and I watched that movie and cried our eyes out for two straight hours.

"It was kinda weird how much we were both moved by that movie," Kim said.

"I know . . . I know."

"What stands out to me is the idea, the way that God is in the ugly things. That's what I remember. How He's there, but He leaves it up to us to find Him—or even look for Him in the ugly things."

Kim didn't think us watching that movie was such an accident. I agreed. The deeper we got into it, the more it seemed that in many ways we were being prepared for Noah's death without actually knowing about it: the gift of such a strong marriage; moving into a home next to the Farsons; what we learned from *Simon Birch* and how it applied to us now. It was as if God had sent us a training video. The message of that movie was clear: God is here. This is about the ugliest, most awful thing that can happen to us, but God is still here. We just have to remember to look for Him. For example, what if they had gotten to Noah in time but he was brain damaged and on machines, and it was left up to us to end his life? I couldn't even imagine the pain of that trauma. How much harder would that have been to watch him suffer? We were spared that.

Worse things could have happened. Keeping that perspective would always be a vital part of our recovery.

Kim said, "We can still have kids." And that made me smile. "As bad as this is," she continued, "we have to look for the good stuff. We have to trust that it's there."

"Okay, but please don't tell me I have to praise God for this, Kimmy. No way I can do that right now," I said.

I imagined myself raising my hands and my eyes to the ceiling in mock worship. "Oh God, dear wonderful GOD, thank you so much for killing my son. You are so wise and wonderful, and I trust You completely. Thank you. I promise to go to church every week now. NO! Every day! Hal-lay-luuuuu-ya."

"I can't do that," I repeated.

Kim's face scrunched up a bit. "Do you blame God for this?" she asked.

"Well, who else is to blame?" I said, raising my voice. I was pissed. Who wouldn't be? I just wanted somewhere to aim it.

"I don't know," Kim shot back, "I guess God."

"Well, I mean someone's to blame," I spit out. "Someone did this. Someone took our son. He's not here anymore. Someone . . . did . . . that."

"God?" said Kim.

"Right! God took him, that's what I'm saying. I blame God. Right now I blame Him. He took him. I'm not ready for all that peace and understanding and praise . . . and thy will be done stuff."

I told Kim that if anyone at the funeral tried to feed me some one-liner, Bible-banger banter that was supposed to make this all better, I was going to freak out. I would go ballistic. I did not want advice on how to trust God from someone with a big happy, healthy family. Not right then. Inside I was thinking, "Let Him snatch one of your kids out of your arms. Let Him change your life forever in the blink of an eye, and then you can quote me your stupid-ass Mathew 8:24 or whatever. But until then, keep your mouth shut. Noah was gone; God took him; it was His decision—that's who I was blaming. Or maybe I didn't blame Him as much as I held Him responsible. Either way, it was going to take some time to wrangle this one out.

"We're good people, right Kimmy? I mean we try to be good people."

Kim nodded.

"We try to do what's right. We live good lives. We're good friends, brothers, sisters, children. And what did that get us? A dead son. You know what I'm saying? I mean, all those times I tried to make the right choice . . . what did I get for it? A funeral. How is that fair? Why did we do all that stuff? We should have just done whatever we wanted to—robbed banks, cheat, lie, turn our backs on our families—if this was going to be the outcome. Right?"

What I was saying was teenagers plop out kids in the bathroom during prom and go back out to do the Electric Slide, and those kids live? But Noah dies? I know a guy who divorced his first wife because he didn't want kids, and when his second wife got pregnant he pretty much told her he would have nothing to do with the child, and he has the most beautiful little boy I have ever seen. How is that fair? For me it would never be about why bad things happen to good people, but the question of why good things happen to bad people that I would never understand.

My mind wandered to those fountains and wishing wells—from Barcelona to Beijing to Boulder—that I had tossed money into over the past 10 years. Every time I asked for the same thing. Not a Corvette, or the lottery numbers, but healthy children. That's all I asked for. Over and over. Always patting myself on the back for being such a grounded guy with such wonderful perspective.

I wanted a refund.

"That's what's got us so rattled," said Kim, "being wrong about so many things."

She was right. I felt like an idiot. I felt so unprepared and clueless. I kept looking back at the man I was until two nights before and I just wanted to slap that guy in the face to get his attention.

God? Fairness? Heaven? Being a parent? What was really important in life?

I was almost laughing at myself when I said, "I don't know shit about shit. I just don't understand any of this."

Why did it happen? Why did God do this to . . . us? Why us out of everyone? What did I do to deserve this? Is it payback for something I did? I didn't think so, but I didn't know for sure. Was it His way of getting our attention? I was confused. Clueless.

"I don't know anything anymore," I said.

"Me either," Kim answered.

I wanted to go back, I really did. I wanted to go back to being that blissfully stupid couple that never had to think about any of this, certain I knew everything, that I had it all figured out. Noah's death would eventually become an enlightening experience for both of us. It would change us completely, but in a thousand different, imperceptible ways. But I would never stop wishing I could go back to the way things were.

We would never be the same because of Noah's death. That was easy enough to understand. The hard part, then, would be figuring out a way to honor Noah in the way we acted from there on. It was going to change our lives. But did it have to ruin them as well? That would be up to us.

So far in that regard the only thing we both seemed to know was we wanted to hit this thing straight on. We did not want to bottle it up, stuff it away, ignore it and then have to deal with it when it inevitably bubbled back up, say, 20 years down the road.

"We're going through this whether we want to or not," Kim said. "We can't just wait for this to be over. Or we'll never be done. Do you understand?"

"Not really, what do you mean?"

Kim sat up. She paused for a moment to gather her thoughts, knowing what a big deal it was. The plan was simple, she said.

"Live," she started. "We have to live. Live each day. Not waste time or wish it away and think that just by mindlessly punching a grief clock we'll get through this. We have to work. We can't just wait to get through this, we have to make it happen. So many people are always saying, 'Oh I'll be happy when I finish school' or 'I'll be happy when I get married' or 'I'll be happy when I have a son, or a car or a boat or whatever.' They waste today, they postpone happiness thinking they'll be happy down the road when life is really now, right now."

I didn't dare interrupt her. It was some of the most important advice I would ever get.

"We have to work at it," she continued. "We can't just go to sleep and wake up normal in two years. Like, 'I'll be better in two years, and all I have to do is watch *Seinfeld* reruns until then, and I'll be back to normal.'"

As good as two years of *Seinfeld* reruns sounded right then, I had connected with what Kim was saying. The one thing we had learned was that nothing was guaranteed—except today.

Kim was adamant that we not wish time away just waiting to be happy again—someday. She believed we had to live for today, to find a reason—no matter how small, a laugh, a memory, a hug, a card, anything—to try and be content *right now*. The only thing we controlled was this very moment. We could wait for it to find us, but then we risked never experiencing it at all.

"Live," Kim repeated. "We have to live."

Looking back, Kim had summed up everything with those four words. Noah's death could do two things: it could ruin our lives, or it could teach us to cherish what was left of them. Which course we took was up to us. Every day from there on out we would have to make that decision.

The first one was approaching rapidly. It was well past 3 A.M. when our little bathroom summit began to break up. We had covered a lot of ground. It would take years to complete our journey, but that night we had covered 90% of the crucial material. I stood up first and helped Kim get to her feet. Then we hugged, holding each other in a new way, as if we might just choose to never let go; a hug without ending.

Before leaving the bathroom, we made a pledge to each other. We promised that one day we would be happy again. We didn't hope for it, or dream about it, or pray to God to make it happen. We would make it happen. That's what we promised. One day we would be filled with as much joy and peace as we were right then overcome by confusion and sorrow.

One day we would be consumed by happiness in the same way that we were then overrun by sadness.

"One day," Kim said, "I promise."

"One day," I repeated, sealing the pact.

꧁꧂

## CHAPTER 7

# Goodbye Sweet Baby Boy

The sky had turned almost purple, and the air was thick and sticky when we sunk into the backseat of Kim's Taurus for the short drive to the funeral home. It felt like rain, which somehow made sense. Bill drove. Dad sat in the passenger seat. Kim and I sat close together in the backseat, holding hands, taking deep breaths, preparing. Bill had come out earlier to turn the car around to expedite our exit, and everyone else was ready to roll the moment we left the house—it was touching the way our families worked so hard to make things easier for us. Our cul-de-sac was nearly deserted, perhaps on purpose. As we backed out of the driveway and inched slowly toward our son's funeral, there was only one brave soul on the street—and she changed everything.

It was Kelsey. Sweet little Beaner we called her. She was alone on the sidewalk in front of her house, frozen still on her bike seat with her feet on the cement and her hands stretched out to the long handle bars. With her thick, short brown hair and tender brown eyes, she looked like a little Dorothy Hamill doll. Jak and Teresa's charming and vivacious second child had the pure heart of a 10-year-old and wisdom far beyond her years. One of the first notes we received after Noah died was from Beaner. It ended with this phrase, written in giant, blue felt-tip letters: NOAH, WE WILL NEVER FORGET YOU. How in the world could a child understand and communicate the exact thing we needed to hear at the exact time we needed to hear it is beyond my understanding. Most of our families struggled to grasp this idea: that what parents initially long for more than anything else is assurance that their dead child won't be forgotten.

Kelsey understood. And her note stayed on our fridge for years. While the image of her on that bike, with her brave little tear-soaked face, will remain with us much longer.

Our eyes locked onto Kelsey, and we twisted backwards in our seats watching her as the car motored past.

Kim and I spun back around, locking eyes. "Stop the car," I said.

Bill hit the brakes, thinking we had forgotten something.

"We're gonna get out for a sec."

Kim walked, then raced over to Kelsey. She bent down and took her in her arms. I hugged them both. We spoke to her without thinking, and the words that came out set the tone for the day. "Everything's gonna be okay . . . everything's gonna be okay . . . it's gonna be fine Kels . . . everything . . . is . . . gonna . . . be . . . oh-kay."

Kelsey nodded back at us as tears dripped from her eyes. There was such utter longing and loss in her eyes. She was communicating what everyone around us felt: a helpless sense of bewildered anguish. We hugged her and dried her face and tucked her hair back behind her ears. We pulled away several times only to be drawn back. When we were finally convinced she was okay, we walked backwards to the car, keeping eye contact with Kels, reminding her—and ourselves—as we went, "It's gonna be okay . . . it's gonna be okay . . . we promise."

We wanted that to be true. But even a few minutes earlier as we dressed in silence, gathered up our things and headed to the garage, it just didn't seem possible. Somehow, though, hearing the words out loud made them real and seeing how much others were suffering along with us eased our own pain. Our grief was like a mountain of pebbles. Today we would begin the task of tearing down that mountain one tiny stone at a time. Kelsey, God love her, was the first to join the line and pick up a pebble. She had steered us away from the natural tendency to play the role of victim. She had forced us to start the day by thinking about more than just ourselves. She had corrected and reaffirmed our path. She had given us someone to be strong for just as we set out for our son's funeral.

Once we arrived at the funeral home, the rest of our families waited on the dark, paisley couches in the sun-drenched lobby while Dad, Kim, and I were escorted into Noah's viewing room.

Noah's coffin was open and positioned at the far end of the room. The giant, empty, windowless space between us made him look even smaller. The air had a manufactured, clean smell to it, like a hotel room. Most of the light came from lamps in the ceiling directly above his coffin. We approached slowly but with no hesitation. It seemed to take forever to get to him. Kim and I stood over him for a moment, overcome by sadness at the sight of this beautiful child, perfect in every way, except one, the victim of some cruel cosmic joke. Then, together, we bent over and kissed him on the forehead and touched his little wrinkled hands. His skin felt more smooth and soft than cold and lifeless. It felt so good to connect with him on a physical level, to see him, smell him, feel him, and create a memory with enough of our senses that it would never fade. Kim and I held onto each other as we embraced Noah. And I liked the thought of the three of us connected as a family.

Despite what looked like a good deal of hair gel, his goofy brown hair was sticking straight up in the back. At the moment, so was his dad's. I pointed this out to Kim, and we both giggled through our tears. There was not a single wrinkle to be found on his little blue jumper. When Kim noticed this she smiled the sweetest smile at me.

Dad stepped forward and made the sign of the cross on Noah's forehead. We had asked Dad to first perform last rites for Noah. It was important to hear the words and witness the ritual. It felt necessary.

Dad then backed away to a far corner of the room to give us time alone with our son. We moved forward and bent onto the kneeler in front of his coffin, lowering our faces to the same level as Noah's. The last time we were on a wooden kneeler like that was at our wedding some four years earlier in Dayton, Ohio. During a large chunk of the service, Kim and I had knelt together off to the side of the altar. During the readings and the sermon we just chitchatted and cracked each other up talking about the day and pointing to the bad outfits, the weird hairdos and our hung-over friends in the congregation. On the videotape we look like two high school kids flirting in study hall.

We caressed Noah's face and hands and I continued to twirl his wild cowlick with my left hand. He had long eyes lashes too, giant ears and little puffy, Popeye forearms. His skin was so smooth and soft. His hair had a natural, clean, cottony smell like the top of Kim's pillow. Each time I kissed his cheeks and his forehead, I tried to lock in the memory, knowing it would have to last me a lifetime.

His thick, brown hair, skin tone, and overall facial structure made him look a lot like Kimmy. As a child, Kim had carried what she called a "crumbly blanket" around with her everywhere. Somehow, she had found the exact same kind of blanket while she was pregnant, and now she tucked the blue silk and soft cotton blankie under Noah's right arm.

"Mommy had a blanket like this when she was little," Kim said softly. "Now you have one, too. And when you get lonely or sad or scared, you just snuggle up with this blanket and it will make you feel better . . . Mommy will always be with you sweetie . . . just like this blanket. We'll miss you. Mommy will miss you so much. But I'm so proud of you, Noah. You've helped us . . . you help Daddy and watch over him.

He misses you so much . . . and before you know it . . . someday sweetie . . . we will see you again."

Kimmy was overcome. I held her for a long time. I didn't say anything. I just held her. Then we turned back to the coffin, and I lifted a miniature white Nike tennis shoe and placed it inside his coffin down by his feet.

"You take this one, Noah," I said, "and daddy will keep the other one. These shoes remind me of all the fun and games and adventures we were gonna have together. You take one, and I'll keep the other and someday, when we see each other again, you'll have a complete pair of shoes, and we'll do all those things we dreamed about. We just have to wait a bit, that's all. But we'll all be together, I promise, you and me and Mommy."

Then I reached up and slid a piece of paper under the shoe. It was a collection of thoughts I had scratched out after holding my son for the first time. One of them was "Am I cradling you, Noah, or is it the other way around?"

Kim was still weeping with her head bowed when I leaned forward and whispered into the coffin, "You've already helped us Noah, and that's the greatest thing anyone can do. Some people live for a hundred years and never have the effect that you've had on people or been loved so strongly." I looked at Kim and nodded, speaking to her as well. "I am so proud of you. So proud. You were so brave and strong. And you've helped us to be brave and strong, and we will always keep you close to us, in our hearts. I know you'll be watching over us. That's your job now, to watch over us. I'm so proud of you. You're my boy . . . Noah . . . and I love you . . . you're my baby boy. You will always be our baby boy."

Then Kimmy added, "you go to heaven now . . . we'll miss you . . . you go to heaven now . . . there are people waiting for you . . . they'll take care of you."

We kissed him some more and caressed his hair. With my thumb, I rubbed tiny circles into his fat forearms. Kim straightened the collar of his outfit. We were in no hurry. Time seemed to stand still inside that room. At first it felt more like we were saying goodnight to him instead of goodbye. After a while we just turned and looked at each other, "Are you ready?" Yeah, we both nodded, "we're ready." We stood up together and slowly closed the lid to his coffin. As the top came down over him, casting Noah in darkness, the weight and finality of this gesture began to sink in. Instantly I was sapped of all my energy. Hope is such a powerful, but fleeting concept; it could sustain me for days and then suddenly and without warning evaporate in a split second.

We moved away from the coffin to another corner of the room hoping the distance would soften the blow. It didn't. We sat for a while on a nice yellow couch, trying to compose ourselves, repeating the things we told Noah and other stuff we had talked about the night before. But having a plan and a philosophy about how to survive something like that is one thing; actually carrying it out is something different all together. Whatever we planned, it was subject to change, completely and without notice. Surviving those sudden shifts was half the battle. Then, for the first time since he died, I had a very heavy sense of hopelessness. I felt crippled, unable to act or to move forward with the ritual of saying goodbye to my son. I just wanted to push pause and stay there with Noah suspended in time, forever, in a place where he wasn't alive but he wasn't buried yet either. The weight on my chest made it hard to breathe. I was unable to speak or to communicate how I was feeling. So we sat in silence for a long time.

When Kim finally asked if I was ready to bring our families in, I cried out loud in a muffled moan, "I don't think I can do this."

Our families were waiting for us in the lobby just a few feet away, and I found out later that they had all heard my plea. I wish they had also been privy to what happened next.

Kim had dried her tears and seemed ready to get on with the day. She had already been forced to deal with letting go of Noah on a physical level three days earlier when doctors literally ripped him out of her belly. Still, she told me to just relax and take my time; that there was no rush and no schedule. And if I needed to sit with him all day then I could have all day, and everyone else would just have to wait. Kim, once again, had taught me an incredibly valuable lesson: that we didn't always have to do our grieving and recovery as a couple. There would be times when Kim was depressed, and I felt great; and other days I might be pissed off while Kim was at peace. What was important was that we gave each other space and support and never resented or tried to manipulate the other person's feelings to suit our mood. This would not be easy.

I needed more time. My gut told me I needed more time. Kim selflessly granted my wish.

"Let's go back," I said.

"Okay," Kim replied with a soft smile and a knowing nod, as if she knew what I wanted before the words came out.

Back we went across that huge expanse of carpet. We lifted the lid and knelt down again in front of our son. If he had been taken from us, then that felt like we had stolen him back—even for just a few moments. We kissed his forehead, his hair and his chubby cheeks. That time it felt different, much more like goodbye. When I held him in the hospital, Noah seemed to still be there inside his warm body. It felt like I was really holding my son—all of him. But now, particularly after coming back to his coffin for a second time, the person in front of us was just a body, an empty vessel. Noah, our son, seemed much more like a spirit now. He was everywhere—above us, in us, all around us—everywhere, except in that coffin. The weight of saying goodbye dissipated because it was clear now that he was already gone.

So we just knelt together and soaked him in one last time. Periodically, we both bowed our heads in prayer. We asked for God to take him now and watch over him. We asked for strength. For peace. For understanding and for some small glimmer of hope.

Strength. Peace. Hope.

I was hunched over forward on the kneeler, praying with my hands stretched partly inside his coffin when suddenly my back shot straight up as if yanked by a cord from above. I turned my head to the right, coming face to face with Kim who had just finished the exact same gesture.

"Did you just feel that?"

"Yeah . . . I . . . I did," she said with a wide-eyed look on her face. "Wow."

"You felt it too Kimmy?"

"Yeah."

"Wow."

"Just warmth and peace and calmness . . . from . . . from above?"

"Yeah," she said.

"You felt that?"

"I did. I did. It just, I don't know, like kinda washed down over me."

"Oh my God."

We both had looks on our faces like the only two people in a crowd who had just seen a shooting star. It was almost an exact repeat of the feeling that came over me when I fell to my knees, alone inside Kim's dark hospital room a few days before. Warmth. Peace. Strength. Hope. I had tried to share that experience with Kim, but it was nearly impossible to describe the depth and power behind it. Now, I no longer had to try to summon the words since she had just experienced the same thing. We had felt it together. We shared it. Teetering on the edge of both our son's coffin and emotional oblivion, our prayers had been answered by a feeling of warmth and peace that, in the end, also felt a bit like a nudge.

Kind of like, *Mom? Dad? Come on you guys, I'm okay.*

"Was that Noah . . . or . . . God?"

"Both, maybe," Kim whispered.

"That's what I felt in the hospital, Kimmy, when I asked for strength and peace. That's the feeling, the exact feeling, that came to me. Just like that. I could feel it. It was so powerful—and real, ya know? I asked for it and it was given to me. Amazing. There was no mistaking that."

Kim looked calm, at peace almost. Then she said, "I think that was Noah. He sent that down to tell us he's fine and that we're gonna be okay. Like he was rooting for his mom and dad and a little bit got through to us."

In our stunned silence, we had both abruptly stopped crying. We embraced. It was a real hug. Before we were more or less just holding each other up, but that was a real exchange. The heavy sorrow and the grief that felt like quicksand had been transformed into warmth, peace and strength. We wanted to share it with everyone.

Together we kissed him on the forehead one last time. Without making a big deal out of it, we closed the coffin for good. Then we walked to the double doors and waved our families into the room. Some people sat down. Some embraced. Some broke down at the sight of the tiny coffin. Some went off to pray. Some wandered around looking at all the flowers. Kim and I made a point of going person to person, looking them straight in the eyes and telling them just exactly what we had experienced a moment earlier.

"We feel at peace," I told my mom.

"We feel hope," Kim explained to her dad. "We really do."

"Please don't be sad for us," we told Greg, "We feel peace; we are really at peace with this. We're gonna be okay, we're all gonna be okay. We really feel that and we want . . . we hope . . . you feel it too."

They were skeptical, to say the least.

Everyone then gathered in a semicircle around Noah's coffin, and we prayed as a family. We moved out to the lobby while William, the funeral director, prepared the coffin and briefed my three brothers on their duties as pallbearers. Apparently Bryan had decided to show up after all. In a moment, the doors opened again. Bill carried the right side. Greg lifted the left, and Bryan trailed behind, touching the back of the coffin. They all wore white gloves. They were all crying. And that made me cry, struck by the symbolism of my brothers united around their nephew, each of them helping to shoulder the burden of my child's death.

There had been some debate on Saturday about whether or not to have children attend the funeral. The thinking was that the sight of kids at our own child's funeral would be an unnecessary, added burden. Kim and I strongly disagreed. Contrary to what we thought would be the case, seeing other kids didn't make us sad. We didn't covet other people's children, we wanted our own, we wanted Noah. Whatever his legacy would be, we certainly didn't want it to be families, and kids in particular, feeling self-conscious around us or worrying that their own joy would somehow bring us pain. Who could begrudge someone else their happy, healthy offspring? Not us. Not Noah. To us, the pure and uplifting presence of children would be a welcome addition at something as traditionally depressing as a funeral. In the end, we told people to do what they felt was best for their children while encouraging them to attend as a family.

After a brief drive down a deserted I-85, under a sky that oscillated between darkness and light, mimicking our own feelings of despair and hope, we turned into the cemetery and wended our way back to Noah's plot. Where the road dead-ended and a thick batch of trees began, Bill pulled over and parked the car behind the hearse. At that moment, the decision to include children seemed prescient. Upon seeing our car pull up, a pack of kids who had been playing in the woods dashed across the road and back under the green canopy that had been set up over Noah's grave. The girls all had on long, flowing summer dresses. As they swept by us, the blue, white, and yellow flower patterns seemed to leave a visible rooster tail of color and energy behind. Kim and I both actually chuckled a bit at the scene. It lifted our spirits seeing those kids bounce by. In fact, that was the first—and one of the lasting—images I have of my son's funeral. The final kid to come out of the woods was Mac, a sweet, goofy boy-giant, who had actually been relieving himself behind a tree.

Had we been cocooned in our own pity and forbidden children from Noah's funeral, we would have missed such a splendid sight. Had we stuck with protocol and left his coffin closed the first time, we would have missed the warm deluge of peace we felt during our second viewing. Had we been unable to see past our own grief in the car that morning, we would have driven right past Kelsey and missed her message. But now, instead of thinking of the exposed dirt around his coffin, the white roses of surrender, the tears, or the phrase "commit his body to the ground . . . ashes to ashes, dust to dust," when I think of my son's funeral, the first thing I remember is Grace and those girls springing by us in a swirl of color and spirit.

The plastic folding chairs that had been set up were already full, and an overflow crowd encircled the tent. Our families were to our left and in the row behind us. Several of Kim's colleagues were in the back, as was Kim's obstetrician, Leedylyn, who was constantly pushing her dark-rimmed glasses up to her forehead to wipe away tears. I was certain she was ignoring hospital policy by attending Noah's funeral.

Standing next to Noah's coffin, facing us, was my dad. My parents divorced when I was in middle school, and over the years a predictable gap developed between my father and me. But when it came time to put together Noah's funeral on a moment's notice, I must say, Dad rose to the occasion and came through with a simple, elegant and deeply spiritual service that honored his first grandson as well as the clergy. When I needed him most, Dad stepped up and delivered. Since that day, no one has worked harder or done more to perpetuate Noah's spirit. And so, out of my son's death came the rebirth of my relationship with my father.

After some silent reflection and a handful of prayers, Dad started in on his homily. "Over the course of the last several years, the Sachs and Fleming families have celebrated some wonderful events," Dad began. "We have laughed at "FlemFest," a gathering of family in Charlotte, to celebrate what we have been, are and can become as a family. We have celebrated in Los Angeles at the wedding of Greg and Trish, and we have given thanks for the birth of Connor. Now we come together with dear friends, adults and children alike, to wonder how can this happen to us?

"Noah has been separated from us—from Dave and Kim. How can this be? Despite our inability to understand all of this, despite our profound grief, despite our pain, we celebrate and take comfort in Noah's new relationship with God and in the things that we do know. We know that Noah is loved more dearly each day by us and by God. We are certain that Noah—as Dave's brother Bill put it so beautifully— knew he was loved. He knew it from his mother's heart, from his father's touch, and softly spoken words as he moved, not always so gently, inside his mother's body. Noah knows he is loved even more now despite our pain, our tears, our hurt.

"Noah is a legacy of love especially, but not only from Kim and Dave, but from all of us. We take away from this awesome pain a renewed sense of caring and loving. That, Noah, is your wonderful and ever-lasting legacy to us.

"On the wall of Noah's nursery room are these words which his parents had inscribed: *I see the moon and the moon sees me, God bless the moon and God bless me.* Oh yes, Noah, you are with God and with us and as you have blessed us, God does indeed bless you."

It wasn't until Dad mentioned Noah's nursery that Kim and I began to weep. The idea of that room—once so bright and full of promise, a place where Kim and I used to go just to sit and daydream about our future family—now being dark and empty, well, that just did it. Dad gave us a moment, then he nodded at Kim, who turned toward the gathering and began reading her message.

"I asked God for strength to say something that would somehow make us all feel better about what has happened, and I am reminded how blessed we are and how we have so many things to be thankful for," said my wife. "We are truly thankful for each one of you, our family and friends. You have been amazing. We can't tell you how much your love and support has meant to us.

"We are so thankful for Noah. Dave and I are reminded of how precious life is, and we would do it all again just to have that one precious moment to hold him. Please remember how precious we all are to one another, especially children. They are gifts from God and, we got to experience that gift for nine months. Noah was strong and bears a strong and proud name. We hope that when you remember him, that you remember his strength and when you need it, ask God for it."

Then, it was my turn: "One of the things that Kim and I believe is that God always shows Himself during the terrible and tragic times, but because of our own grief and shock and perhaps self-centeredness, we forget to look for Him. In so many ways during the last few days, He has shown himself to all of us—and for that I am grateful. I wanted to share a few of these moments with you so that you will see Noah's death as we do: as something more than just tragic, but as something meaningful and uplifting.

"A few minutes after he died, Kim and I got to hold our son. It was at the same time the darkest moment of my life and also the greatest moment of my life. In that moment, I learned that the amount of time and love that you share is not what counts, but more so the depth and quality of that love. In that moment, I got to love my son for an eternity—and for that I am grateful. In the days following Noah's death, the love and support we have received from our family and friends has been something to behold. You have all made a difference. We have friends and family who possess strong character and warm hearts—and for that I am grateful. Also, I did not think it possible for me to love my wife any more than I do, or have more respect for her strength and courage. Yet my love and admiration for you, Kim, has increased profoundly. We will get through this, and we will have a better and stronger relationship for it—and for that I am grateful.

"And finally, to my son, Noah: I want you to know how proud of you I am. You were so brave, and you have given us all the greatest gift: for none of us, from this day forward, will ever be able to take anyone we love or a single moment of our lives for granted, because of the sacrifice that you made, Noah. We will all, from this moment forward, cherish our lives and our loved ones—and for that gift I am grateful . . . to God and to my son."

Our neighbor Susie then stepped forward to sing a sweetly sad church song called, "Be Not Afraid." It was a song Kim remembered from her years of Catholic school; she used to sing it out loud to keep me awake during long car trips. A few years ago, it was also performed at her grandmother's funeral. The song was a symbolic acknowledgment that both Kim's mother, Kathleen, and her grandmother, would be waiting for our son. Although Susie scrambled around town to find the music and had next-to-no time to practice, her rendition was angelic.

Dad then bent down by the foot of Noah's coffin and picked up a handful of the overturned earth. He opened his prayer book and toward the end of this passage he crumbled the dark dirt in his hands, allowing it to fall onto Noah's white coffin. The clumps of earth hitting Noah tapped out a delicate drumbeat, like heavy rain.

*O merciful and loving God, whose blessed son was laid in a holy place in a garden much like this, bless this grave and grant that Noah, who is buried here, may be with You this day and always. . . . In sure and certain hope of the resurrection to eternal life, we commend our beloved Noah to You, almighty God. We commit his body to the ground, earth to earth, ashes to ashes, dust to dust. May the Lord bless and keep him. Lord, make his face to shine upon him and be gracious unto him, the Lord lift up the light of his countenance upon him, and give him peace this day and always. . . . Into thy hands, Our Savior, we commend Thy child, Noah, acknowledge, we humbly beseech Thee, a sheep of Your own fold, a lamb of Your own flock. Receive him into the arms of Thy mercy and into the blessed rest of everlasting peace. . . . Amen.*

Amen.

Laying down white roses as they passed, our friends and family then said their final goodbyes to our son. We stayed seated as the first few families proceeded past us, but when the Farsons approached—Jak held Sam, who was scared and confused by the sight of the coffin and perhaps by our tortured expressions—the urge was too great. We stood and greeted everyone else who passed by with hugs and handshakes.

Then it was our turn. Kim stepped forward and kissed the coffin. I did the same. It was smooth. Cold. Inert. We had already said goodbye. In our hearts, we had already felt him move on. Whether it was exhaustion or some semblance of peace, I'm not exactly sure, but we didn't spend a lot of time clinging to his grave.

"We love you, Noah," Kim whispered.

"Goodbye, sweet baby boy," I said.

And that was that. It was over. Noah was committed to the earth.

As we stepped out from under the shade of the canopy we were greeted by shards of sunlight cutting through the indigo sky. At first, we instinctively blocked the light. Then we dropped our hands to let the golden rays warm our faces.

When we got home, Kim and I sat together in silence on the blue loveseat that faces the bay window at the front of our house. The rest of our families dug into a huge feast of ham, green beans, potatoes, warm, gooey rolls and other dishes prepared for us by neighbors while we were at the cemetery. After a while, Janie peaked around the corner, holding two plates of food. We ate and continued watching through the window as pretty much everyone from the funeral began to congregate at the top of our driveway under the basketball hoop. There was an awful lot of dirt kicking and pacing going on. Inside it was the same way. No one really knew what to do with themselves. Meanwhile, the springy, rhythmic pounding of a basketball began echoing inside our house.

It was Jak. Every so often we watched him leave the group on the street and dribble the ball to the front of our house where he knew all the ex-jocks inside would be tempted by that noise. That would not be the last time that Jak, in his own strange way, pushed me in my own recovery. Sure enough, one by one, my brothers, my dad, uncle Jimmy and even Kim's dad waltzed up to the front of the house to gaze at the hoops court.

I turned to Kimmy and said, "I think they're gonna play."

"You should get out there," she said, nudging me.

"No . . . I . . . couldn't. I couldn't . . . could I?"

"Go ahead. Seriously. Go ahead."

"Maybe I'll just go watch."

It was clear that everyone inside the house wanted to play. But no one was going to move a muscle until I green-lighted the idea. Jak upped the ante by sending his skinny, squeaky blonde-haired daughter, Grace, to our front door.

"Dad wants to know if you guys want to play basketball," she yelled before jumping off the porch and sprinting back to her father.

There were many people, both inside the house and out, who felt strongly that a game of basketball at that moment was totally inappropriate. I understood that completely. But if I had learned anything in the 72 hours since my son had died, it was this: we all grieve in our own unique way, without rules or constraints and without judgment.

More importantly, we are a family tied together at times by nothing more than our love of athletics.

Dad played baseball at Denison University in Ohio and had tryouts with the Tigers and Indians. Bill had played baseball at Albion College in Michigan. A wrestling scholarship paid Greg's way through Notre Dame.

(His 3–2 OT win in the high school state finals is still the greatest athletic feat I have ever witnessed.) How many nights as kids had we spent huddled around the TV in our faux-wood paneled basement watching the Red Wings, listening to announcer Sid Abel over the clanking space heater? Peewee football, baseball, basketball, hockey, track and wrestling—we had played them all, sometimes changing uniforms and equipment in the back of our Ford LTD wagon (with, again, more of that faux-wood paneling) as mom shipped us between practices. People always ask me if I've ever cried at a sporting event. Of course. I used to boo-hoo every time my dad dragged us down to watch his beloved Cleveland Browns in that scrap-metal igloo of ignominy called Municipal Stadium.

We lived a block from a park. How many pickup games had we played there, Flemings versus the world? How many sports had we invented in our own backyard? Pitching games? Hockey? Full-contact hoops? Boxing matches? (Mom finally took away the gloves after Bill knocked me out and not knowing what to do, dragged me into our basement pantry until I came to a half hour later.) How many games of knee football had we played in our living room growing up—the kind that burned holes in the knees of our pants and made the entire house bounce and rattle?

A game of hoops just seemed like the natural thing to do. I turned around to Kim and shrugged my shoulders. "How am I supposed to say no to Gracie?" All the men were in the other room with their fingers crossed.

"Are we gonna play?" someone shouted.

"Yeah, shoot, why not?" I said, raising my voice just a bit. "Let's play."

Instantly, the life returned to our home. It was as if a vacuum had been punctured. Everyone started to talk and then to shout, hoot, holler and trash talk as a mad scramble ensued to find enough shoes, t-shirts and shorts to outfit everyone. Nevertheless, I was still wondering if pickup basketball was the right thing to do just hours after watching dirt fall onto my son's coffin. I still wasn't a 100% sure. Jason and a few others did not play, but everyone else was out under the hoop in the blink of an eye. A row of lawn chairs was even set up so Kim could watch with the rest of the spectators.

For once my instincts seemed to be right. The first time Bill went up for a rebound, Greg yanked his shorts to the ground. Bryan stopped the game once to yell to my mom that we were playing too rough. A few moments later, he called another timeout to warn us that it was "Go time" if anyone touched him when he had the ball. He wasn't joking, but we all still laughed until our sides hurt. Dad took two steps onto the court and twisted his ankle. Ed took out his own frustrations on anyone who dared set a pick. We all poked fun at Uncle Jimmy's blue Navy short-shorts, circa 1979. Periodically I left the court to jog over and kiss Kimmy. No one noticed. I went 1-for-7. My world may have been turned upside down, but at least my basketball game hadn't changed. It felt good to sweat. It felt good to laugh. Both were a cleansing release. It felt good to high-five my brothers. It helped all of us to think about something else for even a short while.

Afterwards I went in to grab something to drink and made my way to the back porch where Kim, Jason and Ed were enjoying the last hour of sunlight. The weather had fluctuated all day. It rained on the way home from the funeral, but by the time we got home, it was sunny. Now it looked like it might rain one more time. I had barely hit my seat and twisted open a bottle of water when the backdoor swung open. It was Bill, still sweating from the game. It didn't hit me at first, but later I would remember the childlike look of wonderment on his face.

"Kim, Dave, you have to see this," he said, waving us to the front of the house.

Kim got up and went with him to the front of the house. I stayed put. I had experienced enough surprises for one lifetime. A few minutes later, though, I could hear Bill's feet pounding their way back toward the porch. Again the door burst open. Bill put his hand on my shoulder with just enough of his FBI agent pressure to signal that he intended to drag me out of my chair if need be.

"Dave, seriously, you need to come see this. Come quick, you do not want to miss this," he said. "Trust me, you do not want to miss this."

The front door of our house was wide open and as I approached, I could see dozens of people standing in our yard with their backs to our house, gazing north, their heads tilted to the sky. Kim was in the doorway, frozen in the exact same position. What was it? I wondered. I followed the trajectory of her face upward.

There it was. Brilliant. Luminous. Breathtaking. Magnificent. When I saw it, and my mind connected the dots, slowly beginning to comprehend the miracle before my eyes, my heart began to pound so hard the pocket of my shirt moved.

Above the tree tops, arcing across the blue sky in front of our house was . . . a rainbow.

Noah's rainbow.

No one moved. No one breathed. No one said a word. As if any sudden movement or noise might scare it away. There were dozens of people standing there, paralyzed by awe. I dared not even blink. I wanted to hold Kim so badly, but neither one of us wanted to take our eyes off the sky. Frozen still and silenced by utter amazement, we found each other's hands and interlocked our fingers. We stayed still and silent. Any gesture would have been ridiculous, any words absurd. We felt wickedly cursed and wonderfully blessed, all at the same time. But if our body language gave off any message at all, it was awe and humility.

A child named Noah. A funeral. A promise. A rainbow. A glimmer of hope.

Now, I know that some people consider rainbows to be nothing more than a very rare optical illusion created by the combination of refracted light and moisture. To others, it's an important symbol of inclusion in our fractured society. And still more people believe the rainbow to be an unmistakable sign from God as described in the Bible. As I understand it, after Noah built his ark, the heavens opened with a downpour that lasted for 40 days and 40 nights. It wiped out everything except for what was spared inside Noah's great ship. When the sky finally cleared, God sent a rainbow as a symbol of his covenant with man: that he would never again cause such destruction.

We took Noah's rainbow as a divine symbol of hope. And we saw it as a promise, sent from our beloved son as he made his way to heaven, that the devastation was over.

⚜

## CHAPTER 8

# Returning to the Monumental Minutia of Life

The morning after I buried my son, garbage trucks came around and collected the trash off our street just like it was any other Monday.

We didn't really want to rejoin the world—"this busy monster, manunkind," as e. e. Cummings once put it—and deal with the monumental minutia of life. But we had no choice. Friends and family had begun leaking out of our house and back to their lives. Tasks had already begun piling up. We had to decide what to do with Noah's room and face one more trip to Elvira to order his gravestone. There was my new job at *ESPN The Magazine* to consider. A toy drive was under way, sponsored in Noah's honor by the sports radio station where I used to work as an occasional drive-time co-host. Through a friend we had also discovered KinderMourn, a support group in Charlotte for parents who had lost children. Kim had already scheduled an appointment for later in the week. Then we were off to a cabin in the mountains for several days.

Janie stayed in town for a few extra days. It helped soften the blow of everyone else's departure. But she needed to stay busy with tasks to keep her mind off Noah. A teacher who works miracles with troubled high school kids, Janie has a self-deprecating sweetness to her. She's also the kind of person whose first instinct when the car breaks down is to clean and scrub the interior before calling a mechanic. As if the car just needs to feel good about itself before it's willing to work again. She can be a neurotic worrier—she hates to fly and she obsessively watches the Weather Channel—so it made sense that, without asking, she assigned herself the job of closing up Noah's nursery. Kim and I were eating breakfast, chatting softly back and forth, when we heard stuff being moved around upstairs.

"Is she in Noah's room?" I asked.

"Nah," said Kim, "why would she be? She wouldn't do that? Right?"

Kim's incision prevented her from walking up stairs, so she sent me to the second floor to investigate. To my utter amazement, Janie was busy boxing up, folding up and locking away the contents of Noah's room. I half-expected to see a new deadbolt, padlock and chains wrapped around to the door.

We had never expressed an interest in closing off his room. We loved that room. We worked hard getting it ready for him, painting the walls, hiring a woman to add a crescent moon mural, finding the perfect crib, toys and accessories. We had spent a lot of time just sitting up there, sometimes lying on the carpet for hours, feeling him kick field goals while daydreaming about our future. Now that he was gone, we didn't want to lock it all away like some solemn shrine. We wanted to experience it and process the empty space. Kim was thinking of donating the diapers, along with some of the clothes and toys, to charity. Some of the bigger items, like the strollers and high-chair, would get put away in the attic. Even that was a heartbreaking but meaningful chore we were glad to do. After that, Kim was planning on buying games and toys and transforming the nursery into a place where kids from the neighborhood could come and play when their parents stopped over. The kids loved it. Kim was right; it was only the adults who were freaked out by our empty nursery.

I went back downstairs and explained what was happening. That was perhaps the only time I ever saw Kim get truly angry in connection with Noah's death. She told me to march back up and stop her mother. I went, but I didn't exactly march, and I didn't exactly stop her either.

You could tell the exercise of stuffing Noah away was cathartic for her—out of sight out of mind—it just wasn't what we wanted. That tug of war over Noah's memory would rage on for years. On his second birthday, Kim's family threw a minor fit when we turned down their invitation to spend the day in the Wisconsin Dells playing golf and "forming new, happy memories." The truth was we all wanted the same thing, we just had different ideas of how to get there.

I leaned into the room, holding onto the doorframe, hovering over Janie, who was on the floor boxing up blankets. "Uh, Janie . . . yeah . . . well . . . see the thing is . . . Kim doesn't . . . actually Kim and I both . . . we don't want to shut this room down," I said.

"Oh I'm just packing some things up, getting stuff out of the way," she said barely looking up. "It'll just help you guys not having to see some of this stuff."

"But Janie . . . that's what I'm saying, we don't . . . uh . . . we want . . ."

In a thunderous voice from downstairs, Kim yelled, "I want you to leave his room alone, mom."

"Okay honey, just let me . . . " Janie yelled past me.

"Mom? MOM! I'm serious. I don't want anything touched up there. Leave it. I'll take care of it. He's my son, and I'll take care of his room—by myself."

There was a long pause as we all stood there, waiting. The way Kim felt about that task was similar to the way I had felt about arranging Noah's funeral. We would only get to perform a finite number of tasks for our son, and we wanted to cherish each one.

I tried to shake my head at Janie as if to say, "Yeah, come on, we better listen to what she wants."

"HEEEEY! CAN'T YOU HEAR ME!" Kim said. "I DON'T WANT ANYONE INHISROOOOOM!" I jumped through the door at the sound of Kim's voice because she had climbed the stairs, stitches be damned, and was right behind me.

"Kim, honey, ooooh, you're not supposed to be walking up stairs, honey. You need to be careful," said Janie.

"Mom, I'm serious," Kim threatened. "I don't want anyone in this room. I mean it. I'll take care of it. Stop it."

With that, we all walked out of his room. Janie was the last to exit, reluctantly leaving behind her unpacked piles. She turned out the lights and closed the door behind her. Kim then walked over and pushed the door back open and flicked on the lights.

As grateful as we were for the support of our families, we were ready to walk the path on our own. Of course, we would never really be alone. Kim and I clung to each other like life preservers. Kim watched me like a hawk. She never let me spiral down too far without a hug, a card or a long talk. My favorite note said: *Love bears all things, believes all things, hopes all things, endures all things, love never ends. I promise you we will get through this, we will have more children, we will be happy again.* It's in the top drawer of my dresser. I read it every day.

What influenced me the most was how Kim, from the very beginning, insisted that we not wish away those days, just treading water until we got better. Honor Noah, she would say, by finding any reason, no matter how small or silly or insignificant, to cherish the day. That attitude had a lasting effect on me. The way it created in me the ability to let little things—a Guinness found at the back of the fridge, a child's smile, a sweet parking space—make my entire day. With all the big stuff crushing my spirit, it wasn't hard to learn how to enjoy the simple pleasures of life. They were all we had.

I thought it was amazing when people came over to pay their respects or drop off a plate of lasagna, that Kim would always go out of her way to ask them how they were doing, to inquire about their lives too. She showed me it was possible to be introspective about it all without becoming completely self-absorbed. And I tried. I really did. Out and about we listened with dead eyes and vice-gripped hands as new parents complained to us about how sick they were of their whiny kids and how exhausted they were from a lack of sleep.

Kim is a brave, strong, independent woman who has lived in Manhattan, traveled the world and advanced quickly in a male-dominated field. After Noah died, though, she was troubled by a new, unfamiliar emotion: fear. She had now been hit by lightning twice in her life and had lost both her mother and her son. It was only natural that she would become scared of losing anyone else. At the beginning, she couldn't even think about me traveling for work without breaking down. Her mind tended to take everything to the worst-case scenario. That way, she figured, at least I won't ever be caught off guard again. Every cold was pneumonia. Every stomachache, cancer. Every plane, destined for a crash. She would struggle with that for a long time. She hated feeling so frail and out of control, so worried all the time. What finally helped her regain her emotional strength was when Teresa and our neighbors Helen and Susie formed a weekly Bible-study/gossip/Noah-recovery group, which I dubbed Scripture Chicks.

That wasn't really my kind of thing. I don't like to admit it, but I lean toward being a bit of loner. Until I get to know someone, I am far too standoffish. What is introversion or shyness, though, is often mistaken for aloofness. Kim had taught me the importance of getting past that, letting my guard down and investing in relationships—in our marriage, our families, our friends and at work. And now I understood why. During that time our friends were amazing. We probably went 20 days without having to cook a single meal. And the sympathy cards and kind notes continued on probably twice as long as that. Our days were filled with flowers, plants, cards, charity donations and phone calls. It was overwhelming. Those things acted like hope vitamins—they would tide us over until we could begin manufacturing our own hope.

Jak literally forced me out of the house to play hoops every few days, usually followed by dinner at the Farsons, who had all but adopted us into their family. Like I said, I'm not sure it was such an accident that we moved in across from the Farsons. You take them out of the equation—the meals, the compassion, the spirit and support they gave us on a daily, sometimes hourly basis—and I'm not so sure we ever would have recovered from Noah's death. By now Jak had stopped knocking before coming into our house through the garage door. It's not uncommon for us to come home and find him on the couch watching HBO while eating a Dagwood-style sandwich. Over the years he's done more repairs at our house than I have. And he seems to be collecting his handyman's fee one meal at a time.

Friends from home, guys whom I grew up with, just refused to let me lose touch. I'd blow them off, forget to return their calls, ignore e-mails, and they'd just keep on reaching out to me. They still do. Mike Burns did the same thing. He insisted we continue our almost-weekly golf game at the course that runs through our neighborhood. Burnsie and I had worked together at *The Cincinnati Post*. He was a sympathetic editor and friend when I was just a lowly stringer answering phones. He was just a solid, down-to-earth, talented and funny dude, who seemed to view life through the same skeptical, ironic lens as I. Most editors in Burnsie's position wouldn't stoop to interact with a lowly stringer, and had it not been for his kindness and guidance, and that of sports editor Mark Tomasik, I may have given up my dreams of becoming a writer. We had a Nerf hoop in the office back then and as we worked to put the sports section together from 10 P.M. until 6 A.M., we'd stop periodically for some knock-down-drag-out hoops battles.

Years later, by sheer luck, we ended up in Charlotte together. Burnsie was an editor for a local Web site, and like most magazine writers, I work out of my home, flying to my assignments while communicating with my editors mostly through e-mails and conference calls. So it was nice to have someone in the business like Burnsie to speak to in person. After Noah died, Mike would drive me around the golf course for hours on end laughing at my game and listening to me spew about the whole ordeal. Listening is a lost art. Most of us just nod our heads waiting for our turn to speak. Not Burnsie. We'd finish our round, and I'd feel exhausted and refreshed at the same time having purged all the thoughts that were bottlenecking inside my head.

What I really liked about those conversations, though, was that Burnsie wasn't just a passive participant. If I stepped over a line or said something stupid or obnoxious, he'd let me know. During one round, I was in a real lather because *Sports Illustrated* was still hassling me for $17 worth of personal calls I had made using my old corporate calling card. They weren't just any old calls. They were the calls I made from the hospital to tell people Noah had died. Up on the tee box I was blathering on and on about the travesty of it all and how I was going to call *SI* and tell everyone off.

Burnsie shook his head. He knew. He knew how good *SI* had been to me over the years, how many people there had gone out of there way to counsel and groom me as a writer. He knew how wonderful they had been to me after Noah had died, and how I probably hadn't thanked them enough for any of it.

"What?" I barked.

"Flem, come on," he said flatly. "That's kinda ridiculous. How are they supposed to know what the calls were for? It's seventeen bucks. You've probably lost that much in golf balls already today. Let it go."

After that round, we met our wives back at Burnsie's house for a cookout. We sat down and immediately Mike's wife, Kim, launched into a long, eloquent speech about grief and recovering from the death of a loved one. In beautiful detail she talked about the stages of grief, the pain, the processing, the sleepless nights—the agony of it all. Tears were welling up in her eyes. I felt like such a self-centered idiot. I had no idea they had been through something like that. She went on for 10 minutes or so until I found a place to interject, "Kim . . . Mike . . . I'm so sorry, I mean, we had no idea you guys lost someone."

"Oh yeah, we've been through this," said Kim Burns.

I sheepishly leaned toward her, asking, "Was it . . . was it . . . a child? I'm so sorry. My gosh. I had no idea. We're only now finding out just how many people have been effected by . . . "

Kim looked at Mike, and Mike looked back at Kim. Something seemed odd.

"Sarge, it's kinda . . . " Mike said.

"Chauncey," Kim Burns interjected. "When we lost her, I went through what you're going through right now."

"Your—dog?" I practically yelled, interjecting the swear words to myself in silence.

"I want you to know you'll get through this."

"Wait."

"But it will go in stages: anger, guilt, acceptance."

I looked at my Kim, and she looked back at me.

"No wait, let me see, anger, denial, guilt . . ."

*Your dog? Your dog?*

Burnsie was waving at her trying to get her to stop. She wanted to empathize with us so badly. No way you can fault someone for that. As a reminder, though, under a couch cushion my own Kim was pinching me in a way that said, "Let it go . . . Let it go or I'll pinch off a sizeable chunk of your leg."

It was all so bizarre. At that point, Noah's death seemed almost straightforward compared to the task of learning how to rejoin the world as grieving parents. Trying to integrate back into the real world was constantly throwing us for a loop. If his death had shown us how unpredictable and uncontrollable life could be, well, we hadn't really seen anything yet. Nothing about his death made sense yet. So it figured that nothing about our recovery would either.

Even getting a haircut was a huge ordeal. Both of us were quite shaggy on top, but we dreaded going back to the people who cut our hair because they had no idea about Noah's death. The last time we left them, everything was perfect and right on schedule. So we knew what was waiting for us upon our return: big happy, robust greetings about our newborn son and anxious hands grasping for pictures. We had no idea on earth how to handle that situation. Who would have thought? Who could have predicted how traumatic it would be to face our . . . hairdressers? We thought about just starting over with new people at a new salon, because, really, at best those interactions would be excruciatingly awkward and tricky for both parties. Even if by some miracle everything would go fine in our delicate explanation, we were still going to wreck their day and leave them feeling like jerks.

It's silly, I know, but we actually playacted the scenario in our kitchen before each of us left. Both went about the same way. The minute I walked in, all the women in the shop stopped what they were doing and came racing over to me with smiles and well-wishes. "Aeeeeiii! It's the proud daddy!" they screamed. "How are you? Are you getting any sleep? Ohhh, did you bring any pictures?" Everyone seemed to be bouncing and clapping and smiling at me. "Aren't babies precious? Show us some pictures! Come on."

I tried to warn them with the blank look on my face. It didn't help.

"We, uh, we lost the baby," I said flatly. "He died during childbirth. We lost him."

Kaboom.

The reaction was like someone had rolled an open can of tear gas into the salon. Everyone went pale, and people fell away to the far corners of the room, holding their hands over their faces. I spent the rest of my appointment explaining what had happened. I spoke loud enough so that everyone who was eavesdropping could make out what I was saying.

You could have heard a pin drop inside the salon, except for periodic sniffles coming from nearby clients and hairdressers. As strange as it seems, though, that turned out to be a really good exercise. I left feeling like I had relayed the news in a no-nonsense style that expressed our pain while evoking hope rather than pity. Sometimes the ideas or mottos we had come up with didn't become real until they were put into action.

Before leaving, I told them about Noah's toy drive, and they promised to make a donation to the already massive collection. The next day, when Kim and I delivered our toys to the station—I also said a quick thank you to everyone on the air—they had practically filled up an entire truck with toys for needy kids. Through the station, I also received hundreds of supportive e-mails. I had some initial qualms about the station using Noah to promote itself, but I felt like the ends justified the means.

Needless to say, by the end of that second week, we were ready for our escape to the mountains, but first we had our initial session with our KinderMourn grief counselor. Her name is Chris. She is a well-educated, extremely thoughtful woman who began working with KinderMourn after her high school-aged son had been killed in a car accident. You could almost see the weight of that loss in her eyes and the creases it had carved into her face. We couldn't help but wonder if that was how we'd one day appear to the world. She had short, corkscrew curly hair, and she usually wore denim jumpers with soft, cotton pastel shirts underneath. She wore KinderMourn earrings (for sale at $19.95 a pair, I think, and tax deductible). The group's symbol was a line that dips then soars. She drank from a Prozac coffee cup.

During our initial call, Chris had encouraged us to join one of their parental support groups. "Every six months or so we form another group of parents who have lost children," she informed us. It was shocking to learn just how many other parents were going through the same thing. That's the whole idea of the group, of course, but we just didn't feel comfortable boo-hooing in front of strangers. Instead, we signed up for weekly one-on-one sessions.

The modest brick KinderMourn home is full of soft earth tones, comfy chairs, Kleenex boxes and hushed voices. Once inside, we were quickly guided to the basement for our first session.

Over the next several months, KinderMourn would become an invaluable resource. The entire organization selflessly wrapped its arms around us and dozens of other grieving families. They helped us get back on our feet and offered support and a place to speak openly about Noah when, just a few weeks after his death, it seemed like the rest of our world was eager to move on. I've spoken at KinderMourn functions, I've written for their newsletter, and their holiday memorial service is a staple on our Christmas calendar.

But what we learned from KinderMourn, more than anything, was what we *didn't* want to be like. In a strange way that may have helped us even more than if we had really taken to the counseling; like how sometimes you can learn more about a picture by looking at the negative. I can't pinpoint it to one person or one event, but the feeling I got inside that home was that people weren't all that eager to let go and move on. Again, those were some of the most kind, understanding, and helpful people we would meet during our entire journey (Chris in particular), but we never felt a deep connection. They seemed to be a part of this thing we started calling Grief Culture: people who had willingly become defined mostly by their loss in a way that was far more overt than I was comfortable with. They seemed to be sad all the time; in part, because that's when they felt closest to their deceased children. I certainly understood that, but I didn't want to feel close to Noah only when I was sad. I wanted to incorporate his spirit into who I was at all times and on all levels so that his memory would be perpetuated through my life—not just my sadness.

To me, at least, the KinderMourners seemed more reactive to their grief, whereas we wanted to be more proactive. Both ways work. We wanted to attack this thing. We wanted to take it on. We wanted to plow through it. That's who we are. They wanted to tiptoe around it, beg it for mercy, and co-exist. We didn't want any special treatment, while some members of Grief Culture make it perfectly clear that they're entitled to it. I'll never forget a story in USA Today around that time, about a group of grieving parents, one of whom practically hissed at the reporter how people would never understand what they were going through so they shouldn't even try.

Grieving is at once both a universal and unique experience. Understandably, many people find solace and support by joining arms with the grand-style grief family that exists in the world. But in the beginning I was terribly uncomfortable with the way they tried to lump everyone into the same group, the way they kept using the familiar "you" as if we were all the same. I felt like it diminished the uniqueness of Noah. If my grief was all I had, I didn't want to share it or try to lessen my own burden by mixing it in with everyone else's.

I'm sure joining up wholeheartedly with KinderMourn would have been the smarter, more mature, and easier thing to do. My isolated path to recovery was in no way the fault of KinderMourn but the result of my own hangups. Until I learned better, my attitude was: this is my pain. My responsibility. My journey. My recovery. And if I made it through, someday, the rewards would be all mine as well. Was I being self-absorbed? Was that the definition of hubris? Did it make things harder on me? Perhaps. But that's the way I felt and, right or wrong, I had to take my own path, regardless of the consequences.

I'm stubborn, contrarian; a skeptic by nature. Eschewing the masses for my own private path felt right. That has always been how I do things. I locate what I hate or people who I don't want to be like—the emotionless male robot; the humorless, angry, world-owes-me-big-time guy; or the sniveling pity-party wimp—and I try to become the exact opposite. It's backwards, and it doesn't always work, but what can I say, it's my process.

Kim was ready for the work; she always was. All she needed was a road map. Just tell me what to do and where to get started, and get out of my way. That's what she was hoping to get from those sessions—grief homework. Instead, KinderMourn's methods just seemed a bit more, well, wishy-washy.

After we sat down, Chris asked me to speak about what I was dealing with. I told her I was having a really hard time in the mornings, working up enough strength and courage to face the day. Occasionally I agonized over my grief to the point that the agony felt more unbearable than the actual grief. I was scared by a strong feeling that seemed to be bubbling right under the surface of my psyche; a sad siren song drawing me down, begging me, enticing me to just quit, give up and stay in bed all day.

How could I face his death if I couldn't even face the day?

"Well," replied Chris, "what would be wrong with that?"

"With what?"

"Staying in bed all day," she said.

"Are you serious?" I said, moving to the edge of the couch.

"If you feel like staying in bed all day and just crying and thinking about Noah, why not do it?"

I could feel my nose scrunch up. "Well, because that would be like giving up," I said. "Wouldn't it?"

"Hmmm. I don't know."

I begged her, "Is that what I should do?"

"I don't know," she replied from inside her coffee cup, "is that what you want?"

"I don't know. That's why I'm asking you."

"Why do you think you need to ask me?"

"I want your opinion."

"Hmmm."

"I'm scared. Is that what you're waiting for? I'm scared, okay?"

"Okay."

"Is that normal?"

"I don't know, does it feel normal?"

We went around and around like that for the entire session and most of the subsequent ones. Afterward in the car, I told Kimmy how Chris reminded me of Donnie. When we moved to Charlotte, we had a real estate agent with the most annoying habit of never really answering any of our questions. (Like I don't deal with that enough already interviewing athletes and coaches for a living.)

"Hey Donnie, does this neighborhood have good schools?"

"Well, some people think they do, and some people think they don't."

"Is siding better than brick?"

"Well, in some cases siding is better than brick, and in other situations people think brick is better."

Arrrggggh.

That's kind of how those sessions would go.

*I'm exhausted.* That's okay. *I'm angry.* Good, you should be. *I'm devastated.* That's normal. *What should we be talking about as a couple?* Anything you want. *Well, any suggestions where to start?* Do what you feel.

*Arrrggggh.*

We wanted answers, direction, and educated opinions about what we were facing. Maybe they didn't exist. Maybe each person had to discover those on their own, and that's what Chris's ambiguity was trying to help us do. Whatever the case, all we seemed to get was unconditional support communicated with a lot of head nods and sympathetic sighs. After a while it seemed like we were asking more questions about Chris and her grief than we were speaking about Noah. Picking up on our frustration for some concrete advice, Chris directed us to their extensive library of grief-related texts. Kim checked out several books she thought might make for good reading on our trip to the Blue Ridge Mountains.

The next day we packed the books, a few bags, and our Lab Scoop and drove several hours deep into the mountains where we had rented a really nice log cabin near a halfway decent trout stream. We got there just as the sunlight was cascading down between the pines. We unpacked, popped open some drinks, and headed to the rocking chairs on the screened-in back porch.

The first thing I read suggested—I swear—that I take my child's corpse home with me for several days, ála *Weekend at Bernie's*. I should dress him up, push him around in his stroller, show him off to the neighbors. I didn't know whether to laugh, cry, or let my curse words echo across the mountainside.

Instead, I opened the screen door and, leaning over the porch railing, flung the *Weekend at Bernie's* book like a Frisbee deep into the woods. If only book flinging were an Olympic sport. Kim sat there in silence.

"Chris was right," I deadpanned, "these books really do make you feel better." I raised my beer and clinked it with Kim's glass.

There are many wonderful, helpful, and moving texts on grief. We would eventually come to cherish them all. But so far, I hadn't quite found what I was searching for. To me, the books we brought to the mountains were either too religious, too clinical, too broad, or too cliché.

I wanted to read about what I was feeling; something real and raw. I was lost, angry, and confused. But what hurt the most was feeling so alone. I didn't have all the answers, shoot, I didn't have *any* answers. And to be honest, I wasn't all that concerned with the entire world view of grief at that very moment. I was a temporarily lost man; an ordinary father trying to deal with an extraordinary experience. Periodically, it felt like I was getting beaten to a pulp by grief. Yet I wasn't the least bit ashamed of my situation. I had hope, love, and determination. I had pride. I guess all I really wanted to read was that I wasn't alone. The grief I was experiencing was nothing like the neat, tidy step-by-step process in the books I had read. For me, it was a maze. An exhausting, confusing, gut-wrenching mess. But according to what I had read so far, I just wasn't smart enough, religious enough, or man enough to heal myself.

During that time, it was very tempting to be drawn to the advice of others while reconstructing myself; to leave the choices and the work up to someone else. To think, "This time I'm going strictly by the book." Yet what I discovered in the mountains was that after losing everything, it was even more important to remember and rely upon what was left of me: who I am at my core.

That's when I put down the "experts" and picked up my own journal. In that first session I wrote until my forearm cramped, and I couldn't grip the pen anymore. During the rest of our time in the mountains, when I wasn't writing, I took long walks deep in the woods with Scoop. I drank piping hot coffee in the morning and beer cooled in a nearby stream at night. I taught Kim how to fly-fish. The air was crisp and clean. The phone never rang. We talked about the funeral. We talked about our families. We spent days on deserted, rocky riverbanks, staring up at the heavens.

I loved how, late in the afternoon, the warm, orange sunlight would trickle through the trees and tickle my eyes. I'd always stop and raise my chin, letting those rays wash over my face, believing they were from Noah. During those moments, the sadness would fade, and oh so briefly a feeling that was a mixture of enlightenment and anticipation would come over me as I glimpsed the rare opportunity I had been given, at 33, to redefine who I was.

In the mountains, we realized there really were three entities grieving Noah: Kim, me, and our marriage. Sometimes we were all on the same page. Sometimes we were all on our own. Managing those differences, balancing and respecting everyone's unique moods and stages of recovery took considerable energy. It wasn't long before the constant query of "You okay?" or "Howya doing?" got really annoying. So inside our cabin, we developed a quick, simple way to check in with each other. Several times a day, Kim or I would just blurt out, "Whatcha got?" or "Whereya at?" and based on a scale of 1 to 10 (one being the night Noah died) the other would shout back their number.

The grief scale quickly took on a life of its own. Sometimes a nod was all we needed to get a number. When we couldn't talk—in church, mowing the lawn, at a dinner party—we signaled with fingers. We were always trying to predict each other's number. Or one of us might come racing up and say, "I just heard something hilarious that I guarantee will get you to a 5."

We were often within one or two numbers of each other. Still, it was an easy and unobtrusive way to keep an almost constant emotional tab going. Rather than letting stuff fester, it really helped to discover quickly if one of us was having a 2 day or if something had shot one of us up to a 6 (which hadn't happened yet). It also prepared us for the inevitable conflict from unbalanced moods. If, say, Kim shouted back that she was having a 5 while I was working on a 2, we'd either work to get those numbers closer or give each other the space we needed.

We both hovered around 4s and 5s in the mountains. It became clear rather quickly, however, that it wasn't going to be the kind of escape we had hoped for. I don't know what we were thinking. Certainly part of it was the naive notion that if we just left the town where he died, maybe we could get away from the pain of Noah's death for a little bit. Not a chance. That's really what struck us both in the mountains: this thing is a part of us now; we can't escape it; we can't drive up a secluded mountain and get away from it; it's left an indelible mark on every cell of our bodies.

That was one of the things we tried to talk about during the trip home. The only problem was that Scoop had spent so much time foraging in the woods on our trip, that he was now passing the kind of gas that could strip varnish off furniture. In between his flatulence, poor, big fat Scoop was moaning and carrying on as if we had fed him White Castles and Tabasco sauce for lunch. We pit-stopped five times before we even reached the bottom of the mountain.

On the sixth stop, that's when I saw "it." I went around to Kim's window and explained to her that we, uh, had an obstruction.

"Behind the car?" she said.

"Neeeeeooooo, behind the dog."

Kim leaned out the window and got a good look just as Scoop waddled gingerly away from the car. "Oh my God," she said. Whatever it was—vine, twig, stem; we referred to it as simply The Obstruction— it wasn't going anywhere (and neither were we) until I, um, assisted it's departure.

A rear-ectomy is what Kim called it.

I begged and begged her to just let nature take its course.

"No," she said.

"Rock, paper, scissors then," I said. "It's the only fair way."

"He's your dog," she replied, rolling up her window and locking the car doors. "Just yank it out."

"Come on Kimmy, seriously."

Kim was howling with laughter from inside the car. Bent over, slapping her hand against the dashboard, she gasped between breaths, "It's like starting a lawnmower."

"Ha ha, honey," I deadpanned, trying the door handle one more time.

Out of options, I found an old plastic bag to use as a surgical glove and, thankfully, without much problem Scoop was back to his cheery old self.

Somehow that Farrelly Brothers moment seemed like the perfect ending to those strange first two weeks without our son. Janie in Noah's room. Chauncey. The hair salons. The Prozac coffee cup. The Weekend at Noah's child-corpse handbook. The rear-ectomy. The world had not gone dark and deserted on us; it was as weird and goofy and loveable as ever. During the entire procedure, Kim and I giggled, snorted, and roared with laughter until our chests burned. After all the crying we had done during the past week, I didn't think anything could have felt as good as that fit of laughter on the side of some secluded mountain road. I don't know what it was that set us off—maybe we were just looking for something to have some fun with—but I laughed harder at The Obstruction than I had at almost any other time in my life. I can't remember every single bout of tears I shed over Noah, but the episodes of laughter stick out like landmarks. That turned out to be fairly typical of how our recovery would go. We'd exhaust ourselves for weeks at a time, sifting through an entire mountain of rubble for one tiny, shiny piece of clarity, hope, or laughter.

There was something pure and hopeful about Kim and me laughing together for the first time since Noah died. No matter how gross or childish it might seem, realizing, after all we had been through, that we could still find something to laugh about in this world—well, that alone made the trek into the mountains worth it.

And if you think we were happy, man, you should have seen Scoop.

$$\text{CX80}$$

## CHAPTER 9

# Back to Work

On my first day back at work, I sat at a table in a conference room inside the ESPN offices in New York, listening as a half-dozen people vigorously debated the NFL season opener between the Philadelphia Eagles and the Dallas Cowboys. Specifically, the significance of Eagles coach Andy Reid's decision to surprise Dallas with an onside kick to start the game—and the 2000 season.

The ESPN offices look exactly like you might imagine. There are TVs everywhere. The floor is a wild mixture of hoops hardwood, spongy track, and Astroturf. The office clock is a scoreboard. It is not unheard of to walk to the vending machines on consecutive days and pass Dick Vitale, Diana Taurasi, and Gary Bettman. The conference room is called The Garage because it's separated by a giant glass garage door. One that could barely contain the discussion I was witnessing.

People were standing to emphasis points; arms were flailing, there was laughing, shouting, and tremendous passion over a kick that went all of 11 yards. The Cowboys, America's Team, was asleep at the switch! That had set the tone for the entire season! Why don't more teams try onside kicks! We need to do a special on kickoffs and special teams! You'd have thought Reid had unveiled cold fusion on the 50-yard line. The enthusiasm, the humor, and spirit—it was pure ESPN. That kind of underdog 'tude and fervor was exactly why I had decided to leave my increasingly stagnant job at *Sports Illustrated* for the wildly successful upstart biweekly *ESPN The Magazine*.

At that moment, however, I couldn't focus on football. I wondered if I would ever be able to. As the Reid debate raged on around me, internally I was still back inside the tiny recovery room of the hospital, my arms heavy from the phantom weight of my son. I was scared to death to speak because what was really on the tip of my tongue was, "How can you all care so much about some stupid, silly-ass football kick when my son, my baby, my sweet little boy is dead!"

It would take me nearly six more months—along with an inspirational trip back to my college alma mater and the example of a truly courageous father at the Super Bowl—before the same kind of enthusiasm would return to my writing. I was incredibly lucky to be working for people who were patient enough to wait for me to come around. The support I received from my new colleagues in the wake of Noah's death made the move seem serendipitous. After a few days off following their child's funeral, most fathers are expected to return to work, stuff everything down, and pick up right where they left off. At a previous job, I had once traveled for 15 weeks in a row covering the NFL only to be denied a vacation request to celebrate my first wedding anniversary. At the same place, after informing an editor about a player who had opened up about his recently deceased father, the guy responded, "I could care less, everyone's dad dies sooner or later."

That's why I owed it to my boss, Max (that's what everyone calls Papanek), to come back as soon as possible. So before Kim and I left for the mountains, I told him I'd be ready to get started upon our return. I was forcing the issue a bit because if I didn't, I might have just stayed in bed until the Super Bowl. Max suggested I start slow with a get-acquainted visit to the ESPN office, and he graciously insisted that Kim travel with me to New York.

Nevertheless, I was still apprehensive about heading into the office. Less than a month after Noah died, I was unfocused and unmotivated regarding work. It was too soon. I just could not summon the same kind of passion I was seeing. I could in the past—if anything, I had been too absorbed in my work—but it just wasn't there anymore. I got through the first day by reminding myself that in six, five, four more hours I'd be free to taxi back to our hotel, see Kimmy, hold her, and concentrate on our son.

Those were the things that consumed my thoughts, not onside kicks, NFC East standings, and groin pulls. Inside our offices, the world seemed out of whack, as if I was the only one not in on the joke. I felt like the odd man out. (After getting to know the staff, the truth was I couldn't have been more at home.) Wasn't Noah's death supposed to teach me how meaningless that kind of stuff was? And with that attitude, how was I ever going to successfully reenter the world?

When it came to work, Kim was more profoundly changed. Although she had skyrocketed through the management ranks of the paper company she worked for, Kim was already contemplating not going back. She thought about working for a nonprofit or volunteering her expertise for some charitable endeavor, and she had not given up hope of someday staying at home to raise our kids. Noah's death had created a monumental shift in how Kim thought about work. It used to be a big part of how she defined herself. And she had done extremely well. Now, though, she could take it or leave it. She was already longing for the day when her official title changed from regional manager to stay-at-home mom.

But for me, work had to be part of the person I was rebuilding. I'm a writer. Or, at least I fancy myself one. I need to write. We also needed to eat and pay the mortgage. I was lucky, workwise, that my job was fun, meaningful, and fulfilling. It would just take a while to understand that caring about work didn't mean I had to stop caring about Noah or what he had taught me. I didn't have to live in a tent in the mountains and eat twigs to prove how much Noah had changed me. The trick, as always, would be to perpetuate Noah's spirit by merging it seamlessly into my life; in this case, my work and writing.

At first I hated the intrusion of the real world into my mourning. Bills? Mortgages? Deadlines? Writing about the NFL? How dare they? Who gives a rat? "I am an enlightened soul now," I thought, "I can't be bothered by this trivial nonsense." I thought all the utter bullcrap of everyday life no longer applied to me. I was on some higher plane. But in the end, it was often those mundane and unrelenting responsibilities that got my ass out of bed when, had it been left up to me, I would have stayed put. Taking that first step back toward the world was the toughest, most important part of my recovery.

Jumping back into work felt a lot like forcing myself to hang out over the edge of a pool until I had no choice but to fall in. I just had to force myself to begin again and trust that I'd find my way, that the balance would return to my life. And so, early on I decided the only way to fail would be to stand still or go backwards. For now, as long as I moved forward—as long as I packed that bag or made that call or sat in those meetings or wrote that story—I was succeeding.

My first trip was strategically planned for my hometown of Detroit, where the Lions were playing the Tampa Bay Buccaneers. Before the game, and during the next several weeks, I was blown away by how much the news of Noah's death had spread amongst my colleagues. Some of the most touching and thoughtful words came from my former co-workers at *Sports Illustrated*. Many people there sent toys to Noah's drive while others made donations to charities in his honor. I received a tear-stained note from the woman who had been my boss at *SI*. Another touching card from a copy editor mentioned that there were arms extending from New York to Charlotte to support Kim and me in our suffering.

Of course, there were a few people who knew Noah was coming but hadn't heard about his death. During the off-season, I had a lengthy conversation about kids with Mike McCarthy, then the offensive coordinator for the New Orleans Saints. The next time I bumped into him, inside the Saints locker room after a big win, he saw me from across the room and came charging my way, a huge proud-poppa grin spreading across his face.

"HEY! How is that little boy? Is it everything I told you? Aren't they great? Oh man, how is the little guy?" I slid up to him sideways, letting my body language introduce what I was about to say. "Aw man Mike, you're nice to remember and ask about him . . . but . . . our son . . . didn't make it . . . he died during birth."

"Whaaat? . . . uhhhh . . . are you okay? Is your wife okay?"

"We're doing okay . . . we're okay . . . I'm sorry . . . It's nice of you to ask, I don't want to ruin your celebration. . . ." By then, other well-wishers and reporters were encircling us. I stepped away, but Mike never lost eye contact, even as reporters began firing questions at him. He seemed lost for words, then he shouted over the tops of their heads, "That's the kind of thing; it puts football and all this in perspective, right?"

Everywhere I turned—in a field where most of the time ego and talent are inversely related—reporters, coaches, players, and media-relations folks expressed those kind of heartfelt condolences. People I barely knew whispered to me in press boxes and locker rooms that they'd be praying for Kim and me.

It was at once both an uplifting and disturbing occurrence. I was touched by the support and compassion, but it definitely felt weird to be so clearly labeled as a "mourning father." Did people see *me* anymore, or did they just see my grief? Is that how bad I looked? Was I emoting sorrow, exhaustion, and anger? Was it permanent? Every time someone saw me now, it felt like the first thing they thought of was THAT'S THE GUY WITH THE DEAD SON. I'm sure I was imagining a great deal of it, but to me it felt like I was no longer a magazine writer or a friend. Now I was just Mr. DEAD SON.

As much as I wanted people to know Noah and remember what we'd been through, I didn't want that. I didn't want to be defined solely by my grief. Thank God, then, that I had pushed myself back to work as soon as I did. If I hadn't, I never would have understood so quickly the importance, or even the possibility, of compartmentalizing my sorrow. It was not all of me. Even in the depths of my anguish, I was more than just Mr. DEAD SON. I would not be defined solely by my grief. I refused. I would not be characterized by what I had lost, but rather what I had left. It was a part of me, a permanent part. Maybe in August I had started out as 99% sorrow and 1% me, but my goal now was clear: to flip those numbers; to someday be about more than just Noah's death. I was a husband and father. I was a friend, a brother, a son, and yes, a writer too. If I was nothing more than just some hunched-over, destroyed human being who invoked pity, how would that honor Noah?

I still felt a lot of guilt going back to work. I figured that concentrating on something as trivial and meaningless as a paycheck or a football game somehow diminished the magnitude of Noah's death and its impact on my life. Peace, like everything else, would only come when I learned how to incorporate the two. The toughest part had always been the travel. Now that was compounded because every time I drove to the airport, I was leaving half (or more) of my strength behind—I felt terribly guilty about abandoning Kim every time my suitcase came out. I dreaded that period of time just before I left; the tug of war between work and family; the feeling that I was doing a poor job at both. Kim was constantly reminding me to do what Noah taught us: live fully for the moment. When you're here, be here; and when you're at work, be at work. A lot of the time, the only thing that got me in the car was that Noah's cemetery was near the exit before the airport, so I could tide myself over by stopping to see him on my way out of town. It didn't always work.

In early October, while walking to a gate before boarding a flight to Minneapolis for a Monday night game between the Vikings and the Bucs, I caught a glimpse of a father with a pudgy, blue-eyed two-year-old boy on his shoulders. The boy was dressed in jean overalls with a baseball cap on his head and little retro Nikes on his feet. Who knows how many times I had seen fathers and sons like that before without even giving them a second glance. But for some reason, that image hit me like a bat to the shins. I stopped dead in my tracks, leaving hurried passengers to swerve around me like a rock in a stream. With each giggle, with each tickle, with each smile they produced, a part of me seemed to break off and crumble to the carpet. By the time I realized what was happening, I was frozen there in the middle of the terminal, snot and tears pouring out of my face.

Oh God how I wanted my son back at that moment. I ached for him. I wanted so badly to squeeze him and tickle him too. The pain was white hot and throbbing in my chest. It felt like it would break me in half. Those whiplash trips back to square one were, by far, the hardest part of the process. I could be flying along fine and, without knowing it, the tiniest thing would trigger a complete breakdown. In an instant, it felt like all the healing I had done up to that point, all the pep talks and all the rules we had promised to follow had been washed away, and I was reminded just how utterly powerless I was against my grief.

I didn't move. I couldn't. I was crying, yes, but with a glare that dared someone to come up to me or shoot me a curious look. (Periodically that kind of anger would spew out of me like lava released from a volcano. During a movie after Noah's death, I walked over and told some obnoxious teenagers to shut up. And when a rather large stranger on the street scolded Kim with some smartass comment after she crossed against the traffic light, I chased the guy down and told him to mind his own goddamned business.) To avoid a similar scene, I dashed into a nearby bathroom and locked myself in a toilet stall. I knew my flight was already boarding, and I'd miss the game if I stayed in there too long. I tried to catch my breath and figure out just what had hit me out there. Anger? That was just a disguise for the weakness and emptiness I was feeling; the unfairness of it all; the pain of missing Noah; the realization of never getting to do something like that with him. There was guilt from leaving Kimmy; self-pity; the exhaustion of grief management. I guess the sight of the father and son headed out on vacation without a care in the world just tilted my delicately balanced brain.

I wiped my face and pulled myself together as the muffled echoes of the flight announcements ricocheted around the bathroom.

"Can't do it, can't do it," I repeated to myself. "Can't do it. Can't do it."

I was going to miss my flight, miss the game, miss my assignment. And what I realized was, once I explained what happened to the editors in New York, no one would say a word to me. *Poor Dave had a panic attack in the airport. He's all messed up. His kid died. Poor guy. What a shame.* I played it out in my mind and hated the scenario far worse than facing that father and son; the indignities of business travel or being without Kimmy for the next few days. Did I really want to cross that dangerous line where Noah would become an excuse for my weakness instead of the inspiration for my strength? No. Hell no.

The toilet paper was too thin to do the job properly, so I just wiped my nose on my sleeve. I splashed some water on my face and bolted to the gate just as they were about to call my name over the PA system. I wanted to see that boy and his father one more time; to smile at them and let them know (and prove to myself) that everything was okay—but they were long gone. I took my seat. I flew to Minneapolis. I finished my assignment and flew back to Kimmy two days later. Maybe ESPN and I would have been better off if, on occasion, I had stayed home to recharge and recover. But after that I was never even tempted to use Noah as an excuse.

In addition to magazine work that took me all over the globe and to some of the coolest sporting events in the world, dating back to the

Atlanta Olympics, I had also written a weekly Internet column called The Fleming File. My annual Turkey of the Year Awards, handed out around Thanksgiving for bizarre and stupid behavior in the world of sports had become one of the staples of the column. After switching jobs, it was decided that this would be my first piece for ESPN.com. As the deadline approached, I was shocked at how easy it was to step out of myself and really let guys like Ryan Leaf, Bob Knight, and Mike Tyson have it in print. The exercise was a revelation: that I could put my emotional bag of bricks down for a few hours and, when I was ready, pick it back up again without feeling any guilt or shame toward Noah. I remember my dot-com editor and good friend, Jon, laughing out loud over the phone at some of the column points and then adding, "I don't know how you're doing this." They ran it on the front page, and Jon called three days later to say that more than a million people had read the column.

It seemed like half of them e-mailed me back. Some loved the work, others welcomed me to my new gig at ESPN, while many others wrote in with some pretty nasty hate mail, I mean, some real electronic sewage. The thing is, I loved it. There wasn't even a hint of pity in those notes. No one in the world had any idea what had happened to me. I had never been so happy in all my life to be called "an f-ing moron." Mr. DEAD SON was gone. They were treating me normal. It felt good. Work had become like a mini mental vacation. It was refreshing to feel passionate about something other than missing Noah. It didn't dishonor him—not even close. Rekindling my passion for work, art, music, sports, all of it was a way to show my son that I had learned from his death how important it was to soak up every bit of life.

From a work perspective, Noah's death had freed me. It made me stronger; it made me fearless—much more unafraid to fail. Once again I found that the ultimate control over my life came from the least likely source: the power to let it all go. At first I was too exhausted mourning Noah to sweat the little things. By the time I got my strength back, it had become a habit: identifying the elements of my life that I couldn't control and just letting . . . them . . . go. (When I realized this approach was baffling and enraging to some of the cutthroat go-getters in my field, I knew I was on to something.) That, in turn, helped me find peace from moment to moment with far less effort. As a result, I'd never felt calmer or more content with work or life.

Simple pleasures seemed to be magnified. I remember when Warren Zevon was close to death during his battle with cancer; someone asked him what he had learned from it all. His response was, "Enjoy every sandwich." That may be the best way to sum up how something like this changes you: the seismic shift that often occurs is that you stop chasing all the big stuff and learn to savor the simple pleasure of a good pb&j. Along with that, in light of Noah's death, I found that I was no longer even capable of getting upset over the stupid little things; stuff like traffic jams or disagreements at work that used to consume most of my days.

Noah had changed my perspective on work in the same way he had shifted my view of everything else: If I can survive the death of my son, then what could work possibly throw at me? After holding my son in my arms until the warmth left his body, how could a deadline or a difficult assignment or a botched first draft be that big a deal?

Work would never be my life, but in many ways it helped me feel alive again.

## CHAPTER 10

# Sparring With The Almighty

St. Peter's is a quaint but vibrant church in the heart of downtown Charlotte. When we moved there, I was immediately drawn to the inclusive ideology as well as the setting. They reminded me of my childhood church in Detroit. Behind the altar at St. Pete's is a beautiful mosaic with intricate shards of red, orange, and gold tiles that make it appear as though Jesus himself is hovering over the congregation. Each time I considered heading back to church, I thought about facing that mosaic and decided to wait another week. Before we knew it, two months had gone by.

Although we hadn't been inside our church for awhile, I was contemplating my faith, beliefs, and spiritual self more than ever before. I was grateful and perplexed, humbled and angry, drawn to and repulsed by the very thought of God—often at the same time. Our first trip back to St. Pete's wouldn't be any different.

We arrived just seconds before the choir and celebrants entered the church. (I hadn't lost my touch in that regard.) Without paying any attention, we slipped into one of the few open pews. Our backs hadn't even touched the wooden benches when . . . WHAM . . . staring back at us over the shoulder of his daddy was a blue-eyed baby boy with tufts of brown hair and chubby red cheeks. He was in the seat directly in front of us, and he had to be about two months old. Kim and I gulped hard, looked at each other, and began to dissolve toward the floor. I spun around looking for a way to discreetly exit the pew for something a bit less challenging, but the choir was already on the move. The music had begun. We were locked in our seats.

That baby destroyed us. He cooed, blinked, and bobbed his head up and down searching for his thumb; and with each glance backward, whatever wounds deep inside us that had begun to heal were tearing back open. We had been adamant about not coveting other babies. But this? This was cruel and unusual. This was us being brave enough to tiptoe back to church and God teasing us like a bully.

Kim was sad. I was pissed. It was then that I glanced up at the altar and locked eyes with the Jesus mosaic. I swear it felt like that picture was snickering at me; as if God himself had sucker punched me in the gut and was now chuckling about it as he watched me gasp for air. I blinked. I rubbed the tears out of my eyes. I squinted and looked back up at him—nothing had changed. Jesus was mocking me.

*Yeah, that's right, I took your son. Right up here. Me. I've torn your perfect little life to shreds, haven't I? Reduced Mr. Know-it-all to a weepy, weak, confused little child. Took everything you valued. Turned your world upside down. Everything's not so funny anymore, is it? The doctors didn't do it. Noah didn't do it. I did it. Me. Right up here. Now get down on your knees and praise me.*

I was doubled over in the pew with my chin on my chest, shaking my head, "No."

"No," I whispered softly, "No."

Kim looked at me, confused. Her face asked the question: What are you saying? No? No to what? No to this pew? No to that baby? No to church? No to God?

No to it all.

I've been to Sunday school. I took the confirmation classes. I was an acolyte. I've read the bible. My dad's a priest, for crying out loud. What I'm saying is that I thought I knew what I was supposed to know when it came to God—all the biggies, at least. Trust Him. Have faith. Ten commandments. Do unto others. Love Him more than anything else. He only gives you what you can handle. Every time God closes a door, He opens a window. The single set of footprints in the sand. Whatever. Those simpleton solutions were great for ashtrays and postcards, but they weren't really helping with my complicated problems.

If God wanted a fight, if that's where we were going, I was ready. I mean, there's only so much you can take, even from a deity. That moment in church felt like high noon in one of those old cowboy movies.

*You're omnipotent, right? You must be because you've been shoving that idea down my throat my entire life. You're the all-knowing, Almighty, right? But how much sense does it make to claim to be in charge of everything and then, when something horrible happens, I'm not allowed to hold You responsible? I'm not supposed to question Your plan? I'm just supposed to have faith that You know what You're doing? I'm not the greatest reporter in the world, but even I can see through that kind of transparent, circular logic. I mean, what a cop-out. You can do any kind of wacky shit you want and Your answer to the tortured soul is: if you really have faith you won't question Me. That's the spiritual equivalent of a kid asking his dad, "why?" and the dad replying, "BECAUSE I SAID SO!" Can't you do better than that?*

I tried to focus my defiant glare on that mosaic, but my view of the altar was partially obstructed by a giant wooden support beam. (That was why the pew had been vacant.) On the beam, perfectly arranged in my line of sight, was a small brass plaque acknowledging that the stained glass window to our right had been dedicated by the Hope family.

I tugged Kim's hand toward the plaque to get her attention. She followed my nod upward and I watched her read the plaque. She bowed her head and pinched her eyes shut in a way that sealed out the tears. We both just shook our heads, baffled. Yes, I was grateful for the intermittent bursts of strength and the peace during my darkest hour. I would gladly fall on bended knee to thank Him for sparing Kimmy. I should have also been grateful that our high-risk pregnancy specialist had recently assured us we could have more children. In my heart, I knew it wasn't right to praise Him one day and curse Him the next. But at times, I've got to tell you, it felt like He had flooded our lives, washed away everything, then just stood over the destruction and, in a distracted sort of way, you know, toothpick twirling in His mouth, half-heartedly dangled life jackets at us.

I sat in that pew with my head down for what seemed like forever, and I asked myself, What do I want? What do I need? Don't be a coward. He's right up there. Ask Him to His face. What did I want? It was right on the plaque above my head. Hope, I finally realized. I wanted to feel hope again. Okay, well, how do I find hope? Where is it? What produces it? Give it to me. Now.

Faith.

He who has faith has hope, and he who has hope has everything.

I had been so concerned with questioning *my* faith in God that I hadn't realized He was probably just as skeptical of His faith in me. I was an ace student when everything was going swell, wasn't I? But at the first sign of trouble, I was ready to bail? To Him, I was that spoiled toddler whining "Why? Why? Why?" to questions that don't have answers as much as solutions: trust. And trust, like faith, like hope and like belief, are meaningless concepts until they've been tested. I knew about faith; what I didn't understand was that living it, using it, exercising it, was something different than just having it.

I know what it's like to jump out of an airplane. I've read about it, watched it on TV, talked to people who have done it, but I've never actually stepped out of a plane into thin air and plummeted toward earth. Knowing about faith is very different than having faith. Until now I hadn't realized they were two different things. For the most part, I had been taking my faith on faith. Until it had been tested, how would I ever really know for sure? If there was some perverse blessing in all of this that was it. While others would be left to wonder about the depth and strength of their faith, I was about to take mine for a test drive. It's petrifying and enlightening at the same time.

I don't remember anything about that service, other than we made it through. It was just before noon by the time church let out and we made our way home. Sparring with God while toughing out that service, especially in the face of that baby, had exhausted us both. Kim and I kicked off our shoes and climbed into bed for a nap.

"I didn't get anywhere," I told her.

Kim laughed. "Don't worry," she said, "God'll meet you where you are."

When we were in New York together during my first trip to ESPN, Kim had gone back to her old stomping grounds near Midtown. "Retail therapy," she called it. But on her way to Prada, she felt drawn to an old, empty church a few doors down. Kim wandered in and sat down. "Did I do something wrong?" she asked. "Was I being punished? Am I not supposed to be a mom?" She wanted answers. She wanted control. But instead, what she felt called to do was surrender. After that, she found her peace with God.

It was interesting how our personalities dictated our paths back to God after Noah died. Kim humbled herself and began to intellectually dissect and study the problem. Out of that came Scripture Chicks. I was more standoffish and skeptical, always the contrarian.

Surrender? That's Your solution? You've got to do better than that. If You're a God, prove it.

While I was at work, Kim sat inside that church for most of the day wondering, "When will I be myself again?" The answer she came up with was, never. We will never be the same again. So we should stop trying. And if it was true that we would never be the same after Noah's death, then God must have *wanted* us to change.

*But I don't want to change*, Kim remembers thinking. Neither did I. To be perfectly honest, I thought I was a pretty good guy before Noah died. I didn't think I needed that much work. I was a good husband. I was a good friend, son and brother. I was honest, loyal, funny, happy. What more did God want from me? Why not teach some corporate thief or some corrupt politician a lesson? Why not take their kid? It gnawed away at me; the thought that had I been more open to the idea of change, maybe God wouldn't have been forced to take our son to get my attention. *You are coming to Me. Now, we can do this the hard way or the easy way, it's up to you.* I, of course, chose the hard way. But was that really the only way He could get my attention? If so, we both need help. I mean, why couldn't God teach us those lessons, or rebuild us, without having to kill our son? He's God, right? He could have figured out a different way, you'd think.

In the end, though, He wasn't the one who was unwilling. The hard truth was that I never would have been changed that significantly had it been left up to me. That, more than anything, is what pushed me in my recovery. I didn't want to make the same mistake twice. The only thing worse than Noah's death would be not learning anything from it.

A week after our first trip to church, I was dreading another face-off with that mosaic Jesus. Sensing that, Kim pulled an audible.

"Let's skip church and go golfing," she said.

"I love this woman," I thought while loading my clubs into our Durango.

With every passing day it had become clear to me just how much of my suffering had been eased by that wonderful woman; by our supportive families; by our compassionate friends; and the freedoms, financial and otherwise, of a good job. My son was dead. No amount of money or compassion could change that, but I was still blessed in many ways.

It was a picture-perfect day. The sky looked like a blue, fresco-painted dome, and we had the course to ourselves. Every deep breath seemed to reinflate my spirit. The second hole is a dogleg right, par 5 with home construction running down one side of the fairway. My tee shot landed in what would someday be someone's swimming pool. Climbing through the chunky, overturned earth, I found my ball, then did a Judge Smails back onto the grass. I pushed a nice fairway wood back into play, then turned to Kimmy and, out of nowhere, I asked her, "Are we gonna sue the hospital?"

"Everyone's wondering that you know," Kim replied.

"Well?"

Over the next six holes we discussed the idea of a lawsuit for the first—and last—time.

No one who loses a child the way we did could ever be satisfied with the care they received. If we were lucky enough to have more children, we had already decided to use another hospital. But was Noah's hospital negligent? Could they have prevented Noah's death? We were expert witnesses in that regard because the whole ugly mess unfolded right before our eyes. What we both felt in our gut was that his death was so decisive, there could be no question of fault. There was no way I could put my hand on a Bible and swear that I thought the nurses or the doctors had messed up. The only altruistic reason for a lawsuit would be to protect other children. If that wasn't necessary, then we'd only be sullying Noah's memory by trying to extract some form of revenge.

This in no way makes me superior to some other parent who decides to sue after the death of their child. In fact, I was grateful in some bizarre way that our situation was so cut and dry. Had there been any question, even the slightest bit of doubt, we would have gone to court. Had we needed money to pay for counseling, had we determined other children needed to be protected or had we just needed to investigate further for our own piece of mind, we would have sued in a second.

We trusted Ed's medical opinion. And he had found no faults. We trusted Kim's doctor. Leedylyn was a friend, a woman of heart and conscience not beholden in any way to that hospital. (She was scheduled to deliver Noah, but was not on call the night he died.) I was certain if something had gone wrong she would have told us.

Still, it was awfully tempting to think about unburdening ourselves by transferring the blame and the pain to others. Handing over the responsibility of creating and keeping Noah's legacy to a lawyer or a court room was a very tempting, but dangerous emotional trap for me. Blame would have been like heroin. Oh how I craved it; just a teeny weeny little bit to unburden my heart or as a way to focus all that anguish somewhere else for even a short while. If I used it once, I knew I'd be hooked.

What would a lawsuit really get us? Cash? A million? A billion? It didn't matter. Any amount they might offer as compensation for Noah's life would be an insult. Any amount would cheapen us both. Was money what we really needed? Was it more precious to us than, say, healing or peace? How would an ugly, drawn-out, disingenuous lawsuit do anything but pick at the scabs we were trying to turn into scars?

I don't want to come across as high-and-mighty because, like I said, in my heart I knew there was nothing to sue over. Still, it's one thing to talk about the value of peace; it's one thing to pretend you don't value money above all else; but it's another thing altogether to put your money where your mouth is. That's what we did. And I was proud of our decision. For some reason, pride is a word no one ever wants to associate with the process of grieving. *Keep your head down. Don't dare to be so bold, or you're just asking for it again.* But for me it was one of the motivating factors of my recovery. I wanted Noah to be proud of the way his dad handled himself. I wanted Kim to be proud of me as a husband. Someday I wanted to be able to look back on all of this and be proud of myself.

We were almost done with the front nine. The final two holes actually run right by our house. The picturesque ninth has an elevated tee above a pond that gives you the feeling you're soaring through the pines. I'm not big on practice swings or any convoluted kind of warm-up, but before chilly-dipping my tee shot into the pond, I stood over the ball for a long time as a single message ricocheted through my head.

*I'm not a hypocrite. I'm not asking you to do something I myself wasn't willing to do . . . watch My only son die.*

Kim was right: God had known exactly where to find me. That brief moment of empathy was a revelation. Clouded by anger, I had missed the obvious. God wasn't an adversary, He was a confidante, a fellow grieving Father; for His own son . . . and for me. I was confused about a lot of things, but I was suddenly certain that no father who had watched his son die in that way could just arbitrarily do that to someone else without being absolutely certain of his reasons—and even then it still had to be agonizing. In a way, I felt sorry for God for being constantly burdened with those kinds of decisions.

I was still wildly curious about the "why" behind the sudden death of an innocent baby. But reestablishing my trust in God made "why" a moot point. If I trusted Him, if I truly trusted Him, then I didn't need to know why. That whole time I was trying to jump ahead in line. I wanted hope, but first I needed to have faith, and to establish faith, I had to start with trust. As the father of a dead child, I felt I was entitled to skip ahead to hope. *Just give me my hope, and I'll be on my way.* That seemed fair. But I had been coming at it from the wrong direction. My attitude had been, "Show me the fairness in Your decision and, if I'm satisfied with Your logic, then I'll trust You enough to have faith and hope."

I had it backwards. It didn't work that way. I was up in the attic, alone and indignant, searching for the meaning of life (as well as death) when God had been standing on my front porch ringing the doorbell.

Fairness? How did I ever come up with that as a starting point for our negotiations? (Again, I saw myself as the petulant toddler, tugging on God's robes, kicking and screaming, "It's not fair, IZ-NA-FAuRR!") Fairness has nothing to do with God or the world. Fairness is a man-made concept. That was a phrase I would repeat to myself a million times in the next year. Fairness is a man-made concept. Imagine how meaningless faith would be if everything was fair? No wonder I was so dang tired all the time. I had been wearing myself out looking for something that didn't even exist.

"You think any of this makes sense, you know, theologically?" I asked Kim.

"Theo-what-ically?" she replied.

"On a theological level."

Kim giggled, shaking her head. "Does that really matter?" she asked.

"I don't know."

"If you ask me, it only matters if you're a theologian who lost his son," she said. What was important was that it made sense to me; that it balanced out in my mind and gave me peace.

I spent the rest of the round chopping it all over the course, far too occupied with those new revelations to even care. I had thought surrendering would make me feel even more powerless and weak. But it had the opposite effect. I felt clarity. I felt reconnected to God and the world. I felt infused by a kind of spiritual harmony that suddenly made a lot of other once-faraway concepts, like energy, hope, and joy, seem much closer.

If only I could say the same for the prospect of breaking 100. After three-putting for a double bogey on 18, we pulled the golf cart back around to the clubhouse. The attendant unloaded my golf bag and quizzed me about my round. I hadn't added up the damage yet, but I was pretty sure it was right around 100—give or take a dozen strokes.

The kid sighed as if to say, "Aw, well better luck next time."

But I was already certain that had been the best round of my life.

## CHAPTER 11

# An Elephant at
# Thanksgiving Dinner

Thanksgiving would be the first major holiday for us after Noah died. Normally we spend it with Kim's family in Dayton. That year, though, we didn't have the energy or the focus to drive the 10 hours to her home in Ohio, and it saddened us to be missing our first Thanksgiving there in more than a decade. So we were elated to hear that Kim's family—Grandbob, Grandjean, Ed, Janie, and Kristen— were going to come to our house for the holiday. In preparation for the visit, Kim was shopping for flowers at a nursery when she spotted a garden stone etched with the word HOPE. She brought it home and placed it in the front corner of our yard. That way anyone who entered our home, be it from the garage or the front door, would first have to pass by that stone and, without thinking, whisper to themselves the ideal that had become more important to us than food, water, or oxygen.

Hope.

Kim and I went a bit further. Each time we passed the Hope rock, we tapped it and said "hope" out loud. It was a reminder and a confirmation of sorts, like football players who tap some symbolic, gilded jock strap as they pass out of the locker room and down to the playing field.

When Kim's family pulled up to our house the day before Thanksgiving in their champagne colored Buick, they parked right next to our Hope rock. Grandbob, in fact, nearly stepped on it as he exited the car.

Grandbob is a lovely mix of Billy Graham and Gomer Pyle. He is a riot, in an old-fashioned, hard of hearing sort of way. Once, when Kim was on a steroid-free milk kick, Grandbob thought our milk actually had extra 'roids and he began complaining that his breasts were growing. "Feel my breasts Dave, feel 'em," he said. He had a penchant for great simple bits of wisdom. To him, the modern toilet is a work of art because of it's simplistic efficiency. He lives in Dayton with Grandjean, his wife of 59 years. I love them both. Grandjean is a matronly, silver-haired former school teacher and a women of great spirit and faith. They are both down to earth, kind, and hopelessly square. They both just say what's on their mind.

"Is that what I think it is?" Bob blurted out, jumping back as if the rock was a land mine.

"What Bob? What do you mean?" I replied. Around us, everyone else was hugging hello and grabbing luggage out of the car.

"You know," he said looking down at the Hope rock, "Noah's grave?"

Kristen overheard his question. She held her breath. Then we both nervously giggled. "Uh, no Bob, no," I said softly, "it's just a rock. Kim bought that a few weeks ago. Noah's buried in a cemetery near downtown. We can go see him if you want. But that's not him right there. That's not Noah."

Because Noah's death was so sudden, Grandbob and Grandjean were not able to make the trip down for his funeral—something I know they both regretted deeply. We did too. Grandjean is one of those quiet but strong people whose very presence has a calming effect on everyone around her.

Bob was exhausted from the trip and a bit out of it, so his *faux pas* was understandable. No big deal. From the beginning, we had pledged not to be hypersensitive about stuff like that. I hated the thought of people walking on eggshells around us, scared to speak because they might accidentally mention something—a child, a birth, a death—that would remind us of Noah.

The truth is I loved being reminded of Noah, even by accident. I loved talking about him. I lived to hear his name out loud, spoken by others. I needed that. We both did. The problem was most people assumed the exact opposite was true, that any mention of Noah would reduce us to rubble. And we hadn't yet become comfortable letting people know where we stood.

Bob had just verbalized something that was on everyone's mind. Noah. His death. His grave. His place in our home and our lives. My guess was Kim's family had spent the trip down to Charlotte talking about Noah and our recovery and creating a game plan for their visit. A game plan that I'm sure was formed out of love and loaded with good intentions. A game plan that was, nevertheless, a horrendous failure. And a valuable learning experience for us all.

Kim's family would be in our home for the next three days, and Grandbob's confusion about Noah's grave was the only time our son's name was ever spoken.

I knew in light of the way Ed had handled the death of Kim's birth-mother that they would be on the conservative side of this process; the less said the better. And I wasn't trying to wedge the boy into every conversation. Honest. I hadn't greeted everyone saying, "Welcome Ed. Welcome Janie. HEY! I wonder what Thanksgiving is like UP IN HEAVEN?!!!" But at that point Noah was constantly on our minds. It was pretty much all we thought about. So it was only natural that, eventually, some of the conversations would come back around to him.

Yet every time we got even close to meandering into the subject of Noah, his death or our recovery, Janie or someone else would hijack the conversation—sometimes physically jumping in between us—to interject something fluffy and light.

It went something like this:

"Yeah, well, work's pretty good but it's hard for me to be away from Kimmy knowing that . . ."

"HEY YOU GUYS, HAVE YOU BEEN PLAYING MUCH GOLF? I LOVE GOLF. ONE TIME A FEW WEEKS AGO, ED AND I WERE PLAYING AND . . ."

Or this: "The holidays are a time to think about family . . ."

"HEY, WHO DO YOU GUYS THINK WILL BE IN THE SUPER BOWL THIS YEAR, HUH? HUH? WHAT DO YOU THINK?"

It was sweet, in a way. If it wasn't so awkward, it would have been kind of funny. We were going to have a shiny-happy Thanksgiving. Even if it killed us.

To be fair, Kim's family was just trying to do what they thought was best for us, which was give us a few days when we didn't have to think about Noah. But that was, and is, impossible. Aliens flying the Oscar Mayer Weinermobile could have landed in our front yard and handed us the winning Lotto ticket, and we still would have been thinking about Noah. His gravestone had just come in a week earlier. It was a classic, shiny, black and gray speckled marble tablet with his name and his birth date etched in simple black letters. At the last second Kim had added the perfect touch to the top of the stone. Two simple words: Our Son. When we traveled down to get a look at it, it shocked us how the grass hadn't even grown back on the dirt where he was laid to rest. He had not even been dead three months.

Talking about our son didn't make us sad. What we quickly found out, though, was ignoring him and reducing him to an elephant in the corner of the room hurt like hell. What stung even more was that we let it happen. I am Noah's dad. I was supposed to protect him and stand up for him—guard his memory, his legacy. Jesus, that task is what got me out of bed most days, yet I was letting him down. And the longer we went without speaking about him, the more that elephant grew, and the more I became crippled by my own confusion, anger and pride.

I kept thinking about Noah watching over us and wondering why no one spoke his name. I wondered if he was sad, if he worried that we had forgotten him already or that we didn't care. I mean, it was Thanksgiving, a time for family, and he had been left out—completely. I was ashamed. I had betrayed my own son.

Kim and I really didn't know how to handle that situation, how to plead to her family or encourage them softly to open up about Noah. We didn't know how to ask people to give us what we needed. And until we learned, we were at the mercy of our guests. Without that ability, we were forced to join in the charade. The elephant in the corner grew into a Tyrannosaurus Rex.

An hour without Noah moved into a day. The more time went by, the harder it became to break free. Kim's family took our silence as approval, a tacit sign that they were correct in assuming we didn't want to talk about him. Empowered, their force field against Noah gained strength.

The first two days came and went. Nothing. Oh, we talked a lot, everyone got along famously, had a great time, but we didn't say anything. Golf. Weather. Politics. Sports. We went to the driving range. We went to the mall. We went on walks. We watched movies. Nothing. We literally talked for hours about the stock market, but we didn't once mention Noah. What was wrong with us?

In bed that second night, I told Kim that the next day I was just going to scream his name out loud at breakfast. She begged me not to. She didn't want to make waves. She is a pleaser, particularly when it comes to her family. Kim was caught in the middle. The good Catholic schoolgirl never wanted to make her family uncomfortable in any way. (Heck, she used to ground herself as a child.) I've always believed she pursued that goal at the expense of my feelings. That was an issue we had been dealing with for years, long before Noah. Now we added a dead child to the mix—and it became toxic.

I felt like she had abandoned us—Noah and me, our family—and plastered a joker's smile on her face to appease her parents. She, on the other hand, wanted to know why I couldn't just go three days without talking about him.

"Because it's Thanksgiving in OUR HOUSE, NOAH'S HOUSE, YOUR SON'S HOUSE, remember?" I shouted.

Kim begged me to be quiet. That just made me more angry.

I pointed to the sky, the words scratching their way out of my throat, "He's up there right now wondering, you know, why mommy and daddy are talking about the weather and your dad's backswing instead of him . . . "

"That's ridiculous," Kim said. "Stop forcing him down everyone's throat."

"Oh come on," I said, "I am not."

"It's too much. Ease up. We're all thinking about him, *you know everyone is thinking about him*, shouldn't that be . . . isn't that enough? Let them grieve how they want."

"But what about me?" I said. "What about what I want? Jesus. I don't want all Noah all the time. I swear. But when he comes up he comes up. Why is that so hard?"

"Your family talks about Noah too much," she countered.

"Oh, here we go. Fine," I yelled.

Kim cut me off. "That's not right either," she continued. "I admit it's weird to not even mention his name, but I don't know what to do. I don't know what to do. What do you want me to do?"

Mourning our son was a daily struggle, an exhausting and nearly impossible task. But now we had to learn how to serve his memory—and our needs—within the often-times messed up dynamics of our families. A death like this only exaggerates and exacerbates pre-existing issues.

I had just assumed we'd all make Noah a part of this holiday, but I was wrong to jump to that conclusion. Some people just aren't all that comfortable chitchatting about their dead grandchild. That was perfectly understandable. In the grand scope of things, Kim's family was as supportive and loving to us as anyone had been in the wake of Noah's death. The timing of Kristen's calls and cards always seemed serendipitous. Late one night in the week following Noah's death, Kim and I were in bed talking quietly when, unannounced, Kristen slipped into our bedroom. Bursting with tears and without hesitating she embraced Kimmy and whispered to her, "I'm not always the greatest at showing it, but I love you so much, and I'm so so sorry you lost your Noah. I think about you guys so much, all the time, and I just love you both, and you'll get through this." It was one of the most pure, honest and touching expressions of grief I have ever seen.

Part of Kristen's message was that Kim's family just did things their own way: with cards and notes and more subtle but deeply loving and spiritual gestures. There is no right or wrong way to grieve. The real mistake was not talking about it and letting the issue fester. I should have trusted my instincts as a parent and communicated my needs to my family.

Instead, I just stubbornly believed when the visit began that we would all quickly make a plan to travel down to his grave for a visit one afternoon. I didn't think it would be a big deal or a huge production. I didn't expect everyone to go, only those who wanted to. But it was Thanksgiving after all. Noah's first. When I couldn't even get people to speak his name out loud—trust me, I tried—I became crippled with anger and resentment. I retreated into a shell.

The NFL. The weather. Christmas. Blah. Work. Blahblahblah. Grandbob. The Farsons. Blah. ESPN. blah. Deep-fried turkey. Blah. College. Blah. Weather. Cooking. Retirement. The stock market. Church. Good morning. Good night. TV. Movies. Blah. Another day. Blah blah endless blah.

Certainly, I thought, no matter what, Noah would be mentioned at the Thanksgiving dinner. It was our home, after all. His home. It had been three days and not a word about our son. By then, however, it was no longer about him. It was about my ego as a father and a grieving parent. It was a contest of wills now. Who would break first.

What I should have done was taken one person aside—Janie, perhaps—and told her softly that we needed to speak his name; we needed to make Noah a part of the holiday, but in a way that everyone was comfortable with. Case closed. Problem solved. Instead, I put my own pride ahead of my son's. I used Noah's memory to be petty. I had a long way to go as a parent.

I'm probably as close to Grandjean as anyone in Kim's family. Yet on that trip, I felt a huge gap between us. We both wanted to talk about Noah. There was so much to share. I valued her opinions, insight, and spirituality, and I wanted to know what she thought or how she was feeling. For me, every time I spoke about Noah to someone, it was as if they were allowed to grab hold of the burden and lighten my load for a bit. Yet we both held back. We never bridged that gap. It was frustrating and sad. At a time when I needed family more than ever, I felt as distant from them as I ever had. I had really missed an opportunity, especially with Grandjean.

I learned later that she had felt the same way. She wanted to talk, but she wasn't sure how to bring him up or if it was even okay to speak his name. She was waiting for a signal from me. And I was waiting for a signal from her. Grandjean felt terrible that she had missed his funeral. She wanted to see his grave on that trip; needed to for her own sense of closure. At her age she feared that she had missed her last opportunity to visit Noah in person. That just broke my heart and solidified for me the real-life consequences of my mistakes.

Three days into what was otherwise a delightful visit, we sat down on Thanksgiving to eat our deep-fried turkey. Ed jumped in and quickly blessed the food. I bit my tongue and fought back the anger and tears.

"Let's eat," someone chirped. By then I had lost my appetite.

I wobbled between rage and laughter the rest of the visit. His name was never spoken. Their Buick had barely gotten to the end of the street when Kim and I piled into our own car to race down to the cemetery.

We had already made mistakes in this process, and we would continue to make many many more. But instead of letting the frustration get to us and dam up our growth, we always tried to analyze what went wrong and learn from it. I have always learned more from my failures than successes. It's just the way I am. I'm a contrarian. Rather than a goal or a role model, I do better with a clear understanding of, *Okay, so this is what I don't want to do or be like? Got it.* On that front, Thanksgiving gave me a lot to work with; which means, in the grand scheme of things, even that bizarre holiday helped move us forward. A few weeks later, Kim came up with the idea to order a dozen or so Noah Christmas tree ornaments and send them to our families so they could hang them on their trees. That way, she thought, it would be impossible to repeat the mistakes of Thanksgiving.

Alone again in the car on the way to the grave, the tension dissipated. I began to cry. I explained to Kim that I was deeply ashamed that I had dishonored Noah's memory. I wasn't mad at her. I wasn't mad at her family. I loved them dearly for coming down to be with us and caring enough to try so hard at willing us to be happy. I was mad at myself. I had the opportunity to change the way things had gone during Thanksgiving, and I had failed. It was my responsibility. We couldn't assume that people who knew us would just naturally know how to help us with something like that. It was clear now that we had to teach our families how to help us remember our son and if we didn't, the person who paid the price would be sweet little Noah.

"Because of me, Noah missed his first Thanksgiving," I said. "I failed him as a father, Kim. It doesn't matter to me why or how or whose fault it is. We betrayed him."

At his grave, the first thing I did was bend down on my knees and apologize. It had been a while since I had cried that hard. I just told him I was sorry; that I had made a mistake; that I wasn't perfect. I was still learning how to be his dad. He had to be patient.

I looked into his gravestone, and I vowed to never again sacrifice Noah's memory to spare someone else's feelings.

"This will never happen again, Noah," I said softly. "I promise."

# CHAPTER 12

# Noel Nadir, The Beginning

Three days before Christmas we were moping around our house dreading the impending holiday like a dentist appointment.

A big part of the Noel nadir was that it was the first landmark, the first time when it was obvious and poignant that someone was missing. When I woke up on November 16th or any other "normal" day, I'd miss Noah with every beat of my heart. But when I woke up around the holidays and he wasn't there, the void became magnified. Even if I managed to get a break for a minute or two, surely a commercial, a song, a decoration, or some kind of ubiquitous, saccharine Christmas crappola would poke at my brain with a fondue fork and remind me of my dead son—just in case I had missed the other 14 million messages about how damn happy I should be at Christmas.

Maybe it's that the holidays are supposed to bring out the kid in all of us. Or maybe it's that everyone who has kids or wants kids daydreams about their first holiday together: putting out cookies for Santa, staying up late to build the kid's bikes and the looks on their faces as they jumped down the stairs in the morning. That is the stuff that makes mourning a child at Christmas like running a marathon with a splinter; every step is more painful than the next.

At a time when most people were out finishing their last minute shopping, we had yet to hang a single light, a single ornament, or a single piece of tinsel. We stood in the front room of our house 72 hours before Christmas trying to convince each other we could get away without the normal holiday decorations.

"What about a tree?" asked Kim. "Are we ever going to get a tree?"

"Screw the Christmas tree," were my exact words.

We eventually found ourselves in the local Home Depot. I pointed to the first tree I saw, the absolute closest living green thing to our car, grabbed that thing by its throat, dragged it to the counter, paid for it, and crammed it into our car in less than five minutes. Once we got home, I threw it into the stand like planting a flag. Kim tossed the lights on. We dropped a few ornaments in place and dumped the tinsel over the top. Had we not been slowed by fits of laughter, the whole project would have taken less than 10 minutes.

The tree was pure Charlie Brown, completely devoid of holiday cheer. It was as if we had picked an arbor that didn't want to be a Christmas tree. Just looking at it made us giggle.

At some point this was all going to get to us. The weeping would come. The sorrow would overtake us. Like the holiday itself, there was no avoiding it. Looking ahead, the thought of suffering through fruitcake, relatives, long lines, and Mr. Chronically-Flatulent-Mall Santa—all of it without our baby boy—well, it was all just too sad and pathetic.

So we took what little control we had and laughed at it all, including ourselves. In both physiology and cathartic release, laughter is a lot like crying. Only instead of surrendering to your misery, it feels like you're controlling it in some small way by saying, "No matter what you throw at me, I'm always going to be able to find something that's funny about it." If humor is the "divine spark" then laughter is the flamethrower. It's the sound hope. And if there was one thing that kept me from going under, it was the squeaky joy of Kim's robust laughter.

The main reason we had come as far as we had in the past four months was because we didn't do end-arounds on the tough stuff. We had faced something like that recently when some friends had their daughter at the same hospital where Noah had died. We knew no one would raise an eyebrow if we skipped the requisite hospital visit. We knew they'd understand. We didn't want to go back there and tip over all that garbage again. But we considered it a challenge—a test. Were we as far along as we said? Had we found peace with what occurred in that hospital? Did we really mean it when we said we didn't want people to feel self-conscious about their own kids because of Noah's death? Well, that was a way to find out; a way to prove it to ourselves.

Kim always liked to say that you can never get milestone moments back. Everyone might understand why we missed a birth, a wedding or a party, but then our absence, and more so, our excuse, would be locked up with that occasion forever. Kim was flexible on just about everything else but on that she was adamant. She didn't want to look back on that one day and feel small and petty for missing that birth. She did not want that to be a part of Noah's legacy.

So we went to that hospital. We held our shaking hands in the elevator. We walked down those very same hallways, past the very same nurses, all the way to where that new, precious baby was, which just happened to be the room next door to where Kim stayed after her emergency C-section. The same place, in fact, where I cold-called funeral homes. We bit our lips. We honored our friends and our son. We did the right thing. Afterward, we felt pride instead of shame; a sense of accomplishment for rising to the challenge.

Had we taken the easy way out of that situation, we would have missed a huge milestone in our recovery. Mourning is all about one step forward and two steps back. Little triumphs like that created failsafes to fall back on. Those milestones of bravery prevented the process from going one step forward, twenty steps back.

Every holiday without Noah was going to be hard, but the first one was going to hurt the most. The only way to compound the problem would be to postpone the pain until next year or the year after. Our theory was: we're going to deal with it sooner or later, so let's not postpone the inevitable, let's do it now while the world is willing to give us the benefit of the doubt. You don't wade into a freezing cold lake; you jump in and get it over with. We would face it head on, we would do it all, and we would get through it as best we could. Then we'd scrape together any blessing we could find and move on. That way, when things got hard next year or at the next holiday, we'd have our failsafe, we'd be able to say, "Well, we got through that first Christmas, nothing will ever be harder than that . . . so we can get through this too."

The next morning we loaded up our presents, our big fat dog, our suitcases—and all our emotional baggage—and drove five hours to the dumpy Hampton Inn we always stay at in (get this) London, Kentucky. We love that place. And there was something fun and oddly romantic about our little hobo holiday. The sport of sneaking in a 130-pound Lab is always good for a few laughs. I enjoy outsmarting a hotel that thinks I'm so dumb they need to remind me to "put curtain inside bathtub before turning on shower." There's also a great diner next-door that makes the nastiest, most irresistible breakfast you've ever tasted. It was Kim and me against the world. We ordered-in pizza, dialed up some movies, and hung the Do Not Disturb sign on the door.

It didn't work. Early the next morning, the nightmare that had been plaguing me since Noah died—the one I thought I had gotten over—came back to haunt me with a vengeance.

The nightmare always begins the same way: I hear a noise that sounds like the front door of our home being broken in. I roll out of bed, suspicious; glance at Kim, sleeping, and make my way to the kitchen. (Our bedroom is on the first floor.) The kitchen is full of flowers, balloons, baskets, and cards, congratulating us on Noah's birth. One of the balloons is that shiny Mylar and as it rotates to the side, in the reflection I see several shadowy figures by the front door. Intruders! (And worse, I suppose, they're clichés.) They're faceless figures dressed in black, hooded robes, and they're making their way to the stairs below Noah's nursery.

Without hesitating—this is the only part of the dream I like—I bolt to the foot of the stairs and confront them. I always get the best of them—at first. I am valiant, tireless. Every blow connects. I am a warrior, the protector of the family. They fold, stumble, fall back. With each swing I can feel my fist hitting something solid behind their black robes. It feels good. Really good. But at some point in the dream, I begin to wear down. Stepping backward, I can't hold back their assault. I know where they want to go, what they're after. But the punches begin to fly right through them. I'm gassed. My arms feel heavy. My punches become slaps, then just useless waves. They're toying with me. I'm losing strength. Another step back. And another. We're on the stairs now. I trip and fall. They're going to climb right over me. Still fighting, though, from on my back. Still trying. Desperate punches. One of them tries to pass me on my left. I dive for his legs and hug nothing but air. The side of my face hits the handrail with a thud, stunning me, and this opens up the lefthand side of the stairs. Some of them quickly float past me, others go straight over me, stepping on my chest.

I am powerless. Crippled. I'm in pain. But more so because I know where they're going, what they want.

With their robes waving in the air, they float into Noah's room. I scramble up the stairs on my hands and knees. I dive into his nursery and stop. The robes say nothing, but their body language implies pity. *You could of stopped this, but you were too weak.*

Then the one farthest away reaches a pointy sleeve into the crib. I cannot see Noah, but there is a baby under the blanket for sure. With a *poof,* the bulge under the blanket goes flat. The crib is empty. I lunge at them, screaming. I fall toward the empty crib, bending over the railing to search the blanket. This is where I begin screaming in agony.

Then I wake to an even more dreadful sight: my wife, next to me in bed, trembling and scared to death by my screams.

When Noah died, I started out thinking I could protect a little piece of myself from this tragedy; that I could somehow keep one little area as it was. I was wrong. That's part of what those nightmares were trying to tell me. Once I felt how this thing attacked my sleep, how it reached with ease into the deepest recesses of my mind, only then did I truly understand that Noah's death had seeped down and whitewashed my soul. It was so much a part of me now, it was in places I didn't even know about.

Obviously, there were things I wasn't processing while awake that had continued to punch through my psyche when my guard was down under the veil of sleep. The night he died, we felt safe and comfortable and without a care in the world in the hospital. And then we were violated, helpless to do anything. When that nightmare occurs, I'm in the warm, safe comfort of my bed (just like the hospital), with my guard down (sleeping) when I am violated in the worst way I can imagine (intruders through my locked front door).

He was gone. He had been taken from me. I was getting a handle on that, but it was the way he was taken that was even harder to process. I never got to fight for my son. As a man, nothing has ever made me feel so worthless.

His death was proof of just how utterly defenseless I am to the whims of fate. For 33 years I believed I had some control over my life. I really thought things were in my hands. That is a hard thing to unlearn. Not because it doesn't make sense, but because, really, who wants to hand it over? Control is emotional currency. It's an illusion, sure, but it's a damn useful one. What Noah's death had taught me was that the only way to be truly strong is to admit how completely powerless I am. And to find peace with that, all I had to do was ignore everything I had been taught about strength during the last 30 years.

In the dark after my latest nightmare, Kim and I talked for a long time. I told her I was having a problem letting him go. She whispered that it was easier for her, in a way, because of how Noah was taken. Because of the physicality of the whole pregnancy, there was no way for her to not accept that he was gone. She had felt him grow for nine months, she was given the chance to fight for him, and then he was ripped out of her in such a way that she couldn't deny that he was gone. She didn't have to learn how to let him go—he was taken from her.

It just wasn't that easy for me. I had been fighting it, and I was losing the battle. I went the first three days after he died without sleep. Then there were times when I couldn't get out of bed. The nightmares were worse. They left me too exhausted to stay awake and too frightened to fall asleep. The first few hours of that night would be the last decent sleep I'd get for a while. It was a harbinger of a bigger battle on the horizon. I was caught between two worlds now: not just sleeping and awake, but between recovery and acceptance, between Noah's world and mine.

I had to let him go or my healing would be stalled here in this holding pattern, between worlds. Until then none of us—Noah, Kimmy, and especially me—would get to rest in peace.

Things began smoothly in Dayton. When we arrived, Kim's family was already decorating the tree in the front room of their house. Karen, Jason, and Connor were there as well. Kristen was home from school. She was on the carpet playing with Connor. I was relieved to see the Noah ornament Kim had mailed them front and center on the tree. One of the traditions in Kim's family is to have each child and grandchild hang an ornament with their name on it. I was shocked and pleased when Janie dug out a blue bulb with Noah's name and asked me to hang it on the tree. In 15 minutes, Christmas had already surpassed Thanksgiving. We had learned from our mistakes and not repeated them. That was progress. It felt good. The teeter-totter had tipped yet again.

I took Janie aside and thanked her from the bottom of my heart for including Noah. It was sweet and brave of her to arbitrate some middle ground for all of us in regards to remembering Noah. It really put me at ease to have this problem out of the way so quickly.

She dismissed the whole notion. "He's our grandson," she said. "Of course we would include him, that's just how it should be. He'll always be a part of what we do."

"I can't tell you how much that means to us," I told her. "I know we're all different, and we're all gonna handle this in different ways. I know Ed isn't comfortable always, you know, talking about Noah. I just appreciate you guys meeting us halfway on this. I know it's not easy."

The rest of the itinerary at Kim's home went pretty much as planned, but something wasn't right. I had worried how I'd react to the sight of the tree and the presents, how I'd be around Connor, or at Grandbob and Grandjean's, even how I'd be in church on Christmas Eve. I didn't want people getting freaked out, self-conscious, or upset if I got emotional.

But I never even considered that this might happen: nothing. I had felt nothing. I had felt that for days now, since our stay in London, Kentucky. I was numb. My life seemed to be taking place underwater. The nightmares continued to plague my sleep, accentuating my already deteriorating appearance. I was scary to look at. (More so than usual.) In pictures that I saw later that were taken during Christmas, I looked like a prisoner who had just been let out of solitary confinement: puffy and pale with dark circles under my bloodshot eyes. I was a zombie. I had grown used to the emotional teeter-totter of our recovery—feeling okay one day and getting smacked back to square one the next. Hopeful in the morning, despondent by lunch. But I wasn't prepared to feel that: to feel, well . . . absolutely nothing.

Before we'd left Charlotte, Kim and I had hung up a Noah ornament on the tree at KinderMourn. Then we drove to visit his grave. We left him an ornament, a few toys, and a half dozen white roses. Kim had brought the rest of the flowers with us to Dayton. Since we would not be anywhere near Noah on Christmas Eve, our intent was to share the remaining flowers with Nan and Kathleen at their cemetery in Dayton. If we could be close to them, maybe it would help us feel close to Noah too.

Kim had never been to her mother's grave. And we weren't exactly broadcasting our plans to her family. We knew they were buried near each other, so we figured it wouldn't be too hard to find the plots. We grabbed the flowers and set off in our car as a light snow blanketed the ground.

"I need to tell you something about Nan's funeral," I said to Kim as we got underway.

"What?"

"Well, my suit was a little tight," I said.

Kim smiled. "Yeah, I kinda noticed."

"See, I hadn't worn the thing in years," I said.

Kim was trying not to laugh.

"So the morning of her funeral, I put it on and, well, it was a tad snug. It was like an hour before we were supposed to be at the funeral home, and I didn't have time to do anything but squeeze into the pants. I was so worried about splitting 'em from ass to ankle, I don't really remember much of anything else."

"Including," Kim guessed, "exactly where Nan is buried."

"Well, yeah," I admitted, "I do remember it was hilly though, that we had to go up a hill right off the road to get to her plot."

I maneuvered the car through the black metal gates of the cemetery. Kim and I looked at the landscape—it was all hills. We chuckled. No biggie. We weren't on any schedule. We had all day. We just wanted to find Nan and Kathleen's graves and in some small, roundabout way physically connect with Noah once more before Christmas.

Because it was snowing, and we were both underdressed—Kim was wearing clogs with no socks and I had on sneakers—we drove around for 45 minutes hoping to jog our memories. We stopped by the caretakers office looking for a map or directions, but no one was around. By then, just enough fresh snow had fallen to make it impossible to read the tombstones from the car.

I took a guess near one ridge and climbed out of the car. One step onto the slick grass and my shoe slipped on a hidden marble slab sending me face first into the snow. Things only got worse from there. For another 45 minutes I sloshed around aimlessly sweeping snow off dozens upon dozens of graves. We moved to another area, and Kim joined me in the search. Another 45 minutes passed. Nothing. Our red noses dripped. Our hands were tucked inside our sleeves. Our feet were frozen to the bone. With each wet step and each new disappointment, Kim and I grew more weary, more confused, and more angry at each other.

Before we knew it, a few hours had gone by. We looked like idiots. I half expected someone to call the police on us for trespassing. I kind of hoped they would. What the hell were we doing here? What were we looking for? What did we hope to gain by coming here? What really mattered to us and Noah? After all that time, was physically connecting with him all that important—or even possible?

We were meandering around in the cold, unmarked world of the dead. Lost. In more ways than one.

"Let's just leave the stuff on the steps of the chapel," Kim suggested.

"Okay, fine," I spat.

We drove to the cut-stone chapel near the front gates. I got out, sloshed up the steps of the chapel, and put the little Noah's ark ornament near the door. Then I sprinkled the rose pedals. It struck me that I was, more or less, just littering. I felt absolutely ridiculous. I felt hollow and unfulfilled. I felt lost. I felt stupid for even needing to do something like that, so desperate now for any kind of physical connection with my son. Why couldn't I just hug him or tickle him or build his bike with the handlebars backwards the night before Christmas like every other dad in the world? Why did I have to perform my own personal Iditarod in that cemetery for one moment of connection and peace? I just wanted to hold him one more time. I couldn't feel him anymore, I couldn't remember what he smelled like, or the weight of him in my arms. I couldn't see him. He was slipping away from me, and I was like an addict hitting rock bottom. I'd take anything, even a frozen gravestone 500 miles away from my home, all just to quench my craving for a connection.

I climbed back in the car and headed for the gates. Kim was crying. I was steaming. The car was silent. I felt embarrassed. Ashamed. About 10 feet from the exit I slammed on the breaks.

Slamming the car into reverse I said, "Screw it. I'm not giving up. Are you ready to give up?"

"No," Kim replied.

I slid the car to a halt in front of the church and rammed it into park. As I got out, I yelled up to the cold, gray sky, "I'll stay here all goddamn Christmas if I have to. Do you hear me? All Christmas. I don't care. I'm either going to freeze to death or deliver these flowers. Frostbite? Yeah, I'm soooo scared. Just try me. It's your choice, big boy." Then I tucked my head back into the car. Kim was smiling. Pleased, I think, to see me fighting—for something; an indication that I hadn't surrendered all of my fierceness. "He's your son," I yelled at her jokingly, "you talk to him and tell him his dad is going to freeze to death unless he helps us find these graves."

I went back up the steps and while collecting all the items, I also had a talk with the boy. "We need your help," I told him. "We need some guidance here. I know it's hilarious watching us wander around in the cold, but help us out, Mo, come on." Kim then came up with the idea to go to a side entrance of the cemetery just in case that's how we all came in the day of Nan's funeral. Maybe that would refresh our memories. We drove out and came back in that way. The car crept along its new path getting deeper into the plots, both of us squinting out the icy windows for any sign.

"Wait," said Kim.

I hit the breaks. "Yeah," I said.

"Let's try this," she said pointing to her right.

"Up that little hill?"

"Uh huh."

I thought that might be it, but after 50 false starts, I didn't want to say anything.

I got out of the car. I walked around to Kim's side. I leaned through her window and gave her a big hug. Then I took a deep breath. I cleared my mind. Without thinking, I walked 20 steps on an angle away from Kim. I stopped to look around when, through the fog of my breath, I could see a gravestone marked with Kim's maiden name, SACHS.

I collapsed back toward the car. I felt weak and wobbly, but triumphant. First the tear in Noah's eye. Then the rainbow. And now this? Kim knew just by the look on my face. Good thing because I barely got the words out. "I found it," I said. "I found it."

Together we walked back to the plots and began sweeping them clean. We sprinkled the rose pedals and placed the ornaments on Nan's grave. Both of us bent down to kiss her stone. We were both drained and frozen numb. But it had all been worth it. When it came to Noah, we were willing to go far beyond our physical and emotional limits for one moment of peace. That's what the last four months had been about. As hard as we tried, we could not find Kathleen's plot. We knew she was close, we felt it. And that, we had learned on that day, was far more important; to feel her in our hearts meant much more than seeing her or touching her or making a physical connection.

"You take care of my baby boy, Nan, okay?" I said before leaving. "You take care of him and make sure he has a good Christmas. Don't spoil him too bad. And no velvet short pants or anything like that."

"Merry Christmas, sweet baby," Kim said.

Back in the car, Kim slid across the seat and tucked herself under my arm. I squeezed her tight and we rode home in peace.

CRBRO

## CHAPTER 13

# Noel Nadir, The End

We were on our way to Michigan the next day. As we navigated the four hour trip, Kim and I tried to get a handle on what I was going through. This was extremely hard for Kim. She was feeling pretty good about things. She was determined to show her family she was okay, and she had succeeded. I was still spinning my wheels. And there is nothing harder while grieving together as a couple than halting your own forward progress to wait for your partner to catch up. It was a huge and selfless sacrifice for Kim to cloud up some of her sunny days trying to help me deal with my Christmas blues.

In the past four months, I explained to Kim, I had battled back to what I considered even ground—a hell of an accomplishment, I thought. Now, though, I was halfway between the destruction of Noah's death and the person I was rebuilding in the aftermath. To move forward, out of Noah's world and back into mine, I had to leave my son behind. He was dead. I was alive. I couldn't live in two worlds at once. I had to decide where I wanted to be. Strangely, it was not an easy choice, because if I wanted to go forward, I would have to do something even harder than watching Noah die. I had to metaphorically let go of his tiny little hand once and for all. We had gone as far as we could together. If I wanted to fully rejoin the real world, we'd have to part ways.

I couldn't stay in his world anymore. And Noah couldn't come with me.

Until I faced those demons, I would be stuck in emotional neutral, in a kind of holding pattern. I felt nothing, yet somehow that was exhausting. Without realizing it, during the past four months, I had fallen into a dangerous habit of feeling close to Noah only when I was sad. Now it was all I knew. Initially, when I felt close to him, I was sad. Somewhere, though, it switched: I had to be sad to feel close to him. Only now, when I wanted to cry, no tears came. I tried music, memories, melodrama. Nothing. Couldn't sleep. Couldn't stay awake. Couldn't laugh. Couldn't cry. I wasn't hungry. Food had lost its taste. I was doing less and was more tired than I had ever been in my life. I was stuck in a gray, colorless existence, between worlds.

We crossed the Michigan border where the deserted, gray highway was dusted by swirling pockets of snow. The closer we got to Dad and Becky's, the more my spirits lifted. I had always felt complete around my brothers, so I was certain they would give me the emotional boost I needed to push through this cavernous rut.

Immediately upon our arrival, however, something didn't feel right. I once again felt out of balance. It was subtle, but one of the things I was picking up from everyone was the idea that they wanted the old Dave back. Jak had expressed the same feelings before we had left. "How much longer until Dave is back?" he asked Teresa. The answer was never. That guy was not coming back. It sounds dramatic, but the truth was, he had died with Noah on August 10th. Back to normal? Normal? What's that? Everyone wanted me to go back to normal, but how could I do that when I no longer had any idea what normal meant?

Pretty soon after we arrived, Greg took me aside to ask how I was doing.

"I'm not really sure," I said. "I still feel numb. I don't think that's right. I'm exhausted. It's been four months, and I thought I'd be getting better, but the holidays have knocked me on my ass."

"You think about him a lot?" Greg asked softly.

I could feel my shoulders drop and my posture bend into a defeated stance. "I can't really think about anything else," I told him.

"It's not getting easier? It should start getting easier, right?"

"I guess," I said. "But I miss him as much, I hurt as much as the night he died. I know people think that time heals all wounds. Right? That's what people think. That's what I thought, too. But I'm not sure that's true."

"Really?" Greg said.

"I know how this sounds, I know how I sound, like a big baby, right? Like I'm feeling sorry for myself, right? I was doing pretty good but the holidays . . . Jesus."

"Just keep fighting," he said, "and don't be so hard on yourself."

"I know," I said. "It's just, you know, Christmas, I mean he's supposed to be here right now. You're supposed to be wrestling with him, making fun of his stinky diapers and teaching him how to hit a slap shot."

"I wish I could take away your pain, Bear," he whispered to me, using my nickname. "I really wish I could."

"You have Greg, that's one thing, I mean, I can't tell you how much you've helped me. I feel like Noah brought us closer together, and that was one of the blessings he gave us."

Greg and I hugged. "Hang in there, Bear," he said.

I didn't want to let him go. I wanted to tell him more about the nothingness I was feeling; how scared I was to be losing hope, to feel it leaking out of me and the paralyzing fear I had of letting little Noah go; how I could almost feel his hand slipping out of mine; how much the idea of choosing between my son and myself, my heart and my head was exhausting me, ruining me. I heard those things inside my head and they sounded like a sniveling baby. I wished Greg would have tackled me and held me down so Bill and Bryan could give me noogies until I passed out. Maybe that's what I needed right then, a swift kick in the ass or an atomic wedgie. Instead, all I said was, "I'm just tired. I'm not sleeping real good. Don't worry okay? I'll be fine. I'll be fine. I'm gonna be fine."

I tried to put myself in my brothers' shoes. It had been four months since their nephew had died. They had never met him or held him. They didn't really know him. Four months is a long time in the real world. The timing went something like this: just as we managed to move on out of our shock, the rest of the world was moving on altogether. So even though I was still in the early stages of my recovery, they had all moved on long ago. Besides, they must have been thinking, it was Christmas, the happiest time of the year. Bill had two young girls, Ems and Meganudo I called them, and he was beaming, a father rediscovering the joys of Christmas through the eyes of his children. It was just unrealistic and selfish to expect Bill—or anyone else—to be able to connect with me about my dead son.

And so in my recovery from Noah's death, I was without my brothers, my closest confidantes.

The divide with my brothers became apparent the next night when everyone was gathered around the fireplace in Bill and Laura's living room. I had already gone up to bed when Bryan began complaining to Kim that I had done, what he called "a really shitty job" of staying in touch the last few months.

He was right, of course. After we buried Noah, I began conserving my emotional energy by streamlining a lot of my relationships. I grew closer to the people who could help me, and I pushed away the people who couldn't. Noah's death gave me a certain sense of enlightenment. But it wasn't always such a wonderful, or welcomed, gift. For the first time in my life, I was getting a clear idea who and what was truly important to me. Along with that, I had lost my taste and my tolerance for anything that didn't fall into those categories. It was wrong and totally self-centered, and I regret it. But I was in survival mode.

Kim sat there, mouth agape, for several seconds trying to comprehend that comment.

"Do you understand what he's going through right now, any of you?" she asked, looking around the room. "Your brother barely has the strength to face each day. This was supposed to be his first Christmas *with his son*. He was supposed to be ice-skating *with his son*. So it takes everything he has to get up and make it through each day. And Bryan, all you can think about is he hasn't called you enough?"

Silence.

"He needs you," Kim said, crying.

The problem was when they did reach out to me, as Greg did, repeatedly, I felt tongue-tied, unable or unwilling to express how the holidays were eating away at me. At other times the thoughts that had been building up and bouncing around my head poured out in a way that didn't make any sense. Worried I wouldn't get another chance to talk, I often tried to get everything out at once. I was all stops and starts and nonsequiturs. What came out was gibberish. So it's hard to criticize people for not reaching out to someone who is unreachable.

The growing disconnect with my brothers only thickened my malaise. They took us out to nice dinners. Nothing. We went to the mall and splurged. Nothing. We went ice-skating, one of my favorite things to do in the whole world. Nothing. We found a great, old used-bookstore. Nope.

By New Year's Day I was hiding in my room just counting the minutes until I could go back home. Everyone else was watching football, eating leftovers, and reenacting big plays on the floor during commercials. I was upstairs on a futon with my hands clasped behind my head. Staring intently at the ceiling fan, lost in my gray world of nothingness, I hadn't noticed Emily and Megan standing next to me. Meg's a super-bright junior attorney with a mop of blonde hair. With her brown hair and soft eyes, Ems seems to be as strong-willed as she is sweet. They were looking through the collection of Noah pictures I kept next to the bed. I jumped up, then tried to act calm. I held my breath, scared that the pictures would traumatize them in some way.

Because, you know, a child's death is such a deeply troubling thing, it's impossible to get a healthy handle on it. Right? Isn't that what I had been telling myself during my downward spiral? I mean, look at me, a normal, stable adult of average intelligence; look at what I was going through trying to comprehend it all.

How could two kids possibly understand Noah's death better than me?

"Is this Noah?" asked Megan with no hesitation.

Emily yanked the booklet out of her hands. "Let meeeeeee see," she cried. "Yeah . . . is this Noah?"

Meg snatched the pictures back.

"That's him, that's Noah," I responded.

Meg and Ems moved together to share the pictures.

Megan ran her finger over his face. "Awww, he's so . . ."

Gulp. What was she about to say?

Dead? Pale? Scary? Fat?

". . . cute . . . he's so cute."

Exhale. Laugh.

"Yeah he's sooooo cute," said her echo.

"Awwwww," they said in concert.

I sat up. For the first time in a week, I smiled.

"He is cute, isn't he?" I said, the volume of my voice increasing. I tried to fix up my matted hair and massage the sleep out of my eyes. In that state, I'm sure I was far more scary to these kids than Noah. Instantly, I was embarrassed and rejuvenated. "He looks a lot like Aunt Kimmy doesn't he?"

"He looks like you too, Unka Dave," Ems assured me.

"Thanks, sweetie," I said. "So you think he looks pudgy?"

They both giggled. "NOOOO!"

"SO YOU'RE SAYING I'M FAT?" I mock yelled while tickling them both.

"NOOOO!" they screeched.

There was a long, silent pause while the three of us flipped through the rest of the pictures. I should have known what was coming. They had puzzled looks on their faces. That meant trouble. They wanted answers. The daughters of an FBI agent and an attorney. I was clearly overmatched.

"Is he . . . sleeping?" asked Emily, skeptically.

"Well . . . uh . . . well . . . hmm."

"He's not sleeping," blurted Megan, bailing me out. "He died. Remember? Remember Ems when we stayed with grandma? When mom and dad went down for his fumernal, fumeral . . ."

"*Fuuuneral*," interjected Emily.

I shook my head in amazement. If it was futile to hide the truth from these girls, how dumb was it to conceal it from myself?

"Yeah, Meganudo's right," I said, softly, "these were taken right after he died."

When I heard the words come out of my mouth, they became real for maybe the first time. I said them again softly to myself. *He died.* My son was dead. I was alive—if I would just choose to be.

"Why?" asked Meg.

"Why what, sweetie?"

"Why did he die?"

My patented answer was, of course, "Oh, you know, he just wasn't meant for this world" or "God just made him so super-duper special he needed him up in heaven right away." But I knew that wouldn't work. These girls were too sharp.

"Ya know what Meg, I really don't know why he died," I said.

Meg pinched her lips together, thinking hard, then she shrugged her shoulders. "Me neither," said her gesture. Emily was still flipping through the pictures.

"So they took these pictures in heaven?" she asked.

Something was shifting deep inside me. I had gone so long without feeling anything, now I was laughing and crying at the same time. My problems, my big, deep, complicated, emotional life and death problems were being solved in two minutes by my two nieces. I bent down onto the floor between them, taking them both in my arms. In return, they both sympathetically patted me on the back.

"Yeah, he was kinda on his way when these pictures were taken," I said.

"Do you miss him?" asked Megan.

"So so much, I miss him so much," I said. "That's my little baby boy right there."

"And that's why you're sad, on, on, Christmas?" Megan said.

"I guess so, yeah."

Emily just blurted out, "You don't like Christmas?"

"No, no, I like Christmas," I said. "I looooove Christmas. I just wish Noah was here. I miss him. It makes me sad that he's not here."

"But he's in heaven," said Megan, once again explaining it all to me.

"Yeah," I said, squeezing them tight, "he's in heaven. I guess you're right."

Without notice, they both started wiggling out of my arms. As hard as I tried to hold onto them, they slipped through my hands and bounced to the doorway, making their get-away. Although I had let them go, the peace they had brought didn't evaporate. It stayed with me.

"Come on Ems," yelled Meg, "let's go play Lite-Brite."

Emily chased after her screaming, "MEGAN! MeeeeGAN WAIT FOR MEEEEE!"

I closed the door behind them and locked myself in the room. Kim was already packed and ready to go. I was supposed to be getting my stuff together too. Somehow, though, I hadn't really felt capable of moving forward out of that room. Until then. Megan and Emily had straightened me out, but good. Although their work wasn't quite finished.

I had been cramming clothes into a bag for about 10 minutes when the locked door handle jiggled.

"Unka Dave?" whispered Megan.

I took a step forward but hesitated. The emotional dam I had been constructing during the last week had finally broken, and I was a bit of a mess. I didn't want Megan to see me like that. I thought it might confuse her or make her think that they had made me sad, when in fact the complete opposite was true.

While I hesitated in silence, a folded up piece of paper slid halfway under the door. The girls had not been playing Lite-Brite. They had been drawing me a picture. I moved to the door and bent down to my knees.

This was it, really. The time had come to make a choice.

The door between us was locked. The picture lay there on the wood floor like an invitation, halfway between the two worlds. Inside was Noah's world. Death. Outside was the real world. Megan. Emily. My brothers. My wife. They were all out there. As was the new life growing inside Kim.

I was staring at the paper, repeatedly reaching out for it then pulling back when Megan's tiny little voice startled me.

"Sorry about your baby," she said before her little feet tapped out a retreat on the wood floor.

I grabbed the picture, pulled it toward me, and unfolded it slowly. Tears were streaming down my face, but they were damming up on top of a smile. The picture assured me it was time to let him go. I unclenched my grip so that Noah could be in his world, and I could return to mine. *Goodbye, sweet baby boy, goodbye.* And as I did this the picture fell to the floor in front of me.

Meg had traced the imprint of her own hand, then she and Ems had filled it in with the colors of Noah's rainbow. I had let him go. And now, staring back at me, was a picture of a tiny little rainbow-colored hand waving goodbye.

CSBO

## CHAPTER 14

# The Balancing Act Begins

Every doctor we had talked to, every book we had read, every grief counselor we had spoken to suggested that a year seemed to be the minimum amount of time needed to recover—emotionally and physically—before getting pregnant again.

We made it four whole months.

When I got back from a long road trip covering the NFL playoffs, Kim was waiting for me in our living room with one of those infectious, flat smiles spread across her face. At that moment she was a snow-covered volcano. Trying hard to restrain her joy, but not managing to do a very good job, she looked like she was going to burst. I knew the second I saw her.

I dropped my luggage and backpack. Kimmy stood up and handed me a rectangle jewelry box.

"Oh, I hope this is that gold bracelet I've had my eye on," I joked, prying open the lid.

Inside was the pregnancy test Kim had taken a few days earlier, the marker for positive still clear as day. I wrapped my arms around her. Kim was crying. I was laughing. She whispered to me that the same day she took the pregnancy test, Leedylyn had called to tell her that all the blood work recommended by the neonatologist had come back in the normal range. I closed my eyes and wondered when I would return to my own normal range.

I fell to my knees, hugging her waist and, speaking into her belly button, introduced myself to our second child.

I was thrilled. But I was apprehensive too. I hated that, hated how it had become hard for me to just feel joy, pure joy, without worry creeping into my thoughts. But I couldn't hide it. A part of me had vowed to never be taken by surprise again. Kim was feeling it too. I mean, was that it? Was I now just supposed to stop missing Noah? Was I just supposed to pretend that it all couldn't happen again? The hurt wasn't gone. I wasn't sure it ever would be. After realizing what was in the velvet box, one of the first thoughts that came into my head was, *I'm not done yet. I'm not done mourning Noah. How can I get excited for our next baby when I'm not done processing what happened to our last? If I had barely survived one child's death, how could I possibly handle two?* (I couldn't even allow myself to consider the risk of losing Kimmy.)

I had just assumed that I couldn't juggle such polar opposite feelings as horror and hope. Couldn't finish saying goodbye to Noah while saying hello to this one. Couldn't grieve for one and celebrate the other. Couldn't spend one birthday at the cemetery and the other at Chuck E. Cheese's. After getting through the holidays, my recovery had begun to pick up steam, but this ratcheted up the pressure. We had painstakingly said all the right things since August, yet that didn't mean I was ready to actually *live* by all that stuff. Action was the only thing that could give all those words meaning. But when I had originally come up with that brave, enlightened notion, I was sure I'd have at least a year, maybe two, before I ever had to put it into practice. What if I went backwards? What if I was still a basket case when this child got here? I looked to Kim. Her attitude all along had been: so what? So. What. If we waited for the absolute right time to have another child, well, that day might never come, and that would be far more tragic than anything we had been through with Noah.

My face was a question mark when I looked up at Kimmy and said, "What if I'm still thinking about Noah?"

"Is that what you think, that you have to stop thinking about him?" she replied.

"No, but I want to be fair to Noah, to both kids."

"You will be, of course you'll be," she said, smiling softly to me.

Kim went on to explain the simple, hard truth of the situation. It wasn't in our hands anymore. The ball was already rolling. I needed to get with the program whether I felt I was ready or not. She was right. Sometimes that's how life works; it takes off without you and you just have to catch up. So it was silly to anguish over a decision that had already been made. You can't decide not to ride a roller coaster halfway through the first hill.

Almost immediately I realized how easy it was to hold and handle two such completely different emotions. I had sold myself short—again. One of the most significant gifts Noah left behind for me was the realization that I was much stronger than I ever imagined. His death helped me find a deep resilience, an inner faith I never knew I had. Would balancing two kids be difficult? Would it be hard to bridge the gap between a death and a birth? Would it be painful or scary? Those were such relative terms now in my life. Because if I could survive Noah's death, I should be able to handle anything.

Several times during this journey our layers of protection had been stripped away and while standing at a crossroads we had to make decisions that reached down to the core of our being. Would we do an end around or would we attack our grief? Would we sue the hospital or accept what had happened? Would Noah's death ruin us or change us? This was one of those moments. Could I live with two dead children? I wasn't really sure. But, more importantly, could I live the rest of my life as a coward, someone who, burned once, had become too timid to risk life's greatest reward: children? Could I live with myself knowing that the legacy I had created for my son was cowardice? No.

After Noah died, my faith in God had returned rather quickly. But it wasn't until my turnaround at Christmas that a faith just as important had begun to reemerge: faith in myself. I was believing in myself again, trusting my instincts. Right then, no, I wasn't certain I could make it through another pregnancy. But I was positive that the strength would eventually come. I'd find it or manufacture it or just fake it until I found an equilibrium that would serve both my children. Once again, the biggest challenge was summoning the courage to get started. And in this case, I didn't really have a choice.

"You ready for this?" Kim asked.

"I will be," I promised.

Our big secret lasted all of 15 minutes. Jak had seen my car pull up, and he was in our kitchen eating Pop-Tarts double-fisted when he noticed the bracelet box I had left on the counter top.

"Hem, whabs dis?" Jak said with his mouth full, opening the box. He fumbled and bumbled trying to pretend like he hadn't seen the contents. Kim and I just broke down giggling. "Comfrabulations," Jak said, crumbs falling out of his mouth.

The following week we found ourselves back inside our doctor's drab, eggplant colored waiting room. We both just shook our heads as if to say, "Here we go again." In a way, it seemed like nothing had changed. Had the last five months actually happened? I was just beginning to recall our last visit there, the one that green-lighted us to check into the hospital. The snag that started the unraveling of our perfect lives. Then the receptionist called our names.

Leedylyn had already been in contact with our neonatologist, and she explained to us that steps could be taken to significantly lower the risk of a repeat placental abruption. (Even though, after crapping out on 1-in-5,000,000 odds, statistics meant very little to us.) Beginning at 24 weeks the plan was to monitor the baby with weekly ultrasounds and nonstress tests. At 32 weeks they would increase the frequency of the tests to every three days. One of the few things the doctors did know about placental abruptions is that repeat PA's tend to happen at the same gestational period. That meant the closer we got to full term the faster the time bomb inside Kimmy's tummy would be ticking down to 0:00. At 36 weeks our neonatologist, Dr. Shaver, a soft spoken but confident man who conducted himself with the magnanimity that seems to have evaporated from the medical profession, would perform an amniocentesis to check the maturity of the baby's lungs. As soon as the oxygenation levels were to the point that the baby could breathe on its own outside the womb, the doctors would yank that kid out of there as fast as they could make the first incision.

I could see Kimmy doing the math in her head: thirty-six weeks would be 10 days after the anniversary of Noah's death.

Leedylyn then asked her to lay back on the exam table. She took out her small black microphone thingie and placed it on Kim's belly. We held our breath as she moved it around searching for the heartbeat. *Oh God, not again.* At that moment, part of me wished we had listened to the experts and waited a little longer, like 10 years. Every millisecond of silence was pure torture. *Could we really be back here, doing this all over again?* More static. I closed my eyes, and the green, square heart, the one that was flashing on Noah's fetal monitor, hit me so hard my head rocked backward. What were we thinking? We weren't ready. My stupid, massive ego had taken a leap my heart wasn't ready for. Tick. Tock. Silence. With each breath, the deep, freshly healed scars were slowly beginning to tear open all over again.

The tidal wave was returning, all the memories flooding back. Dark storm clouds. Pain. Uncertainty. Helplessness. Death. And then: Whoosh. Whoomp. Whoosh. Whoomp. Whoosh-Whoomp. Whoosh WhoompWhooshWhoomp. There it was. Oh God. Leedylyn squeezed Kim's hand and nodded at her with both compassion and confidence. WhooshWhomp. WhooshWhomp. Another child. There it was. So strong. Wow. I was crying and laughing at the same time. Sniffling on the inhale, scared to death, then guffawing on the exhale, expressing pure joy with each stuttered chuckle. It was a bizarre physical quirk. One I'd be repeating a lot in the next several months as we layered the pain of Noah's death with new memories and the hope of our second child.

The balancing act had begun.

While all the exams, the sights, and the sounds would be eerily familiar, from the beginning this pregnancy felt distinct from Noah's.

For starters, Kim was much more sick this time. At 18 weeks we went in for our first ultrasound and with the first wave of that wand over Kim's belly, this pregnancy officially became unique: we were having a girl. Kim waved me in, and we hugged while she was still up on the table. We stayed there a long time, rejoicing. We didn't say a word, but we were both celebrating the same thing. If that strong heartbeat was the first layer, that ultrasound was the second. Oh how different that felt compared to the last ultrasound, the one we had watched the night Noah died. Moment by moment we were adding steps in the bridge between the horror of our past and, just maybe, the hope of the future.

We both agreed that another boy would have been wonderful. Somehow, though, this just seemed right. Absolutely unscripted, but perfect. It gave Kim the chance to shop for a whole new wardrobe of cute baby clothes. We got to add sprinkles of pink to the nursery. It added an air of excitement to the phone calls we made back to our families. And it gave us something to celebrate on our annual post-NFL season vacation.

The timing and the location of this getaway could not have been more perfect. For the first time since Noah died, we actually felt like we had something to celebrate, and we felt fortunate, once again, to have the time and the resources to do so. All of our milestones as a couple seemed to have taken place on the beach. We got engaged in Hilton Head. We honeymooned in Virgin Gorda. And the secluded, lazy tropical setting of the appropriately named Point Grace resort on the Turks and Caicos islands in the British West Indies felt like one more new beginning.

Kim had splurged on our accommodations, and besides all the piña coladas, cappuccinos, lobster, and exquisite personal service I could handle, Point Grace's oceanside pool featured the coolest double-wide lounge chairs I have ever seen. They weren't really chairs at all. They were more like all-weather, queen-sized, canopied beds. Kim and I probably spent half of our time snuggled up on those things talking about the past five months and the next 50 years. (The rest of the time I spent snorkeling in the island's world-class reefs, four-wheeling in a rented Jeep, and tossing down Red Stripes while watching local cricket matches.)

Kim came up with the name Ally while on our chair/bed. I liked it too. And once I realized I could call her Ally Oop, that was all she wrote.

The next five months would be the most intense, yet content, times of our lives. The truth was, hey, we had nothing left to lose. By simultaneously looking forward with hope while looking backward with growing peace, we had found a new level of balance and clarity to our lives.

With each moment now we had to make a choice: sadness or serenity? Panic or peace? Baby 1 or Baby 2? That was a constant part of our lives now, the decision with each breath and each new thought to focus on the darkness of the past or the promise of the future. The antidote to worry is thankfulness. We called the act of choosing between the two "flipping." Every time we were scared to shivers by the thought of another lost child, we would flip that thought by remembering how lucky we were to at least have the chance to try again. Every time I got sad about never getting to watch Noah play football, I flipped it to think about someday playing Barbies with Ally Oop. Every time I thought we had been picked-on, I remembered stories from families far worse off than us. For a long time I was far too absorbed in my own grief. I couldn't see past my own tiny bit of suffering, but in Turks and Caicos I was able to step back and put our loss into some greater context, and it eased a lot of pain. Things could have been so much worse. No one who loses a child will ever consider themselves lucky, but certainly there were things I needed to be grateful for. Noah had sacrificed so much to teach me so many lessons. The trick was to focus on those blessings by remembering to flip my worry to thankfulness, thereby honoring Noah.

Ally's impending arrival also helped me through my final stages of intense grief for Noah. There was a part of me that wanted to prove to the world how much he meant to me by letting Noah dominate my life. When I'm passionate about something, I tend to overdo it. (Kim kept joking about how I was going to start collecting rainbows and arks like other people obsess over ceramic unicorns and clowns.) Focusing only on Noah, though, wasn't healthy or fair to Ally. I had two kids now. I needed to secure a reasonable place in my everyday life for Noah in order to prepare and make room for Ally. I especially needed to find some peace with Noah's death or else I risked burdening Ally with the final step in my healing. My peace could not be contingent upon Ally's safe arrival and happy life. It would be cowardly to saddle a child with such a responsibility. I couldn't ask Ally to heal my heart, but I certainly could let her motivate me to heal it myself.

After 10 days in Turks and Caicos, we ended our time in paradise with a stroll down the island's sugary sand beach. Walking hand in hand as the crystal clear waves crashed at our feet, Kim wondered out loud if "Noah was happy about having a little sister." We turned to continue walking and there, stretched out across the horizon, was another one of Noah's rainbows.

∞

## CHAPTER 15

# Back in the Arms of
# Mother Miami

When the invitation arrived asking me to take part in an event at Miami University featuring distinguished alumni, Kim joked that the school must be selecting people based on a random lottery. "I guess they're on the F's now," she added. She probably wasn't that far off. In February when I returned to Oxford, Ohio, for Eye on Alumni, the first thing I did was take a nostalgic stroll around the bucolic red-brick campus. Down a slanted walk near the dorm where I lived as a freshman, I came upon a poster for the event that featured my picture and the ESPN logo. I had a hardy chuckle when I saw that they had spelled my name wrong.

Over the next two days I spoke to English, creative writing, and journalism classes. I also attended group seminars, was interviewed by the tiny newspaper in nearby Hamilton, Ohio (the same one that, smartly, wouldn't hire me after I graduated). I toured the campus, tipped a few back with fellow distinguished alumnus Bill Hemmer, the CNN reporter and 1987 Miami graduate, and snuck a case of beer in for Kristen at her freshman dorm. The two-day event culminated with a panel discussion in a packed auditorium.

At the beginning of our recovery process, Kim and I moved forward with tiny baby steps: fighting, talking, and exhausting ourselves for days at a time for small glimmers of hope or understanding. But the longer we stayed with it, the easier the process got. And now I seemed to be moving ahead by leaps and bounds. Kim was getting over her morning sickness. Every day that Ally grew stronger, so did I.

The KinderMourn symbol is a line that dips then climbs to even greater heights. As I drove from the airport to campus, I realized I was feeling the same way. It was hard not to with the ego boost of Eye on Alumni. The way students were so interested in what I did for a living was invigorating. Miami has always been a special place for Kim and me. The trip back reminded me that on some level, Noah's death was just one bad day in what had otherwise been a pretty great life. On campus I felt important. I felt lucky and blessed. I felt funny again.

"I've only been gone 10 years," I said after being introduced at the opening night cocktail party. "But in that time they changed our nickname (from Redskins to RedHawks), they cut the wrestling team, and I think part of my fraternity (Sigma Chi) just burned to the ground. Now if someone tells me that (my favorite bar) Ozzies is closed, I'm leaving." Later, a student asked me what my greatest accomplishment was at Miami. "Finding my wife," I responded, to a chorus of sighs.

On campus was the first time I could hear Noah—or rather the things he had taught me—coming out of my mouth and reaching others. It was like an out-of-body experience, really, the way I could listen to myself speaking for Noah. "It's really happening," I thought. "He's living on, changing people, through me." Until then, it had only been a theory or a wish: now it was reality. It gave meaning to his death and to my life.

I advised the students to be bold and to take chances in life, to gamble on themselves, to not be afraid of failure. With graduation a few months away, the chronically over-achieving eager beavers at Miami, a place that fancies itself a "public Ivy League school," seemed obsessed with getting on with their perfect little lives and wonderful little jobs. It all sounded so familiar. Relax, I told them. Over and over. Just relax. Live for today. Enjoy today. Don't waste it. Don't be in such a hurry. Don't wait to be happy or fulfilled. Don't leave it up to your future job or your future house or your future BMW. Find joy now. Trust me, your life will take a million twists and turns that you won't ever see coming. But those twists and turns, that's life right there. Don't miss it. In the past I had followed that exact advice. So in a way I was forcing my own hand. Because if I didn't get back to that myself, then I'd just be one more blowhard phony. Like the world needed one more of those.

"They might not invite me back for saying this," I said when asked for a final comment at the end of the panel discussion, "but what I've learned—recently—is there's so much more to life than your job. You just won't understand that until you get one. But it's true. Don't get me wrong, having a job is important, enjoying what you do is important, but what's more important is just every day; just absolutely squeezing every last drop out of life that you can."

The students politely listened to everything I had to say. I'm sure they absorbed as much as I would have when I was their age, and I too already knew everything about life. In the end, though, I think I inspired myself more than anyone else.

After the panel discussion, the students who organized the event took the old fogies out for a few drinks. When I got back to my room, I typed up a Valentine's Day e-mail for Kim.

*Okay,* I wrote, *I've had several beers and a few kamikaze shots, and it's almost 2 a.m., but now that it is officially Valentine's Day, I wanted to be the first one to ask you if you would do me the great honor of being my Valentine. NOW WAIT BEFORE YOU SAY NO. Hear me out. When I think of this place and the feelings that I have for you and how they changed my life and transformed me as a person, I am truly overwhelmed. When I got here, the first thing I did was go to the bookstore and look for things to buy and, of course, right? I ran smack dab into the Miami baby stuff, and I nearly lost it because I was so sad that I would never get to take baby boy to a game or bring him here for a trip in high school and all that. It's times like these that I miss him so much it's hard to describe. But the feelings I have for us and for you that stem from here are just so strong, they just overpowered everything else. I owe you my whole life. I owe the perspective that keeps me in balance to you. Everything I love in life is alive in you, Kimmy. I feel like the last few days, in very subtle ways, I really did get to introduce Noah to Miami. I could just hear the lessons he taught us coming out of my mouth and touching other people, and as I walked campus and thought about him and what he represents—all that is great from each of us—I realized that is why I can't wait for babynordstrom because (she) too represents everything that is wonderful about our union. You are the most amazing person and the one thing I pledge is that I will cherish every day of this pregnancy and every day that I share with you for the rest of my life. I have never been happier, and it is because of the light in you Kim. It is because of your spirit. All the lessons I told the students are things that you and the boy taught me. All the things that impressed people about me are the things that you created and nurtured in me. I so wish you were here to share this with me because it was all a tribute to you and to the boy. I am rambling Nord, sorry, but I am forever indebted to you. I learned to love my life again because of you. I am, despite it all, the happiest, luckiest person in the world because of you. I have survived the darkest moment that anyone can experience and, because of you, have become a better person for it. I have two great accomplishments in my life, that is one of them. My marriage to you is the other. Our next baby will be no. 3 because the greatest joy in my life is, and always will be, watching you as a mother. Our kids are so lucky to have you, as am I. But none of that means anything if you won't be my Valentine. So, what do you say? Please?*

Far too early the next morning I drove around campus one more time before heading to the airport for my flight to Baltimore. For an upcoming piece in *The Magazine,* I was scheduled to hang out for a few days with Super Bowl XXXV hero, Baltimore Ravens kick returner Jermaine Lewis. But before leaving Oxford, I cruised around and let all the great Miami memories wash over me one more time. The fun. The friendships. The challenges. The setbacks. The promise. Kimmy. And finally, the person I became when I was there. That was, after all, the kind of person that someone like Kim fell in love with.

The car came to a sudden halt.

"I'm still that person," I thought.

"Whadaya know?" I said to myself, chuckling, shaking my head inside the car.

"I'm still me."

CBEO

## CHAPTER 16

# Two Fathers

As I would later write for ESPN, the Jermaine Lewis story was something I knew I had to do. Both he and I had lost our infant sons during the previous NFL season and the minute Lewis became the star of Super Bowl XXXV, sitting in the press box in Tampa, I just knew I was uniquely qualified to tell his story. Still, editors at *The Magazine* repeatedly cautioned me about ripping open my own emotional scabs in order to write the piece. I wasn't sure either how it would work out, but I did know that every single time Kim and I had challenged ourselves to step out of our comfort zone during this process, the healing, understanding, and growth we experienced as a result were truly magnificent.

A month earlier, in front of a world wide audience of 700 million, the 5'7", 180-pound Lewis sparked the Ravens victory in Super Bowl XXXV with a spectacular 84-yard kickoff return for a touchdown. It was one of the most moving moments I've witnessed in the 10 years that I've been covering sports on a national level. Right next to Muhammad Ali lighting the Olympic torch, playing pickup hoops inside Beijing's Forbidden City, and watching a scrawny benchwarmer from Toms River, New Jersey, win the Little League World Series with a home run in his mandated final at bat.

When Lewis reached the end zone in Tampa, he pointed to the sky in honor of his son, Geronimo, who was stillborn on December 13. Later, for a piece in *The Magazine* titled "Daylight," I wrote, "Lewis had somehow found the strength to rise above the sudden death of his son to create a loving and lasting legacy for his child. . . . In an instant, a father's prayer was answered: his son would not be forgotten . . . and certainly, somewhere in that global audience, there were grieving parents—struggling with a similar ordeal, fighting just to face each day—who now had a role model."

I, of course, was one of those parents. And that was how I approached that story: more as a father than a sportswriter. Jermaine's story was my story—and that of a thousand other fathers.

He picked me up at the airport in his white Lexus for a quick trip back to his hometown of Lanham, Maryland. Jermaine's tragedy had gotten so much attention during the media circus that is the Super Bowl, I wasn't sure if he even wanted to talk about it anymore. About 15 minutes into our ride, I told him about Noah, but only as a way of saying to him I understood what he was going through and if he didn't want to talk about it that was cool with me.

My disclosure had the opposite effect. Jermaine seemed as eager as I was to talk to another father. When we arrived in his old neighborhood, he pulled over to a shady part of the street and put the car in park. He leaned back in his seat, rubbing his hands over his face, and the memories just seemed to wash over him. He sat up every so often to hit the repeat button on song by 8Ball & MJG, a somber, thumping tribute to a fallen friend that, Jermaine swore, was written just for him.

* * *

I had been doing the exact same thing with U2's latest album. Just like it had done for Jermaine, music was the first mainstream passion to return to my life after my son died. It was a lucky coincidence for me that only a few months after Noah died, my favorite band, U2, came out with what critics said was a masterpiece of powerful songs about rebirth, hope, and grace. It opens with "Beautiful Day," a song about someone beaten down by life who finds hope in a new day. "Reach me," Bono sings. "I know I'm not a hopeless case." Near the end of the song there's even a reference to a rainbow. "After the flood, all the colors came out . . . it was a beautiful day."

After hearing that album for the first time, the color seemed to return to my landscape as well. Now, did I wish it was some great work of art that created that spark? Some novel or painting or poem instead of a pop/rock album? Or did I wish I had been inspired the way Kim was by her Bible-study group, her volunteer work, or her tireless medical research? Sure. But in the end all that mattered was discovering something to push me out of my mental and emotional hibernation. The what didn't matter. It could have been lawn care, body piercing, or checkers. In my case it was music.

Whatever the inspiration, it felt good to finally feel strongly about something besides missing my son or worrying about my daughter. The album became the soundtrack to the final stages of my recovery.

Kim understood that before I did and when dates came out for U2's 2001 Elevation tour, she pushed me to see as many concerts as I could get to. I wore a hat to most shows that had Noah's picture taped under the bill. In May, Kim and I saw U2 in Charlotte, and the next night Burnsie and I drove to Atlanta where we watched from the front row. Afterward, Burnsie and I went to a nearby pub until 4 A.M. Then, while butchering "Elevation," stumbled back to our hotel through some not-so-safe parts of town. Somehow we didn't get mugged or lost or, worse, signed up for American Idol. "This proves the kid is looking out for us," Burnsie said the next morning while retracing our steps.

A few months later, while working on a Donovan McNabb feature in Philadelphia, I raced down to Washington, D.C. to see the band one last time. That night Bono improvised a new ending to Beautiful Day where he celebrated his own newborn son, referring to him as the "golden soul."

That was Noah, all right, and Geronimo, too. The two of them: our Golden Souls.

*    *    *

Jermaine stayed silent for several minutes, but then in a gravelly, shaky voice he began. "After the doctors said, 'We can't find a heartbeat' I remember not being able to keep it all in. I was in shock. I was in intense pain. I remember being mad. Mad at God. I remember thinking, 'Why?' I remember saying to myself, 'God took him for a reason' I just have to find out why."

I couldn't believe what I was hearing. That was almost word for word, my exact reaction to Noah's death.

Jermaine continued, "I had a nickname for him: G-Mo."

"This is weird, man," I said, interrupting him.

"Why?"

"We called Noah . . . Mo," I said.

"G-Mo and Mo," Jermaine repeated softly to himself.

"Hey, let me ask you something. What do you tell people when they ask if you have any kids?"

I had trouble at Miami being consistent with how I answered that question. Sometimes I said, "no," then I worried about what Noah would think. Sometimes I said, "yes," then I worried what to say if they asked a follow-up question. Sometimes I said "We had one child, a son" and just left it at that.

"Different things," he said. "I tell different people different things."

"Yeah."

Then Jermaine spoke about finding refuge in the hospital cafeteria. How he'd go there, order a bunch of food he had no intention of eating, and sit in the corner and cry. He still didn't like to break down in front of his wife, Imara. He wanted to stay strong for her. But he didn't know where else to go.

"I cry when I cut the lawn," I told him. "Pull my hat down low over my eyes, put some headphones on, and just let 'er rip. You're sweating already so no one really notices."

Jermaine smiled and nodded his head. "Yeah man, yeah," he said.

We talked like that—back and forth, comparing notes, ideas and theories, two broken fathers sharing their sad secret code—for almost an hour. And then, after speaking to his high school track coach, we drove to a live-seafood store to buy some Maryland blue crabs to cook up for dinner. Lewis was discussing his recipe with the guy behind the counter—sometimes he used Jack Daniels, sometimes he used beer—when he saw me leaning over the bag.

"Be careful man, those crabs will . . ."

Too late.

"Yeeeeoowch," I screamed.

The little guy on top practically pinched my damn pinky off. I jumped and skipped around the shop in tight circles, shaking my hand, my face bright red from the pain. That, of course, sent everyone into fits of laughter.

Finally I came to a halt. Still waving my throbbing finger I said, "Ha ha ha. I'm throwing that little dude into the pot first."

Jermaine was still chuckling about my mangled digit when we pulled onto his country estate located on several acres in Boring, Maryland. Once inside, he needed to make some phone calls about a charity foundation he had started in Geronimo's memory. So his wife, Imara, gave me the grand tour. Before heading into his office, Jermaine shared Noah's story with her. "They lost their baby too," he said. Imara showed me the wraparound porch, the nursery, and the trophy room. On a sun-splashed table in the corner of their den, we came across the tiny silk box that held their son's effects. I stood over it, dazed and frozen.

This is what I wrote: "I knew, at that very moment, back in North Carolina on the second floor of our home on top of a changing table inside an empty nursery, sat the very same box. Inside the box are the purple ink imprints of (Noah's) little feet, the blue and pink striped stocking cap he wore, hair clippings that perfectly match his mother's thick brown locks, the tiny hospital wristband he never got to wear, and several pictures of my sweet, pudgy little fullback."

It was clear to me then just how much I had missed by not interacting with other bereaved parents. By going it alone, I had indeed made things much harder on myself. I had been so certain that I was the only one in the whole wide world grieving a dead son. I had been so proud and so stubborn about my unique grief. All that created in me was an even greater sense of isolation. After listening to Imara and Jermaine, I realized how wrong I had been. There were thousands upon thousands of parents just like us. (A fact that was reinforced by the response to the article.) I had discovered, a tad late, that it is possible to gain and give support to others without compromising the uniqueness of your own situation or intruding on the things you don't wish to share with others. I don't really consider that a mistake, but a personal preference. I could have jumped in from the beginning and defined who I was from within that group, but that wasn't me. I needed to figure out who I was on my own before joining the larger, greater brotherhood of bereaved fathers.

"It all comes down to a constant, daily battle," Imara said, shaking me out of my thoughts. "Of whether you are going to triumph over this or succumb." I just shook my head back at her in amazement. My knowing smile caught her off guard.

"What?" she asked.

"That's nearly the exact same thing my wife and I say to each other," I said.

"In the end we had to do this story, he and I," I later wrote. "We have the same haunting memories (of holding our sons for the first and last time); the same fears (that time does not, in fact, heal all wounds); the same refuge (in music); the same dreams (to see our kids again someday, perhaps playing together); the same hopes (we both wanted to try to have more kids); and finally, that we were both profoundly changed, and motivated by our loss."

Outside of Kimmy, I probably related to Jermaine more than anyone else in the whole process. For all that people like Jak, the Farsons, and Greg had done for me, I kind of wished that wasn't true. But there's just no comparison to the deep connection you make with someone who has actually been through the same thing.

Heading up to the mountains to fly-fish early one morning, Jak asked me how often I thought about Noah. Right away I thought it was an odd question.

"How often do you think of your own kids?" I asked him.

"All the time, I guess," he said.

"Me too."

"Really?" He replied without hiding his incredulity.

"Yeah, really . . . what, you think I'm lying?"

"Well, no, I just wouldn't think . . . I don't know," he said.

No, he didn't. I guess that's the point. As much as he cared, as hard as he tried to, he never could completely understand.

Jermaine was proof for me that I was on the right path. I was moved by his willingness to serve as a role model for other dads; the way, in light of Geronimo's death, he still called himself blessed; the way he kept his son on his mind while refusing to be defined by that grief; the way, like most great athletes, he never seemed to be bothered by things he couldn't control; the way his loss had seemed to make him stronger, bolder, tougher as a man; the way Geronimo had changed his attitude about life. When I asked him how much he worried about getting hurt during a kick return, what with 250-pound guys hurling their bodies at him at breakneck speed, he replied without hesitation, "I've already survived the worst thing a person can go through. To me, a kick return is nothing."

Those were the creeds I lived by as we got closer to Noah and Ally's birthdays. *I've already survived the worst thing a person can go through. To me, a second pregnancy should be nothing.*

Later in the day we moved out to the deck to sample the crabs. I asked Jermaine about the team's upcoming Super Bowl ring ceremony. His answer served as the ending to my story:

*Lewis said he might wear the ring only once and then put it with the rest of G-Mo's things. "After everything, sometimes it just doesn't seem real," he said. "The touchdowns, the wins, the Super Bowl . . . everything, all the success, I've just been blessed." Lewis' voice then trails off a bit, and he turns to stare out into the 11 acres of woods that surround his house. "Of course," he whispers, "I'd give it all back in a second."*

We hung out for another day, and I spent some time interviewing his teammates and coaches. We never promised to stay in touch. It just seemed obvious that we would. Then I jumped into a cab for the Baltimore airport. Stuck in traffic, I tried to remember the last time I had strung together so many positive and fulfilling days. I couldn't think of one. Miami. Jermaine Lewis. Work. Noah. Kim. Valentine's Day. I felt sustained strength, clarity, balance, and purpose for, maybe, the first time since the boy died. Everything up to that point had been such peaks and valleys, only then did I feel like I was on a steady, even path. There was, finally, some momentum to my healing. I wanted to share it all with Kim, but my flight was already boarding when I reached the gate. After we took off, the urge to talk to her was too great. I ignored the $25-a-minute charge and pulled the Airfone out of the seat in front of me, swiped my credit card, and dialed our home phone.

It was the best $287 I ever spent.

"Kimmy?" I whispered.

"Hey, how's it going?" she answered. "Are you okay? Where are you calling from?"

"I'm great, Nord. How are you feeling, how're my girls?"

"We're good. The interview went good? It sounds like you're underwater."

"It was amazing, I learned so much," I said.

"Good. Hey, you're on an air-phone, an airplane phone?" she laughed. "Your flight left okay?"

"Yeah," I said. "I just had to call you, Nord. The Miami thing was so cool."

"I know. I read your e-mail, thanks . . . got your flowers today, too, thanks."

"Well?" I asked.

"Well what?"

"What's your answer?"

"Valentine? Yes. I'll be your Valentine." I knew she was smiling on the other end. So many of my odd phone calls on the road had begun with me telling Kimmy I was hurting. Not that one. Not anymore.

"Alright."

"Jermaine, how was he?" Kim asked.

"He was awesome, really open about everything."

"I'm so glad."

"It was just so good to talk to another dad," I said. "We talked like two dads. I can't believe how much of the same things we're going through. I'm so glad I didn't back down from this story. They have the exact same kind of little green silk box as we do."

"Really?"

"And the stuff that I thought was weird or bizarre or whatever? Like I was the only one feeling that? He's dealing with the exact same stuff."

"I'm so glad everything went good," Kim said.

"Me too."

"*Kimmy?*" I said.

"Yeah, what is it?"

"I want to tell you something."

"Okay, sure. What is it?"

I paused for a few seconds, turning toward the window of the plane for some privacy.

"I feel . . . I feel . . . normal," I announced, exhaling a slightly incredulous laugh. "I feel normal again, Nord. How 'bout that?"

For me, normal was huge. It meant I was beginning to think as much about Ally and our future as I was about Noah and our past. It meant for the first time since our son had died that Kim didn't have to worry about me. It meant balance, emotional balance, and strength— the kind I could begin to seriously build on for whatever was in store with Ally. I could sense Kim's relief. I think she had wanted to push me harder to get there, but instead gave me the space and freedom to reach it on my own. She must have been feeling now just how monumental normal was, because even at 33,000 feet, I could hear her crying softly on the other end of the line.

## CHAPTER 17

# Spring Comes Again

From the window of the ultrasound room, I could look out across a parking lot then up several stories and see the outline of the hospital room where Noah had died. This was our life now: a constant balancing act between our two kids. Actually it felt more like juggling. I had placed the palm of my hand on the cold glass, reaching out to the boy when the technician swung open the door and asked me to draw the blinds. "See ya, Mo," I said softly as the room went dark.

I turned toward the ultrasound screen and waited to see my daughter. I was so grateful to be able to attend those appointments because the ultrasounds allowed us to literally watch her grow on an almost daily basis. Eventually, I'd end up sitting through so many of them that I could take the measurements and punch them into the computer myself. For the early morning appointments it was my job to wake Al by tickling her feet, singing to her, or rattling a can of pennies on Kim's belly button. Oh how Ally hated that. She would kick at the sound, kick at the ultrasound wand, kick kick kick. If babies can have attitude, Al had one. A few minutes later we'd watch on the screen as Ally stretched out to go back to sleep. With her legs extended and crossed at the ankles, Ally looked like she was lounging poolside. Her chubby little cheeks gave her the cutest, most delicate little doll-face profile. We watched her suck her thumb, and the nurse pointed out a wisp of hair growing on top of her head. It was important for us to see her like that every few days, to trust what was on the screen, and not become blinded by fear and grief. She was so strong and unafraid it seemed silly for us not to be as well.

"Everything's perfect," the ultrasound technician would say.

*It was with Noah too*, we'd inevitably repeat to ourselves.

When Kim found out she was pregnant, I thought maybe it would be hard to fall in love with this little girl knowing that I could lose her too. Instead, it was the easiest thing in the world. Learning that I could lose those I adored didn't make me scared or guarded with my emotions—it made me want to love them more, love them fully, to give all of myself to them, always, without ever wasting a second. And so during each ultrasound I tried to remind myself to push back all the fear, to surrender this innate appetite for control, and just trust what I was seeing.

It wasn't easy. The battle between the heart and the head never ceased. We lived with the reminder that she could be gone in two minutes, just like Noah. I had to constantly wrestle with the thought in my head that one morning I might pull back the sheets and see blood. Of course we had spells of anguish, worry, and doubt. Sometimes the thoughts were so all-consuming, I'd blink and half a day (or night) would be gone. At other times I was sure the clocks in our house were spinning backwards, that we'd never get to August. We spent hours upon hours with Kim on the couch and me sitting on the coffee table facing her, our legs creating a human bridge between us, talking each other down, "flipping" all the dark thoughts, infusing all the hurt with hope. Our lives had become a minute-by-minute choice between fear and hope, control and peace. For the most part, though, we had turned it all over. All that stuff we had said? All those conclusions, revelations, and promises? They weren't just words anymore. We were living them.

At that point, if we had any questions about the straightforward, open, and somewhat relentless way we mourned Noah they were all gone now. Whatever confidence or peace we felt with Ally was a direct result of the hard work we had put in with Noah. Life had thrown us down, and we were climbing back higher than we had ever been before.

Midway through Kim's pregnancy, Leedylyn announced that she was leaving her practice and moving her family to Maryland. She actually volunteered to put those plans on hold until Ally was born. Kim and I desperately wanted her to stay but couldn't, in good conscience, hold her back. Before leaving, she referred us to another doctor, a friend of hers whom she trusted. Leedylyn shared our entire history with Dr. Vuong and it made for a smooth transition.

Until we got around to meeting everyone in the new practice, however, it was shocking how often doctors would come in to speak to us without so much as a clue about what we had been through. It seemed impossible, but more than a few times we heard, "Looking good, everything is looking good, let's just keep it up, and we'll see you when it's time to deliver at 40 weeks." That did not exactly assuage our skepticism or our fear, the fact that so many doctors would treat us without even taking 60 seconds to read the front page of our chart, which was clearly marked with the words "placental abruption" and "fetal death." No one's life is in my hands, yet I'm pretty sure I'd be fired if I ever showed up so unprepared for an interview.

Once again it would have been easy to feel entitled to a hissy fit—and trust me I was close on a number of occasions—but whenever possible we chose peace instead of panic. We had become pretty good at making the best of a bad situation. When faced with something like that, here's what we always boiled it down to: Is Ally still alive? Yes? Is she okay? Yes? Then I don't really care where Leedylyn moved to, who the new doctor is, or how many times we have to explain our situation. If Ally is okay, nothing else matters. We did that not because we were enlightened or above it all but because, honestly, what other option was there? We had another child to live and be strong for. It was not some scary movie where we could close our eyes until the danger passed. Kim would not allow that. Anything less would make us hypocrites. I would not allow that.

In what amounted to a daily prayer, Kim was constantly saying, "We have her now and that's all that matters. We have her now and that's all we can be sure of, so let's make the most of today. Our whole life is today."

The truth is my grief had turned me into something of a 12-stepper: committed to staying off the addictive combination of pity and the fear. I lived in the moment. I lived my life one day at a time, trying to cherish everything I could—reading to Ally, singing to her, feeling her tiny feet kick against Kim's belly button. I took nothing for granted. I tried to turn the things I could not control over to a higher power. That time of our lives reminded me of a John Steinbeck quote. When faced with the "desolate impossibility" of writing an entire 500 page novel, Steinbeck would always become haunted by a sick sense of failure. Then he'd write one page. Then another. And he'd keep on writing, but without ever considering the possibility of finishing. Before too long, he'd be done. That was how we had approached Kim's second pregnancy; let's just focus on today and not even think about finishing. Let's just do this one minute, one hour, one ultrasound at a time.

Outside in the parking lot after the latest exam, I stood in the shadow of Noah's hospital room with a grainy black and white ultrasound picture of Ally in the palm of my hand. She had gotten high marks across the board on all her tests. In the picture she was asleep, sucking her stubby little thumb. She was strong, safe, and at peace. So were we. It was a crisp, cool day but nice enough that if you stood still for a moment the sun would warm your face. You could smell the sour bouquet of dogwood trees beginning to bloom. The moment was short-lived. It blew away with the next rustle of wind, the next moment of uncertainty. But for a few precious seconds I felt peace. It lasted no longer than a few breaths but it seemed to mean far more than anything I had ever felt before. Later, it made me wonder if before Noah died, when I was so clueless, if I lacked the perspective to ever be truly happy. If my understanding of peace and happiness was incomplete because they had never been balanced by real life doses of confusion and agony. If back then had I even known, or valued, what it was to be content? Or had I just been another one of the ignorantly blissful masses who just figured I deserved my wonderful little life?

As we walked to our car, Kim began rubbing her hands in smooth circles on either side of her stomach as a way of comforting Ally after the appointment. It was such a gentle, instinctive, and loving gesture; one she had used all the time with Noah. That day, though, was the first time she had done it with Al. I went around to unlock her door, but first I pulled her close to me. She tucked her head on my chest with her ear against my heart. I stood tall, wrapping my arms around the top of her shoulders; her protector. I could breathe with ease. I closed my eyes but could still see orange and gold rays from the sun, and I filled my lungs with the fragrant air with such little effort I was sure I wouldn't need to breathe again for the rest of the day. Ally was in my hand. Kim was in my arms. Noah was in our hearts. My family was in balance. I was living perfectly in the moment.

And for the first time since my son died I was certain that spring was about to return to our lives.

CぴびD

## CHAPTER 18

# Sunrise in the Cemetery

Inside the cemetery, just before dawn on the day of Noah's birthday, the sound of our car doors sent the sleeping birds in the nearby trees fluttering off into the inky darkness.

As we had hoped, the cemetery was peaceful before sunrise. No planes were flying overhead. There was no traffic on the way there. We had the entire place to ourselves. It would eventually be a hot and muggy day, but for the moment it was cool and pleasant. There is something solemn and soothing about the quiet calm of the early morning, even in a cemetery.

We followed the usual routine: I kissed the O in his name, and Kim kissed the already lipstick-stained A, and then we both bent down and began cleaning off the grass, dirt, and bird droppings from his gravestone. We do that, I suppose, because it is our only chance to be like other parents who dab a bit of spit on their finger in order to wipe some crud off their kids' face.

"Happy birthday, baby boy," Kim whispered sweetly to him.

Over the year, just as Kim had predicted, the collection of trinkets at Noah's grave had become quite large and unsightly. There were seashells, some Miami stuff, several little toys, a Super Ball, and a bunch of other stuff that had become faded and dirty. So we pitched most of it, and I collected the rocks we had placed at the base of his grave as mementoes every time we visited. As always, we said hello to Mildred (who was buried on his left) and greetings to Chico Ray (buried on his right.) I couldn't even guess how many times we had been there during the last year. (The trail of tiny rocks we had left behind wrapped all the way around his headstone.) Sometimes I went there several times a week and other times I went 15 days between visits. I do know that as the year wore on and the more I incorporated Noah into my everyday life, the less I needed to go there to feel close to him.

Once our housekeeping chores were done, we laid out a blanket and proceeded to have some birthday cake. The cake was chocolate on chocolate with green frosting that said: Happy Birthday Noah! We talked to our son about how proud we were of him. We spoke of the now second annual toy drive and from that collection we gave him a tiny stuffed bear with a rose in its hat to remind Mo about all the good he had done. We thanked him for helping us stay so strong, teaching us so many lessons, and giving us so many blessings. We also thanked him for acting like a good big brother by looking out for his little sis as she grew inside Kimmy's tummy.

The leaves of the maple tree behind his grave swished and swirled in response.

Around Christmas I had finally begun to accept Noah's death. What I had concentrated on since then was figuring out what our relationship would be like. And what I had come up with wasn't quite the earth-shattering, complicated concept I had thought the situation required. Different. My relationship with Noah was going to be different from what most dads share with their sons. But different wasn't necessarily bad. Thank goodness I had been taught from a very young age to respect and crave diversity. I just never imagined it would manifest itself in that way; giving me peace and pride in my unique relationship with Noah. Different could be okay. I could live with different.

That's what I had to keep telling myself, at least. Every day of my life I miss and mourn my son. I've learned to deal with it better perhaps, but the ache has never eased. And so every day since he died in my arms I have had to coax myself off a ledge with little pep talks like that one—our relationship is different than most fathers and sons, but different was cool. I don't fight it. Or argue. I accept those mental calisthenics now as part of my daily life. Like brushing my teeth.

No, I would not get to experience all those things dads and sons normally do together. There would be no games of catch. No fishing. No hiking. No ball games. No naps. No manly talks. No Tigers games. No weddings or college move-in days or first beers or Stanley Cup playoffs. And the thought of that still periodically crushes me. No, I would never get to watch him dive into that double-chocolate cake and smear it all over his face on his birthday. I'd never get to do that.

But on his birthday I could look at my reflection in my son's shiny, marble gravestone and be proud of the man staring back at me. I had not only survived the hardest thing life would ever throw at me, I had triumphed over it, and in doing so had given my life a newfound depth and meaning. I was sure that Noah was proud of me. And I wouldn't trade that for anything in the world.

I was sad, of course, but what I felt more than anything at his grave was peace. I was ready for wicked grief. Sorrow. Pain. Anger. Confusion. Despair. A year of tears ready to run down my face. The dam to crack open once again. Another flash flood that left me weak, lost and nearly drowned.

Instead, I felt peace.

Just as that feeling of contentment came over me at Noah's grave, rays of light from the rising sun began to peak through the tree branches. It is a powerful metaphor to watch the sun rise again and warm the stone that marks your child's grave. We sat there in silence with him for a long time. Just soaked him in. We were not to the point yet where Noah's memory didn't make us sad, but we were getting there, we were on our way. Not too long before, pole-vaulting to the moon had seemed more reasonable. Now it was within our grasp.

Noah had become such a part of our everyday lives that the trip to his grave wasn't all that traumatic—even on the anniversary of his death. It felt normal. Routine, even. There were no great revelations that morning, but that's what we had been working at for the last year. Acceptance. Contentment. Peace.

We finished our cake. Kissed him a few more times and whispered happy birthday before heading back to the car.

As we drove out of the cemetery—both of us crying softly with Bono singing "isolation, desolation . . . let it go . . ." in the background—we saw the orange orb as it climbed above the treetops for the first time, bathing the day in gilded light. As badly as I wanted the world to stop on the anniversary of my son's death, to be plunged into darkness on every August 10, life just didn't stop. The sun rises. The dew dries. The birds sing again. Life goes on. We drove out onto the main road and saw school buses motoring by and commuters on their way to work. The groundskeeper for the cemetery was already riding his mower. He tipped his hat to us, and Kim and I smiled back at him and then to each other.

## CHAPTER 19

# Noah's Gifts

The sunrise visit to Noah's grave turned out to be a wonderful and meaningful beginning to a great day. Kim was smart enough to schedule things on Noah's birthday so that we wouldn't have too much idle time. By the time we got back home from the cemetery, there was just enough time to pack up the toy-drive bags and head back downtown to the hospital.

That year's scaled-down toy drive gave everyone we were close to a chance to turn their feelings of helplessness into something action-based and positive. I guess when you get right down to it, that had been the theme of the entire year. The idea actually came from Granjean. She nearly broke my heart a while back when she explained how every time she was out and was sad because she wanted to be buying Noah a little toy, she had decided to go ahead and buy that toy and then donate it in his honor to a needy child. We decided to follow her lead and spend one full afternoon roaming the aisles of a local toy store, filling basket upon basket, then taking all the loot to a children's hospital in downtown Charlotte.

My dad had done the same thing in Detroit. But when he got to the register he said the total was close to $500. Dad stopped, and with the cashier and the people in line behind him listening in, he looked up and asked Noah if it would be all right to maybe take some toys back.

"Sure gramps," my dad said Noah replied. "Ya big cheapo."

Even my mom joined in. Now, this is a woman who would rather take a package and hitchhike across country with the Hell's Angels rather than pay to overnight it. Yet on the day before Noah's birthday, a FedEx package full of about 50 tiny, stuffed animals arrived.

"We have experienced many, many miracles this year," I said, laughing at the sight of the package. "But this one—my mom paying for FedEx—it may top 'em all."

We pulled into the parking lot of the hospital and went to the lobby to wait for the volunteer from the children's wing to meet us. The receptionist saw Kim and asked her if she needed a wheelchair. "No," Kimmy laughed, "not yet." When the volunteer appeared, Kim took one look at the little book cart she was pushing, smiled a wide and warm grin, and said, "You're gonna need a bigger cart."

Indeed. The nurses, the staff, the kids, were all elated to see the piles of new toys. On our tour of the facilities we began to understand why: inside the playroom the shelves were half empty and the toys they did have were old, dirty, and broken. Noah had struck again.

"We are set for a year on toys now," said a volunteer.

As we continued our tour through the unique floor—complete with lowered doorknobs, bright colors, and cartoon characters painted on walls—we saw a child being wheeled to her room by her mother. Her shaved head was the telltale sign of a brain tumor.

When I saw her I instantly felt terribly shallow and self-centered being so caught up in my own problems, which were now a full year old.

As the girl rolled by us, a nurse said to her, "Sweetie, these are the people who donated all the toys." The child looked up, her eyes dark and sunken deep into her face, and her cracked and dry lips straightened as she tried to smile. All she could manage was a whispered, "Thank you" over her shoulder as her mom wheeled her by.

Seeing that little girl in the hospital that day reinforced the notion I have that everyone, every last one of us, if you look deep enough, we all have terrible things to deal with and heavy burdens to carry. We have Noah. That girl and her family have their own nightmare. That past year, after my story on Jermaine Lewis came out in *ESPN The Magazine,* we learned of hundreds of parents who had been through similar situations, some much, much worse. In a week I would learn of a friend from high school who had recently given birth to a baby boy and then, a few hours later, died of complications. She left behind two kids and a grieving, broken husband.

Every night on the news there seemed to be some new horrific tragedy to report: natural disasters, famine, terrorism, genocide. Thinking of those and seeing that little girl did not trigger a misery-loves-company kind of feeling. Not even close. That was just a reminder that whatever I was suffering through, other people were going through things just as bad; and in many cases much worse. One of the last things to return to me was my sense of perspective. I had not been picked on. I had not been singled out. I was not alone with my grief on some island in this great big happy world. Quite the opposite, actually. We all have heavy burdens to carry. Grief? Sorrow? Suffering? They don't discriminate when it comes to race, religion, economics, or geography. In fact, they are one of the few things that link us together as human beings.

Hanging on the wall about 10 feet past that girl was a giant, felt rainbow quilt. I thought of Noah, the power of his legacy, and how the day and the past year had gone. I thought of that brave little girl smiling at us.

I put my hand on the quilt. I felt Noah's little hand on the other side.

I looked up.

The quilt said, "Always look for rainbows."

Once again, we had found ours.

CRBED

## CHAPTER 20

# A New Kind of Tears

When we got back home, Kim and I sat in the front room of our house holding hands and looking out at the street. We saw Kelsey come out of her house. She was racing back and forth to the houses on our street. On each trip she'd stop to crane her neck, peering hard into the western sky behind our house where the sun was beginning to set.

"What is she doing?" I asked.

"Oh, sweet little Beaner," Kim said, squeezing my hand.

"She's looking for a rainbow."

The cookout that everyone was calling "the Noah Dinner" started at 6 P.M. in the Farson's backyard. A muggy day had turned into a pleasant evening with a slight breeze, nice enough so that most everyone stayed outside chatting, laughing, and eating. Occasionally we talked about Noah, but for the most part it was just nice to be together in his honor. By 8 P.M. or so most people had finished cooking their dinners on the grill, and I was helping Teresa make homemade ice cream out on their back porch when Jak jumped up on his just-finished retaining wall behind their house.

He asked everyone to come together for a moment. This was particularly poignant on two fronts.

First, Jak and I had spent the better part of the past 12 months working on "The Great Wall of Jak." From shoveling the dirt to pouring the concrete to laying the cinder block and red brick to the final cosmetic touches of steps and trim, it had been a backbreaking project. But somewhere between the re-bar, the red clay, and the final few bricks, we had managed to build an impressive 50-foot wall and solidify an even stronger friendship. I channeled a lot of my pain, sorrow, and helplessness into that wall, which, I'm sure, was Jak's plan all along.

We had often joked that in 100 years the only thing left standing in our neighborhood would be that wall.

Secondly, Jak would rather cut off his hand than speak in public. But there he was up on top of the wall waving for everyone to be quiet. All the kids from the neighborhood took a seat next to him.

"I just wanted to say a few words," he started.

Kim and I found each other and held on, looking up at Jak.

Jak had played golf earlier in the day and when he explained to his buddies what they had planned for that night, they looked at him as if he had lost his mind. "Why would you want to do that?" they asked him. After the way the past year had gone, Jak told them, it just felt like the right thing to do. Not to be sad, but to celebrate. "The guys still thought I was crazy," Jak said. "What Noah has meant to us, that's what we're here to remember."

Kim and I squeezed each other close. I recalled how a year earlier, locked in our bathroom on the night before his funeral, when we first realized the notion that how we conducted ourselves would be Noah's only legacy to the world. If we were bitter, his legacy would be bitterness. If we were weak, his legacy would be weakness. If we were angry or withdrawn or joyless, that would be how people would remember our son. At times, we were all those things. But if we were strong and full of faith and hope and open to the many, but often deeply hidden blessings, then that could be part of his legacy as well. It was up to us. That was something we had always strived for but were never sure we had achieved.

Now, here was a friend of ours confirming, on the anniversary of Noah's death, that we had done a decent job of handling ourselves. That we had been able, in some small way, to make that year as much about what we had gained as opposed to what we had lost.

I will always consider that to be one of the greatest accomplishments of my life.

Just then I noticed a dish rag covering something on The Great Wall of Jak. Jak bent down and pulled the towel away and announced, ". . . And so, uh, in honor of all that . . . we wanted to, I guess, dedicate this wall to Noah."

We were shocked, to say the least, and we shook our heads and gulped back the tears for as long as we could. Jak leaned down and read the small gold plaque.

*"In Loving Memory of Noah William Fleming on his birthday, August 10, 2001."*

Kim and I collapsed into a hug. We were both crying now. But it wasn't rooted in sadness. The tears that day all felt different. I couldn't explain it then, but they were different in a significant way. We held hands and walked down to hug the Farsons. Then we read and touched and kissed the plaque. I'd never get to watch Noah graduate or get married or win the Nobel Peace Prize or, who knows, be the Employee of the Month at Burger King—but there's no way a dad could be prouder of his son.

We barely had time to digest the plaque when the kids, still sitting on the wall like a row of Sesame Street characters, waved us over, and Beaner handed us a box with a ribbon on it. I'm guessing everyone else knew what was coming because immediately the yard went silent.

"Oh gosh, you guys," I said, more than a bit embarrassed by the gifts and the sentiment, which exceeded my wildest expectations. "I don't think I can take anymore."

Everyone laughed. But boy, was I wrong.

Abby Farson is your typical first child: a studious, self-motivated, overachiever. She has the rare ability to take what she does very seriously without ever taking herself too seriously. Abby doesn't just learn to play the guitar, she masters it. She doesn't just try debate, she makes it to nationals. She doesn't just start a Web page, she creates one better than most companies. She didn't just think of our family on Noah's birthday, she organized and helped create the single greatest gift I have ever received. During the previous few weeks, prodded along by Abby and Kelsey, the kids in the neighborhood had each created a one-page tribute to Noah. Beaner then collected the drawings, poems, and letters (that's what she was doing when she was racing from house to house) and the girls put them in an album bound together with three rainbow-colored ties. On the cover was a rainbow made out of construction paper below the word Rainbows.

I wanted to read each page out loud, and I actually started, but Captain Sappy couldn't even make it through the dedication. So I handed it back to the kids and one by one, they read and explained their pages, which turned out to be much better.

There were hand prints in purple paint. A giant heart painted like a rainbow. Several self-portraits. A few Noah's arks. One page was a whole gang of Jesuses—all of them standing below a stick-figure drawing of a baby with a halo above his head—Noah. Another rainbow had four flowers underneath it: one for Kim, me, Ally, and Noah. One page just said, "We will always miss Noah." Beaner had done a watercolor of a rainbow with the inscription, "Noah, sweet child of God" underneath.

Beaner then took the book and turned to the final page where she read the same passage from Matthew that we used at Noah's funeral. Funny how at that moment the connotation seemed so utterly different than a year ago. "Let the little children come to me, and do not hinder them for the kingdom of heaven belongs to such as these."

Never more so than at that moment. We stepped toward the kids. We all came together for a giant hug at the foot of Noah's wall with the Rainbow book in the middle.

"We will never be able to tell you just how much this has meant to us," we said. "Thank you Abby. From the bottom of our hearts, really, thank you all so much."

In that moment our greatest prayers had been answered: In the obvious way that he had touched those children's lives, Noah did indeed have a deep and meaningful legacy. And if that day was any indication, he would never be forgotten.

Stunned, overjoyed, and well, exhausted, a little while later we hugged all the guests as they left the Farsons, and then Kim and I walked back across the street to our house. We sat together in the great room with the Rainbow book resting in our laps. As we leafed through the book one more time, we both cried softly. The tears were, again, different than what we had expected on that day. Not pain. Not sorrow. Not grief or regret or sadness or pity. It was something else altogether.

Periodically throughout that year, when frustration had set in or we had lapses or low points, Kim or I would shout out the very valid question: "What is our reward? What is our reward for not being bitter or withdrawn or spiteful? God would understand, right? He knows everything, right? And our friends and family, they would give us as much leeway as we needed. So why are we doing this? Why are we taking the grief head on? Why analyze it and study it and strategize it and conduct ourselves this way? Why not just give in? Why be constantly exhausted by this? Why not take a break? Why not sleep all day and cry and whine and bitch and moan? Why not hate? Why not give in? Why not quit? Why? Why? Why? What is our reward?"

I looked down at the Rainbow book and the bridge that it made between our two laps. I turned to Kim.

"This is it," I said. "This is our reward."

Kim shot me a puzzled look. She had been unusually quiet that day, choosing to just soak everything in. Just 10 days away from the birth of our daughter, Kim was the picture of serenity and calm confidence.

"These kids have been changed by Noah," I explained. "That means he'll live on in them, and in their hearts. Some of them, they won't forget Noah, I don't think, and that means he'll outlive even us. People have been changed by him . . . so this is our reward. For doing things as best we could, this book is our reward."

A long time ago Kim and I agreed that at some point in this process we would be able to think of Noah and his death and the thought would not tear us to shreds. Even when we formulated that goal, we couldn't actually fathom a time that might actually come true. But if it did ever happen, we agreed we would be well on our way to being healed.

As we talked about Noah's first birthday, we both continued to cry.

"You know what these are?" I asked Kimmy, pointing to the tears on her face.

She smiled at me. I smiled back. For the first time in a year, I didn't feel the urge to wipe the tears off her face. We had craved these kinds of tears for a long time. I didn't want to get rid of them.

"Tears of joy," I whispered.

There was a long, silent pause and then Kim took my hand in hers. She arched her head toward the sky and with her eyes closed whispered, one last time, "Happy birthday, baby boy."

# CHAPTER 21

# Okay God, Bring It On

I want this to be part of the permanent record. One person among all our friends and family was completely certain Ally's lungs would be mature the first time around. There was only one true believer among us. Not the mom. Not the doctors. Not the neonatologist. Not the grandparents or the godparents. Just one person. One person of such incredible character, unshakeable faith, and unfathomable intellect that he never wavered in his belief that Ally was going to be born on that day.

Me.

(I'm joking, of course. If you've stuck with me this far you understand that—I hope.)

Everyone else was hedging their bets as we checked into the hospital and settled into our room in the maternity ward. Patting Kimmy on the hand, they all repeated the same kinds of things. "Now, lets not get our hopes up too far . . . it's no big deal . . . there's no way of predicting if her lungs are mature or not."

Not me. After a year of thinking everything through, after analyzing each action and always making sure to balance ourselves and limit our emotional exposure, I had had enough. Or maybe I was finally close to some kind of peace and clarity with Noah's death, because what I felt in the 10 days between Noah and Ally's birthdays was a growing sense of, "Okay God, bring it on."

*Whatcha got big guy? Come on. I'm ready. We're ready for whatever You've got in store.*

"What do you think?" Kimmy asked, sitting up in her hospital bed. Looking back at pictures from that morning, Kim was radiant. She seemed to glow with peace. I appeared, well, clammy and pale, but I always look that way.

173

"She's coming today, sweetie," I said. "No question."

That made her smile. At times I may be half the man she deserves, but I have always been able to make Kim smile.

When we arrived at the hospital early that morning, Dr. Shaver performed an amnio to see if Ally's lungs had matured enough to breathe on her own. The results were not due back for another hour or so, and everyone else had stepped out for some breakfast. We were alone in the hospital room and kind of enjoying it. No phones. No magazines. No figidity grandparents. Just us.

At that moment we had nothing, and we had everything.

A year before, geez, you should have seen us making our way in from the hospital parking lot. We looked like we were boarding a cruise ship for a two-week sail around the Mediterranean. We toted in two big bags of clothes plus a diaper bag and a backpack that included outfits for every occasion, style, and climate. I think I even brought a tie and something like three pairs of shoes. We had a stack of magazines and books that a library would have envied, a CD player with 20 or so carefully chosen discs, a disposable camera, a regular one, a digital and a camcorder. I had three different kinds of batteries. I had two cell phones, a calling card, a scroll of phone numbers and, had they allowed me to bring it in, a bullhorn, a satellite dish, and a sandwich board to help announce Noah's birth.

A year later we sat alone in our hospital room with practically nothing. Equipped with only what we needed the most—peace, hope, perspective, and each other.

Grasping Kim's hand and scooting onto the bed with her, I told her, "Today Kimmy, she's coming today . . . I guarantee it."

"Like what percent?"

"One hundred, Nord. One hundred percent. Have you seen the way she kicks? The way she moves? How strong she is? How she, like, responds to our voices? How she looks on the ultrasounds? All that fetal breathing? Man, she's ready. We're ready. Her lungs are ready. I know it. She's coming today."

"Promise?"

"Guaranteed."

I bent over and spoke into Kim's navel. "Help daddy out, Al. Come see us today Baby Nordstrom . . . or you're grounded."

Just then the door to the room swung open. But suspecting that is was a grandparent, neither Kim or I looked up.

"She's mature!" the nurse practically screamed, swinging back the curtain in dramatic fashion.

That sure got our attention.

"Whaaaaaaaat?"

"Her lungs are mature. You daughter's lungs are ready! She's coming today."

When emotions are pure and powerful, it's almost as if they take on a physical form. At that moment the energy between Kim and me felt like a tempest in the room; a swirling, electric wave that seemed to wrap together like a helix, drawing us together. How many life-changing moments had we been through in the past year? And how many more were yet to come on that day? But through it all, that was the one we both seem to especially cherish. *She is coming today.* Greatest words we have ever heard. Another world-changing sentence made up of four simple words. Words that meant freedom, the finish line. Most of the milestones and blessings in this process were so subtle they were easy to miss. But those words from the nurse were a powerful, explosive affirmation.

So maybe that's why we reacted the way we did, with such warm hugs and flowing tears; why we allowed ourselves a few golden moments of release and joy and vulnerability. As each grandparent trickled back into the room, we burst out: "SHE'S READY! SHE'S COMING TODAY!" There was so much joy. We had learned to soak it up while we could. The grandparents all seemed a bit apprehensive, though. There was some hard swallowing and chest patting, as if to slow down their jittery hearts. But we had learned to enjoy her right now, knowing we weren't guaranteed anything beyond that moment. We were ready. For whatever was to come. We had worked hard to get to that point and we were just so happy to be moving forward out of our holding pattern.

Okay God, bring it on.

*If everything had gone wrong a year ago with Noah, it all seemed to be going right this time with Ally.*

After a year of living moment to moment, breath to breath, time just started flying by. The nurse handed me my blue paper-thin operating room scrubs and told me to change and get ready. Each of the grandparents then handed me their cameras to take into the operating room. In less than an hour, I heard the nurse explain through the bathroom door, Kim would be taken back and prepped for a C-section and if everything went right, Ally could be here before lunch. *This was actually happening* I thought *and happening fast!* I kicked off my shoes and with my emotions now swirling in every direction—sad, happy, scared, nervous, confident, back to Mo, thinking of Noah, connecting to him as I looked at his picture, the one I carried in my pants pocket—I turned quickly and was struck by my own image in the bathroom mirror.

Several times that day I would be on the verge of losing it. At times my peace of mind evaporated and I'd be frozen by the fear of losing another child and the risk of losing my wife along with my own will to live. And then I would be taken aback by my own reflection—in a car window, a vending machine, a hospital mirror— and shaken to clarity and focus by this one thought: *I'm watching you, Daddy.*

That moment alone in the bathroom staring at my reflection, like I had done so many times with Noah's shiny, marble gravestone, triggered so much in me.

*Don't let Noah down,* I thought. *Don't let yourself down. Not now. You've spent the last year running the race of your life, don't go tripping over your shoelaces and falling flat on your face with the finish line practically in view.*

I nodded my head, *yes,* turned and left the bathroom.

The scrubs were great, but they had one serious design flaw: the belt on the pants was never meant to hold up under the weight of three cameras. Seconds away from the most intense moment of my life, my mind was completely occupied by one horrifying thought. *My pants are gonna fall down.*

*When they go to hand me my daughter, I will release my hands from my waist to cradle little Oopie and—plop—my pants, weighted down by those stupid cameras, will fall to the floor, nurses will faint, and moments later I will be shackled and billy-clubbed and taken away on indecent exposure charges.*

Kimmy was wheeled away to get her epidural and be prepped for surgery. There, at Kim's request, the nurse hooked her up to the fetal monitor one more time. Ally's heart was pumping loud and strong, right at 150 beats per minute. Her heart was beating so strongly the nurse had to turn the volume down on the monitor.

*If everything had gone wrong with Noah, it all seemed to be going right with Ally.*

Meanwhile, the grandparents and I were led to a waiting room that was basically a broom closet with a sink, toilet, a few chairs, some lame, pastel paintings, a clock (one that, I swear, seemed to be going in reverse), and some magazines left over from the cold war. Everyone was pretending to either be totally relaxed or reading.

"Aren't the nurses so nice here?" asked Janie.

M-hmm.

"And I like Dr. Shaver and Dr. Vuong, don't you?"

Yup.

"How are Kimmy's spirits?" asked Becky.

*Fine, fine. We're doing fine.*

"We're ready," I said. "For whatever happens. Good or bad. We're ready."

*Wrong answers, Dave. At least for this crowd.*

The room fell silent, except for the tock-ticking of that backwards clock.

It was hard for all of us to sit there and worry, away from Kimmy. After all, she had kept us calm, positive, and upbeat for so long. For going on a year she had been the rock of this extended grieving family: the person we had all taken our cues from, the one who reeled the rest of us back in when we wanted to lose it. Now she was off alone by herself once again getting strapped to a gurney with a giant needle stuck into her spinal cord. It was one of the few times we had been apart during the last year. We all needed her. But Ally needed her most.

Ten minutes went by. My four (okay, it was five) years of college seemed to have zipped by faster.

*Noah had died in a third of the time. Is she okay? Is Al okay? Am I okay?*

A few idle moments are all it took for a year's worth of worry and fear to pop through the mental barriers I had set up—like holes springing in a dam. It's a frightening thing to experience. How after one minute of mental wandering—BAM—I am whiplashed back to square one, back to the frail, scared, confused, blubbering mess I was the night Noah died. One thought, one image, one scent or one sound can take me right back to square one, shredded emotionally into a thousand pieces that have to be put back together all over again. There was no way to know what things would take me back there. No way to side step it. I just had to accept those trips, brace for them, ride 'em out, and recover.

*Two dead children? What if Kim dies this time too? Could you live through that Dave? Nope. I don't think I could. I mean, I barely made it through Noah's death. How much longer? Shoot? How much longer? Strength and peace, Lord. Strength and peace. Breathe. Remember to breathe. You with me baby boy? You with me?*

When I was a kid I used to walk across rows of parking curbs pretending to be on some cliff's edge. As I neared the end of the curbs, I had to fight the urge to just try and sprint the last 10 feet and get to the end because the extra speed would always cause me to lose my balance and fall off and blow the whole thing. That's what I was feeling. I had walked with balance and purpose for so long and now, with the end in sight, I was fighting the urge to sprint the rest of the way, abandon everything I had learned, and risk tumbling hard off the path.

*Is Kimmy okay? Is Al okay? Are you watching over them, Mo?*

To break the clatter in my head, I stood up and went into the bathroom. I washed my hands and splashed some water on my face and, leaning with locked elbows against the sink, I looked up for some towels and was struck once again by my own reflection in the mirror.

*Are you completely full of it? Huh? Answer me? Or did you really mean all the things you'd said this past year about how Noah had changed you, given you peace and strength, made you a better man? Did you mean all that or are you just a good talker? A phony? Are you a phony? Somebody who talks a good game? I wonder. Well, it's time now. Time to find out who you are. Time to become the person you rebuilt during the last year. It's now or never. This is it.*

I regained my composure, wiped my face, and dried my hands on my pants.

*I'm watching you daddy.*

"Thanks, baby boy," I said out loud looking to the ceiling. "You are such a good boy. You keep looking after us Mo, okay? That's what big brothers do, okay?"

A short while later the nurse stood at the doorway.

"You ready, dad?"

*I'm ready. You hear that God? Bring it on.*

"I'm ready," I said, heading for the door without much fanfare. I slapped Dad on the shoulder and shook Ed's hand and waved goodbye.

"We'll be back in a few minutes," the nurse said.

Down the hall we went. It seemed like we were the only ones in the hospital that day.

"You nervous?"

"Not really," I told the nurse. "I'm cool."

*You're not cool; you're a big fat phony, a big fat phony.*

She guffawed. I laughed.

*I'm cool? What was that? Doofus. You are such a doofus.*

We took a right turn, headed through two double doors, and then paused outside the operating room. The cameras were now pulling my blue scrubs down to the verge of indecency.

"Pull your mask up," said the nurse. "Here we go."

*Here we go.*

Deep breath. Pants begin to fall.

*Grab pants. Stop thinking so much. Let's do this. Strength and peace, Mo. Give me strength and peace. And hold my pants up too, baby boy.*

The nurse stepped to the side and guided me into the room with her left hand on my back, sort of spotting me just in case I passed out. Somehow she had seen through my veneer of calmness.

Inside there seemed to be at least seven or eight people. Bright lights and shiny metal things everywhere. Lots of crisp, blue sheets, too. Everyone in blue and green and pink masks. To the left, the anesthesiologist sitting behind an array of tubes, knobs, controls, and gadgets that looked like a Willy Wonka invention. To the right, a gaggle of pediatric intensive care nurses waiting around an empty bassinet. I nodded and then turned my head away from them. I had seen enough empty bassinets in my mind the last year.

*Push that from your mind ... strength and peace, strength and peace.*

Oop was going to be born a month early. We had agonized over that decision, but everyone agreed that if you charted out the safety of the baby, her development, and the risk of a repeat abruption, the lines all seemed to cross at 36 weeks. Still, our greatest fear was that we would put our daughter in danger trying to assuage our own fears about losing another child. So, best-case scenario, we expected her to be frail, blue, and gasping for breath. And we prepared ourselves for the image and the long, scary nights in neonatal intensive care. Not to mention the guilt and the agony of watching another child suffer in great pain, having still not fully recovered from the first one.

The best thing about the operating room was that the fetal monitors were turned down and out of sight. No more fetal monitors. Thank God.

Straight ahead was my wife.

She was looking up to the sky, her lips barely moving. I knew what she was doing: whispering Psalm 23 to herself over and over. *Fear no evil.* A few minutes before I had come into the room, the doctors asked several questions about her scar from Noah's C-section. It was higher than usual. It was raggedy and there was a lot of scar tissue. The doctors said they would try and clean it up a bit this time.

*That's what we're here for in more ways than one. To clean up the scars.*

Kim was covered from her neck to her feet in blue sheets except near her navel where the nurses were putting something that looked like orange cellophane on her skin. Both arms were strapped in a supine pose to gurneys that extended out in each direction like a crucifix. The tubes, wires, sheets, lights, needles, and instruments surrounding her were too numerous to fully take in. I caught a glimpse of a row of something that looked like shiny, stainless steel barbecue tongs and quickly looked away. *Push it, push it from your mind.* I took a seat in a chair next to her head and leaned in cheek to cheek with her. I did this partly to be close and feel her strength and partly to get under the curtain that was stretched across her chest so I wouldn't be able to see them cut her open.

*You're such a wimp. Be a man goddammit.*

Kimmy's thick brown hair was already soaked in sweat and pressed against her forehead—she was in a zone then, all business. She was relaxed and focused. She kept her eyes staring up at the ceiling most of the time. She was a warrior about to head into battle. Her teeth were clenched. She looked fierce and fearless. The strong one. Always the strong one. My biggest concern was blabbering like an idiot or jumping for joy and getting depantsed in front of everyone and here was my wife, about to get sliced open, the picture of clarity and laser-like focus.

*My God, she looks so much like Noah right now.*

She was short and curt with me, as if to say, "Focus Dave, no blubbering or crying or cracking nervous jokes; focus with me right now, get serious, get ready . . . or get out."

"Hi, sweetie," I said, kissing her forehead.

"Hi."

"You okay?"

"Fine."

"Hang in there."

"Mm-hmm."

"Everything is going to be fine. I am so proud of you. You are so strong. So strong. So strong." *Dude, please, just shut up.*

She just shook her head and pinched her eyebrows into a V, which is code for, "Dude, please, just shut up."

Get tough. Get serious. Get ready. Or get out.

*This is it. It's time to become everything you worked on during the last year.*

I got the message.

Just in time, because a few seconds later, Dr. Vong announced, "Here we go." And let me tell you something: you need to be focused, ready, and strong when the smell of a laser cutting open your wife wafts into your face. Kim had gone white after catching a glimpse of the procedure in the reflection of the overhead lights. I was only two shades behind her and paling fast. I wasn't prepared for the amount of physical force a C-section required. The two doctors standing over Kim's midsection were tugging and yanking on her to the point that the table rocked back and forth, and Kim's head jerked side to side like someone on a subway. I kept my head tucked down next to Kim's. I said little. *Strength and peace, strength and peace.* But our eyes were locked on each other and we exchanged smiles. I broke with protocol and kissed her repeatedly on the forehead.

The tugging seemed to go on forever. It made me nauseated—and I was just standing there, no one was yanking on my innards like a knotted up garden hose.

"Gosh, the traffic was bad this morning?" Dr. Vuong said to her partner across the table.

"I know," he replied. "I just got back from vacation. Forgot how bad it is in the city in the morning."

"Well, how long'd you go for?"

"Ten days," he said.

*Jesus Christ, are we at a cocktail party or a C-section, people?*

"BP's fallen just a bit but still good, heart rate is fine," said the anesthesiologist. "Looking good. How we doing, Kim?"

"Good, good," she said. "How's the baby? Her heartbeat?"

"150. 148—doing great."

Kim shook her head. I touched her cheek and tucked her hair behind her ear—*she freakin' hates when you do that*—and then quickly untucked it.

"Hang in there Kimmy, doing great."

A tug.

A yank.

A push.

The movements were so violent, Kim's head and neck shook. If the bed was on wheels we'd be in the parking lot by now. If this one seemed invasive, I couldn't even imagine what Kim went through a year ago.

"Okay Kim, everything looks great, your uterus looks great."

*What the?*

"Here we go . . . we're close now . . ."

". . . we can see the baby . . ."

*That was so quick. I've been waiting a year for this—I felt like I could account for every excruciating second of the past 12 months—and now all of a sudden it's caught me by surprise, how did that happen?*

"Everything looks good . . ."

*Breathe. Breathe. Breathe.*

"Okay, getting close . . ."

The nurse who brought me to the operating room came over and tapped my hand and squeezed my forearm. I looked up and she was giving me a warm, calming smile. Knowing our situation, the doctors never let more than a few seconds go by without an encouraging word or gesture. Then, without warning, the anesthesiologist was tapping me on the back, saying, "This is it dad. If you want to see your daughter being born, *stand up*."

Gulp.

The first shove from the doctors produced nothing but a tidal wave of fluid and blood that pooled up below Kimmy's abdomen. *Woa boy.* I swayed. I steadied myself on the back of the chair. And for the briefest of moments I was transported back to the night when Noah died, when the nurse pulled the sheet back and the bed was awash in crimson.

*Push that from your mind now, push it. It's time.*

*Okay God, bring it on.*

"Doing great, everything's great," said Dr. Vuong. "Little more, Kim, just a little more."

Kim nodded.

*She's so strong.*

She turned to me, and we locked eyes in a kind of serious, go-get-'em nod. Mentally we had been standing side-by-side at the edge of a cliff— sometimes teetering, sometimes wanting to jump, sometimes enjoying the view—and that look was us clasping hands and taking our leap of faith.

*I'm ready. For anything. Okay God, bring it on.*

The doctor's hands disappeared inside Kim's belly and when they reappeared they were holding Ally's arms. She slid out, face up, a bit pale and covered in blood and slimy yellow and white puss. She was alone. (Until the end I had held out a goofy hope of twins as a kind of cosmic two-for-one makeup.) All the colors seemed the opposite of what I had expected. The umbilical cord was light brown, purple, and red. The slime was yellow. The baby, too white. The doctor put his left hand under her for support and they went about cutting the cord and getting her to the neonatal nurse as soon as possible. Because she was coming 28 days early, there would be no pomp and circumstance around the cutting of the cord.

"Looks good," said the doc. "Oh, she looks good. Everything looking good, Kim."

*She's beautiful.*

I ducked back down to Kimmy's cheek, partly to be with her and partly to get away from the gore.

"She's here. She's perfect . . . she's strong. She's fine. She's doing fine."

But that's not what Kim wanted to hear. Me either.

Kim's dry lips barely moved as she whispered, "I want to hear her cry."

"I know," I said. "I know. She will sweetie. She will."

As if on cue, as if it were an instantaneous answer to our silent prayer, that strong, beautiful little girl, our miracle, gathered up just enough air in her preemie lungs to let out a tiny chirp, like a baby bird. AUrrrrrrtt! And when we heard that noise Kim and I rejoiced, cheek to cheek. I reached up with my right hand and hugged her head. We both exhaled for maybe the first time in a year.

Like any task, when we started out on our climb, staring up at a mountain of grief, we used a few goals and dreams to keep us moti- vated. When we tired and became frustrated on our climb, we focused on two things: we wanted a birth certificate, that had become our defacto diploma, and we wanted to hear our baby girl cry. Most parents want their kids to shut up, but at that moment, hearing her cry was a joyful noise; an earthly manifestation of a year's worth of work and prayers.

*If everything had gone wrong with Noah, it all seemed to be going right with Ally.*

I left Kim and walked toward that glorious sound over to the neonatal station to see my daughter. She was the opposite of everything I had prepared myself for. That hadn't happened in a long time—about a year and ten days to be exact. She was solid, not skinny; she was pink and healthy; not bluish and pale; she was kicking and clawing, not flaccid and lifeless; she was wheezing and coughing and squeezing the air into her lungs, determined to breathe on her own. *She's strong and beautiful . . . just like Kimmy.*

The nurses continued to clean her off and collect vital signs, and the breathing specialist stood by with one of those masks attached to a bag at the ready to help Oop catch her breath. After a while we all stood there watching, inhaling and exhaling right along with her. *That-a-girl. Come on, sweetie. You can do it. Daddy's right here, sweetie.* She was wheezing a bit, struggling to catch a full breath, like a motor gasping— huh-huh-huh-huh-huh-shhhhh—before it turns over on a cold morning. I stood there in awe again, watching her tummy push up and down, such a fighter. Her eyes squeezed shut in battle, the skin pulled taut over her puny little ribs, her precious hand and her porcelain fingers balled into a little fist of fury. *My little Kimmy.*

"You can touch her," the nurse said, nudging me. "You can talk to her."

I stroked her leg and touched her cheek and bent down under the heat lamp and kissed her tiny, perfect hand, each finger, each crease, every hair follicle, living proof a million times over of a God that I had been taking on faith the past year. I slid my finger into her palm and she grabbed that thing and squeezed with so much vigor I thought the nail would pop off.

"Woa!" I said. "She squeezed it hard. She's so strong. Wow. Cooooool."

The tears trickled. The nurses giggled.

*She looks like you, Noah. You did great. You're a good big brother. So different. Everything feels so different.*

"Breathe, baby girl, breathe," I whispered in a singsong. "You can do it, sweetie. Daddy's right here. Hi baby. Keep going. You're doing great. Breathe, baby girl, breathe."

Yanked into this world four weeks early, little Oop would never need a single bit of help breathing. I'm not sure she would have accepted it, anyway.

I just couldn't move. I couldn't take my eyes off her. I was mesmerized. She had a hold of my forefinger, so I bent my thumb around and stroked the top of her hand with it. And then I realized: we were holding hands. Daddy and his little girl, holding hands for the first time. Then she opened her eyes, blinked and, following my voice—the one that had been reading to her and singing to her and lecturing her through Kimmy's navel about sports, art, and current events—she turned and looked right at me, right through to my soul.

On the morning of Ally's birth, with Kimmy and Scoop still asleep, I walked outside to watch the sunrise. At that moment the only fear I had was what my emotional state would be like once Oop was born. I was scared I wouldn't be able to hold it together and take care of my girls. After all, who knows what 54 weeks of grief, soul-searching, nerves, anger, fear, joy, growth, and prayer look like when they come out? Are we talking a truckload of tissue? A fist through the wall? Running naked through the streets? Catatonic crying? That's what I figured. Uncontrollable weeping and release. The emotional dam, the pressure building exponentially each day during the last year, finally giving way. Release. Peace. Joy.

Instead, though, what I felt was expansive and unfathomable growth—in my heart, my scarred, rebuilt, heart. In that moment it had changed back from the green, cubed sharp heart of Noah's fetal monitor to a real, live, beating pumping muscle. Once again during the past year I was reminded that I am capable of so much more than I ever imagined. When Ally looked into my eyes, my soul expanded. Whatever I had assumed was my maximum capacity for love before that moment no longer existed.

My happiness and joy, my strength and confidence, my spirituality, with one look from my daughter they had all just expanded a 1,000-fold.

My journey had ended. The search for peace, strength, hope, and joy was over. I had found it all right there in that little girl.

CSBO

## CHAPTER 22

# Ally's Birth, Our Rebirth

Someday I may regret this, but I never once considered pulling out the cameras that were tugging my pants to the ground and snapping a picture during Ally's birth. It all seemed too pedestrian, too routine, too casual, like I was some dorky tourist on a Birthing Ride at Disney World. Nope. Too intrusive. Too typical. Too common.

A child being born is a miracle. That word is so overused nowadays. A miracle weight-loss shake! Miracle moisturizing cream. The Miracle on Ice. But when I put my child's hand inside mine and examined that intricate, tiny, delicate, yet perfect mechanism, I cannot come up with a word more fitting than miracle. Maybe it's great that nowadays a child being conceived, grown, and born healthy is taken for granted. Until I saw Ally, I hadn't fully understood that it took a miracle to bring a child safely into this world. But once that thought hit me, Noah's death instantly seemed easier to take. It seemed more, well, reasonable. God didn't forsake us. We didn't do anything wrong. No one was picking on us. We didn't get what we were asking for; no, but what we had asked for was quite a lofty request: a miracle. In the end, we got everything we had ever prayed for. We just got it in a way that made it clear to us someone else was in control of the plan. As crazy as the notion would have once seemed, it all felt perfectly planned.

The warm, salty tears streamed down my face.

*Ah, tears of joy.*

I made no attempt to wipe them away.

I looked down at my daughter. Ally then took a deep breath and seemed to hold it. Her chubby bottom lip pushed out and rolled back over, down toward her chin. Her eyes pinched shut. *Was everything*

185

*okay? She looks like she's in pain. Is she okay? Why isn't she breathing? It looks like she's pushing? Boy, she's getting awfully red isn't she?*

All these worries and questions screaming inside my head and then . . .

A veritable fountain of, well, pee sprang out of her, arched into the air and tinkled back down into the blanket below her legs. We all gasped first, stepped back and let out a hardy laugh.

"Oh God," I said. "Oh my God! I have to tell her mother!"

Holding my pants up with both hands, I shuffled back over to give Kim a full report.

"Oh Kimmy, she's so strong. She's breathing great. She looks great. She's pink and chubby and a fighter and . . . she just whizzed all over the place," I said. "It was a pee-pee fountain."

"Are they taking her to intensive care?"

"She's got a little bit of wheezing and coughing, and she struggles sometimes to get a full breath, but she's doing great, she looks great."

"The NICU, Dave, are they taking her there?"

"No, right now they don't think she needs it. She's here Nord, she's here, she's actually here. It was a fountain, a whiz fountain I tell you, a pee-pee fire hose into the air!"

Not fully appreciating my bathroom humor, Kimmy turned away for a moment. She blinked and went off by herself for a few seconds. She seemed to be releasing a year's worth of anxiety. I could sense her rewinding back the past 12 months—the millions of battles we had fought to get to this place. Every tear, every last second, it had all been worth it. Kim had carried this family during that time. Now she was setting down that burden. When her eyes reopened they were filled with utter contentment, happiness, and love. Her eyebrows unpinched. She smiled up in the air as if directing it to Mo, and then she turned her head back to me and whispered, "I love you."

As if saying it for the first time, I told her, "I love you too."

"She's so strong and beautiful Kim . . . just like her momma."

Kimmy smiled at me, finally.

"Congratulations," said the doc.

"Thank you," we said back.

The head neonatal nurse then asked me to do the honor of informing the grandparents. Then they were going to weigh and measure Al.

"I'll be right back Kimmy," I said. "I'm gonna go tell everybody and come right back. Are you okay?"

She shook her head.

"You wanna close your eyes, sweetie?"

She shook her head.

I bent down and kissed her forehead and touched her cheek. I looked up at the anesthesiologist, and he shook his head softly back at me. "She's fine, go ahead," he seemed to say.

Now here's a first: After I practically floated down the hall to the waiting room, I jumped through the door and then I just, well, I just stood there for what must have seemed like forever to the grandparents. I was speechless. Totally tongue-tied. I didn't know what to say or how to convey what had just happened. I had never described a miracle before. Everyone stood, their eyebrows all raised in anticipation. Mouths agape. Waiting. Waiting. And I just stood there, smiling, shaking my head, trying to push a sound, a cough, anything, from my mouth.

"She's beautiful!" was all I managed to blurt out. "She's great. Kimmy's fine. And Ally is great. She's beautiful and strong, just like her mother."

I told them how everything went, her little chirp and the raspy coughing she was doing trying to catch her breath. I explained that I was going back in to pick up their granddaughter and that they could meet me at the nursery to watch her getting weighed and measured. Then she was going to see her momma. But the fact that she was okay, the fact that we had made it, hadn't really sunk in with them either.

"You're bringing her out?" asked Janie.

"Yup."

"Wait," said Ed. "No NICU? No oxygen? She's coming out?"

"Right now?" asked Becky. "Already?"

"Yes, you guys, come on down and see her. Come see your granddaughter!"

Silence.

Freeze-frame.

Sinking in now.

*Here it comes.*

*Bingo.*

Now I was getting mobbed all over again.

The four of them now hugging and rejoicing, crying and laughing and hugging. You'd have thought we had just won the World Series.

"Oh wow!"

"Hahahaha."

"Oh my goodness"

"Okay you guys, I'll meet you down there," I said. "But first, here, take these dang cameras back."

"Did you get some good shots?" yelled Becky.

I hollered back to her over my shoulder, laughing, "Yeah yeah, tons, just wait till you see 'em, they're awesome."

Back inside the operating room, I sat down next to Kimmy who was resting with her eyes shut as they continued to sew her back together. The neonatal nurse then brought Ally over all bundled up like a cotton burrito with a fluffy, pink knit hat on her head. She leaned in and without hesitation or warning, handed my daughter to me.

*Hey! Wait. I had never held a newborn before. Let alone a preemie or my own daughter. What do I do? How do I hold her? Wait. Wait. Stop.*

But I never spoke up; instead, I stood, moved my hands into position and took that girl into my arms. Sometimes the real work starts once your prayers are answered and your dreams actually come true. Life could be eminently more frightening than death. Maybe my journey wasn't over, but just beginning.

*This is life. This is your child. You are a dad. You stand up and take that baby. Your child needs you. Do it. Simple as that. The rebuilding is over. Finish the project. Become the person Noah died to help create.*

Ally was so much smaller than Mo. A tiny little thing. Noah required two arms to support. Ally felt like you could hold her in your palm. The pink hat struck me for a moment. I bent down and kissed it. I inhaled the smell, a mixture of warm skin, lotion, and her mother. A year ago I had taken Noah's hat and put it in my pocket. *I can't have this one, Ally needs it to keep her head warm. Wow. Cool.* The juxtaposition between the two births—the polar opposites in emotion, life and death, cold and warm, joy and heartbreak—it was stunning in its power and scope.

*If everything had gone wrong with Noah, everything seemed to be going right with Ally.*

On each exhale she hummed a little like a content kitten. I, of course, took that as a sign of her deep, deep love and confidence in her father.

She had the tiniest, most delicate little features. The nose. The ears. The curvy little, microscopic doll lips. I sat down in the chair with her and leaned as far over to my left as I could so Kim could get a look at her. That was torture for Kimmy, though. She was in great pain and extremely drained. Having her that close and not being able to touch her or kiss her was hard. So I stood and left with my daughter, and the nurse and I took Ally down to the nursery to have her weighed and measured. The sooner we got that done, the sooner Kim could hold her.

I've never stepped with such pride and joy; such strength, such total peace. The smile on my face, Teresa would tell me later, was like nothing she had ever seen before: it seemed to glow with the power of pure and utter joy.

They unwrapped Ally, placed a blue paper cloth down, and set her on the scale. The numbers came up 6.01. We had hoped for five pounds. Four was fine. And here she was more than six. Then they stretched her out and measured her lengthwise—18 and ½ inches. As they were measuring her, Ally was growing impatient and a bit angry. She reached up with one hand, grabbed that blue cloth, and balled it up in her tiny fist. And then, for good measure, she kicked the side of the scale. She was a little mighty mite. A six-pound, one-ounce ball of life, power, and vigor.

I laughed. Just laughed and laughed and laughed. The sound of hope. *Look at her up there, all six pounds of her with tufts of blonde hair and truckloads of 'tude. Remind me again what I was worried about?*

The nurses took her back and while they finished their measurements and paperwork under the watchful eye of the grandparents, I slipped off to go be with Kimmy. When I found her in the recovery room, the color had come back into her face and she was sitting up. She was beaming.

I kneeled by her side and took her hand in mine. "Oopie's so strong," I said. "She's so beautiful. Don't worry about her, she's so strong."

"Really?"

"You should have seen her getting weighed, Kimmy. She was mad. Oh she was mad. And that little girl—you think she's so tiny and fragile—she grabbed the paper on the scale and crumpled it up into her little fist like she was shaking it at the nurse, like, 'Put my clothes back on!'"

"Ooooh."

"Yeah, she's a fighter Kimmy. A little fighter."

A tear fell from Kim's eye.

"When can I see her? I want to hold her."

"Soon sweetie, so soon," I said. "And then after that, for the rest of your life."

Kimmy dosed off for a while, and I stayed there, holding her hand. A few minutes later, I looked up and there was the back of a nurse, wheeling Ally's bassinet up to Kim's bed. The nurse lifted Al out and handed her to her mother.

I stood back and soaked in the scene, the most powerful and beautiful thing I have ever seen—a mother and her child staring into each other's eyes for the first time. The instant, deep, connection. The soft smiles. The warmth. Really, the personification of motherhood and life itself. A mother and a child who had given life to each other. Ally had opened her eyes the minute she had smelled and heard Kimmy, and she was arching her face up to get a better look. God, they were twins.

For once in my life I stood back and said nothing, just taking it all in. Kim bent forward and kissed her on the forehead and Ally blinked her eyes shut and leaned into the embrace as if that kiss was transferring love and energy from mother to daughter. They had been connected by flesh and blood for nine months—well, a bit less actually—but now they seemed closer than ever.

If I were allowed one moment to keep and was forced to erase all others from my memory, I think I'd take that one.

*If everything had gone wrong with Noah, it had all gone right with Ally.*

Then it hit me: She's here, and she's healthy because we took her out early and we took her out early because Noah's death warned us about going full term. Noah's death is what saved Ally. In a way, Noah gave his life to save hers. He died so that we could appreciate life. He saved his sister. He saved us all.

Noah's death had hit us like a giant tidal wave, washing away everything unnecessary in our lives and sending us off onto a completely uncharted course. Kim and I sailed away from everything we had been and everything we had known, barely moored to this world. Our marriage. Family. Friends. Work. God. We set off to reconstruct ourselves. Summer turned to fall. Thanksgiving gave way to Christmas and out of that deep, dark plunge came a turning point. A child. Sailing back now. Moving back toward the world. And just like we were promised, spring did come again. It gave way to summer and summer warmed us with HOPE. Noah's birthday brought peace. Ally's birthday became our own rebirth. Back to rejoin the world. Different. Changed. Forever. But for the better. Trust had restored our faith. Faith had given us peace. Peace grew into strength. Strength created hope and from hope, we found joy.

My prayer had come true. I was never going to be the same because of Noah's death but maybe, I had honored him by becoming better. A year before, my life was about the foolish quest to bend and manipulate the world to accommodate my whims. The past year had brought me something of a Galileo shift about the center of my own universe. That I am the one who needs to readjust in order to find peace in this world—a world that took away my son, but also gave me my daughter. A world that trains us to be selfish even though all our rewards come from being selfless. When I look at the world, I don't see myself first anymore. I see Kim. I see Noah, and God. I see Ally. I see my family.

The past year had been something like how they must have created that mosaic at St. Pete's. We started blank. Wiped clean. Devoid of color. Empty. And with every thought, every conversation, every lesson, every revelation, every surviving breath, we added a piece to the canvas. But until Ally's birth, I hadn't taken a step back to gaze at the new portrait of myself.

I found strength I never thought I had. I found a depth to love I never knew existed. I now possessed balance, peace, and contentment when, not too long before, I wasn't all that concerned with finding them. I now have a hard-earned, unique, and valuable perspective on life. Noah taught me more than how *not* to be afraid of death. He taught me how not to be afraid of *life*. I was given the toughest test of my life, and I survived. Now I am free to live the rest of my days knowing nothing I'll ever face will be that hard. I am a better husband. A better father. In many ways Noah's death is what completed me as a man—made me full and free.

Would I give it all back for one more moment with my son? In a second.

I'll never say that I'm better off because of Noah's death. Never, But I will concede this: pain can sometimes be a blessing. I have a friend in the NFL whose son is afflicted with a neurological disorder that blocks him from feeling pain. At first he thought it was the greatest thing in the world, that his son would go through life and never have to suffer or be in pain. It was just the opposite. He burned himself on the stove. He broke his leg jumping off a slide. He was so reckless on his bike his parents had to take it away. Without pain that little boy couldn't understand fear or consequence or what it meant to injure someone else—and that made it hard for him to relate to others. It didn't take long for my friend to realize just how much we all *need* pain—to learn, to grow, and to gain perspective. As crazy as it sounds, pretty soon he was praying that his son would one day be able to feel pain.

I too will always be left to wonder if I could have grown the way I did without having to suffer the death of my son. Could I have changed so much without such torment? Could I have gained such perspective without experiencing such pain? If I'm honest, probably not.

But could someone else? God I hope so.

We will never stop missing Noah. That hurt never dissipates. His death is a wound that will never completely heal. We're going to grieve him every day, for the rest of our lives, and in the same way whether we have 10 more healthy kids or none. Ally's joyous birth wasn't a make-up exam meant to somehow lessen the sorrow of Noah's death.

Sometimes when we think about him on his tippy toes, wearing a hat and a Kool-Aid smile, leaning into Kimmy's lap to kiss his little sister, saying, "Hi Allwweee!," we ache for him more than ever. But a truth we cannot ignore is that if Noah was here, then Ally probably wouldn't be. That fact makes it impossible to love Ally fully without first accepting what happened to Noah—because one could not have happened without the other. It also doesn't seem right to curse God for taking my son, then praise Him for giving me a daughter. One made the other possible. They are connected. I see that now. And so somehow it all feels okay. Not great. Not even right. But okay. Enough to make peace with it. That is everything.

I had always imagined that peace or grace just floated around and landed on certain people. But the truth is you don't find peace. You don't wait for it to fall on you. You go after it. You track it down. You make it. It's a choice. A daily struggle.

Peace ain't easy.

I had to go through that entire ordeal to understand the most important thing: the final goal isn't complete understanding, knowledge, or fairness. It's not an answer, finally, to the great question of WHY? I'd never get that. But I didn't need it. So I had to stop searching for it. But what I could get, what I could make as my ultimate goal was peace. To find peace with what happened. That's it. Not knowledge. Not enlightenment. Survival. To be changed by death and not ruined by it.

Peace.

That is everything.

I haven't dropped a single coin in a wishing well since Noah died, and I don't think I ever will again. Wishing or wanting seems silly now. Life is more about accepting. I have accepted Noah's death. Mainly because along the way I discovered that I don't have to be better off to find peace with it. I don't have to be able to say or get to a point where I think, "Thank you God for taking my son. You're just the best, Big Guy." No, if I can just see and be touched by some of the blessings from Noah's death, then I can find enough middle ground to trust and understand God's plan. I don't have to like it. I don't have to approve or be happy. Honestly, what kind of a God would expect me to be? I just have to find peace with it. And that, I think, is what Ally's birth had given us: she was the one, crucial piece that transformed the mosaic from a collection of broken pieces into a clear portrait.

She gave meaning to our suffering. She gave us peace.

I had been trying to figure out all year long how Noah's spirit would fit into our lives. And there it was plain as day. What had we been repeating since the night he died? That a person's true character comes out in the toughest times. Well, on Ally's birthday Noah's true character had come out. Sure, the sappy, narcissistic side of me wanted big signs, huge symbols, giant gestures, and national media coverage—a rainbow everyday! Instead, Ally's birth showed me just how and where my son's spirit would fit into our lives. Noah would always be right over our shoulders, in our hearts, and in our silent reflections, instead of right in front of our faces or tugging on our legs. Noah would always be strong and steady and with us every step of the way, but his spirit would be silent and soft and subtle.

Just like it was that day—on the greatest day of our lives.

The day before, at the cemetery, I used a blank piece of paper to take an impression from Noah's gravestone. When we got home I tacked it to a wall next to the computer in my office. From straight ahead it looks like a blank piece of notebook paper. But if you peer closer, or from a different angle, you'll see the imprint of Noah.

In many ways I think all parents who lose children are like that piece of paper. On the surface I may look exactly the same as I did a year ago. But if you take a closer look, or a deeper glance from a different perspective, you'll see there is a significant and deep impression that says, simply . . .

Noah.

C33 8

## CHAPTER 23

# Her Name is . . .

We had been alone as a family for only a few minutes when there was a knock on the hospital room door.

Kim and I looked at each other—as grateful as we were for everyone's support, we were really craving some time for ourselves. At that very moment, though, yet another caravan of cars was traveling down from our neighborhood to meet Oopie. We understood what that little girl meant to so many people. Every night during the past nine months, Jak and Teresa's six-year-old son, Sam, had prayed for Ally before going to bed. Now, this is a kid who can "forget" to shower for weeks on end but when it came to looking after Al, he didn't miss a single day.

Still, we had barely been alone with Ally since she was born.

"After this," Kimmy said, seeming a little tired, "maybe we should stop with the visitors for just a little bit."

"Honey, I'll just tell them no," I said. "I'll just tell them no, okay?"

Kim shook her head, saying, "I guess one more would be okay." She was right. So many people helped us get to that moment, how could we deny them now? In a way our squeaky, perfect, adorable, little girl belonged to anyone who had been with us on the journey.

I stepped toward the door and said, "Come on in."

Through the crack in the door peeked a smallish woman dressed in nurse clothing holding a clipboard in her right hand.

"I have a few questions for you, if you have a sec," she said.

"Sure," said Kim, waving her in. "Questions about what?"

"Your daughter's birth certificate."

Oh. We looked at each other. *Oh.*

Our heads spun around, and our eyes crashed into each other's. We were both smiling and shaking and already fogging up with tears. Ignoring the nurse, we paused for a nice long, family hug. That poor woman just stood there patiently, having no idea the magnitude of that piece of paper.

That was our diploma. That was our finish line. That was our gold medal.

A birth certificate. That was the last sad memory from Noah that we had yet to layer with something new from Ally.

* * *

Alone in the hospital in the early morning hours after Noah had died, Kim was sleeping, and I was staring out a window down the hall from the nursery. That's when a nurse stepped up softly and asked me if I could I follow her back to the nurse's station.

"We need you to sign the fetal death certificate," she said, sliding the form toward me.

"Does he get a birth certificate, too?" I asked.

"No, Mr. Fleming, I'm sorry, he doesn't get one. I'm so sorry."

"Why not?"

"It's policy."

"What policy?" I said, looking for a fight. "He was born."

"Mmm-hmmm . . ."

"I mean, he came into this world. He was *born* into this world."

"Yes I know."

"So I want a birth certificate. Can you get me one?"

There was a long, drawn-out pause during which I formulated a different approach.

"I'll just take a blank one and fill it out myself, okay, would that work?"

"I can't do that, sir," said the nurse.

My words were now coming out in short hot bursts, like gunfire. "I don't understand," I said. "Can't you just give me one, can't you just do that, can't you?"

"Well," she said, looking back and forth, perhaps for reinforcements before leaning in close and continuing in a hushed voice, "it wasn't a live birth, per se."

*Per se?*

I felt a wild, throat-bursting, glass-shattering scream building in my gut and burning the back of my throat. I choked it back, like hot bile. I'm not sure what I was after. Maybe, I thought, if I had gotten angry before, the world wouldn't have messed with me. It would have moved on to someone else. Maybe I wanted someone to acknowledge that my son had been here, because it felt like he was already disappearing, fading, dissolving on me, as if I had imagined the whole thing. Maybe I wanted something in writing so that the heavy burden of perpetuating his spirit wouldn't fall on me.

"I'm really so very, very sorry," she said, whispering in a way that invites you to keep your voice down too, thankyouverymuch, "but I have to ask you to sign this for us."

"Where?"

"Right here."

Father of deceased child: David P. Fleming.

I signed, writing hard enough to make three copies just like the paper asked. My first official act as a father was to acknowledge, in writing, that my son had died.

I bowed my head and steadied myself against the counter like a drunk would against a bar. I waited there, staring at the floor for a long, long time, the tears kerplunking on the ground below me. I could feel a dozen eyeballs burning into me from around the nurse's station. Pity. Worry. Fear. Some crying, some ready to cry, and others deciding how long it would take security to get here if I freaked out.

But I was exhausted. I was defeated. I was out of anger. I was a zombie. I was alone. Five hours earlier my son had died right before my eyes. I felt the life ebb out of his body—and mine. No form would allow me to go back.

I scribbled my name, put the pen down, and slid the form back across the counter.

"Thanks."

"Yeah, sure."

She separated the copies and slid the pink one back to me.

"This one's yours," she said before catching herself.

I just shook my head in utter amazement. The anger and vitriol gurgled in my throat once again. I bit down hard on my lips trying to lock it in. But for God's sake, a receipt? A receipt? A fucking receipt? Give me a break. I didn't want a *receipt* for my dead child, as if I might return before 90 days and demand a refund. "Well, if only you had saved your receipt. . . ." I wanted to break something so bad. I wanted to break myself. (I didn't know it yet, but I was already shattered into a thousand jagged, mismatched mosaic pieces.) To break the world, then. To break God. I wanted to put my hand or my head through a plate glass window, to feel anything but that. Anything. Instead, I walked away and left that hideous piece of paper behind. The nurse smartly did not call after me to pick up my copy. She let it sit there. For all I know it stayed there, on that nurse's station, for the last 54 weeks.

* * *

But if everything had gone wrong with Noah, everything had gone right with Ally.

Now, all we had was a few more questions to answer, and Ally's birth certificate would be finished.

"Mother's place of birth?"

"Dayton, Ohio."

"Father's?"

"Dearborn, Michigan."

"Is her weight and length correct?"

"Yup."

"And she was born . . . at what time?"

"12:46 p.m."

After each answer we just giggled and laughed and celebrated more and more. Looking back, all those things we theorized about a year before on the cold tile floor of our bathroom had all come true. Except for one thing. We had promised one day to be as full of joy as we were, at that moment, filled with sorrow. But the exchange didn't turn out to be even. Not even close. The warmth, happiness, pride, and fulfillment I was now feeling far surpassed the horrors of Noah's death.

The poor nurse just rolled her eyes. She had a job to do. She had seen so many births, they had become routine to her. She had grown blind to the miracles performed right before her eyes every day.

"Okay, um, last one," she said, clearly losing patience.

"Uh huh . . ."

"What is her middle name?"

We hadn't finalized it or talked about it, but we both knew.

On his way to heaven, Noah, our sweet, pudgy little fullback; our beautiful, brave, baby boy, sent us the greatest gift we have ever received in the form of a rainbow—the gift of Hope. And that is what kept us alive.

Rejoice in your suffering, we are told, because suffering produces perseverance, perseverance character, and character hope. And so from that moment on, hope became our most valuable possession. Because without hope, we learned, you cannot heal, you cannot grow, you cannot breathe, you cannot face the next moment—you cannot live.

Hope is a rock, the unshakable source of strength we rebuilt our lives upon. Hope is a prayer, the silent wish that we focus on what we've *found* through all this as well as what we've lost. Hope is a compass; the thing that guided us as we tried to create a loving and lasting legacy for our son. Hope is a goal that we will be defined by more than our grief. Hope is a candle, a steady flame that warmed our heavy hearts and reminded us that we were never alone in our suffering. Hope is the sound of laughter.

Hope is a pledge and a promise we once made to Noah: We will never be the same because of your death, but our prayer is that we can find the strength to honor you by becoming better. To do that, above all we needed hope.

That's why in the world we rebuilt since being demolished by Noah's death, hope was every*where* and hope was every*thing*. You can live without food. You can live without water. But to go on without your child, you cannot live without hope.

Hope is the centerpiece of our mantel. It is the word I superimpose over my own reflection when the bathroom mirror fogs up. Hope is etched into a rock by our front door. Hope is the family name on the brass plaque near our pew at church. Hope is the comforting warmth of my wife's soft and steady hand. Hope is the ray of sunlight from our son that trickles through the tree branches behind our house and tickles our eyes.

Hope was laying in Kimmy's arms.

And it was well worth the year-long journey we had taken to discover it.

We turned to the nurse and spoke in unison.

"Hope," we said.

"Her middle name is Hope."

# About the Author

David Fleming is a senior writer for *ESPN The Magazine* and columnist for ESPN.com's Page 2. Prior to joining ESPN in 2000, Fleming covered the NFL for six seasons as a staff writer at *Sports Illustrated*. A graduate of Miami University in Oxford, Ohio, he and his wife, Kim, live in Davidson, North Carolina with their daughters, Ally, 4, and Kate, 1.